Aeschylus.

DUCKWORTH COMPANIONS
TO GREEK AND ROMAN TRAGEDY

Series editor: Thomas Harrison

DUCKWORTH COMPANIONS
TO GREEK AND ROMAN TRAGEDY

Aeschylus: Persians

David Rosenbloom

Duckworth

First published in 2006 by
Gerald Duckworth & Co. Ltd.
90-93 Cowcross Street, London EC1M 6BF
Tel: 020 7490 7300
Fax: 020 7490 0080
inquiries@duckworth-publishers.co.uk
www.ducknet.co.uk

A catalogue record for this book is available
from the British Library

ISBN-10: 0 7156 3286 8
ISBN-13: 978 0 7156 3286 4

Typeset by Ray Davies
Printed and bound in Great Britain by
MPG Books Ltd, Bodmin, Cornwall

Contents

Preface

I first read the *Persians* twenty years ago and some of my intuitions about the play have held firm over the years: the *Persians* is more a tragedy of defeat than a celebration of victory; a crucial condition for its conception is the nascent Athenian empire; its integration of poetry and spectacle, word and image, reveal a playwright at the height of his powers. As the earliest extant tragedy and first product of western culture to deal with eastern despotism and imperialism, the *Persians* is also an invaluable historical document.

It is my pleasure to acknowledge those who have taught, helped, and supported me in this project. Pride of place belongs to Froma Zeitlin and Josh Ober. I could not have been blessed with better teachers, critics, and friends. Simon Goldhill, Kurt Raaflaub, Deborah Boedeker, David Konstan, Victoria Wohl, Jon Hesk, André Lardinois, and my colleagues at Victoria University of Wellington, Matthew Trundle and Arthur Pomeroy, have all helped to improve this book. The Duckworth team – Thomas Harrison, Deborah Blake, and the press's anonymous reader – have my praise and gratitude for their work. I would also like to thank the students at Princeton and Victoria Universities who read the *Persians* with me and helped me to see the play with fresh eyes. Thanks also to Sarah McMillan, who helped with the maps.

I dedicate this book to my parents, who gave me the gifts of life and love.

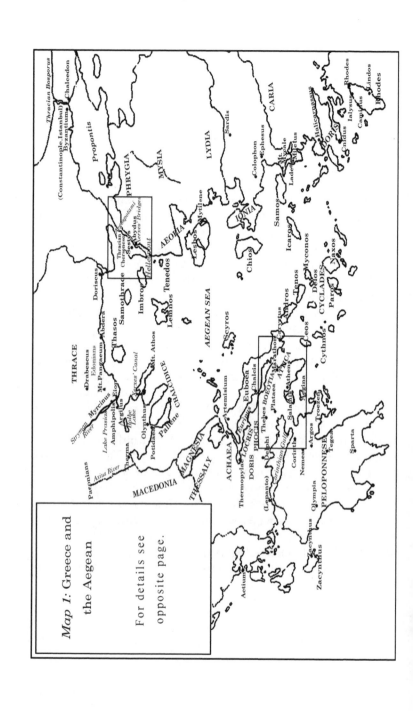

Map 1: Greece and the Aegean

For details see opposite page.

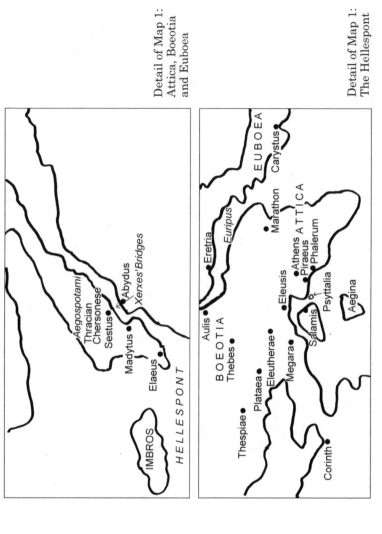

Detail of Map 1:
Attica, Boeotia
and Euboea

Detail of Map 1:
The Hellespont

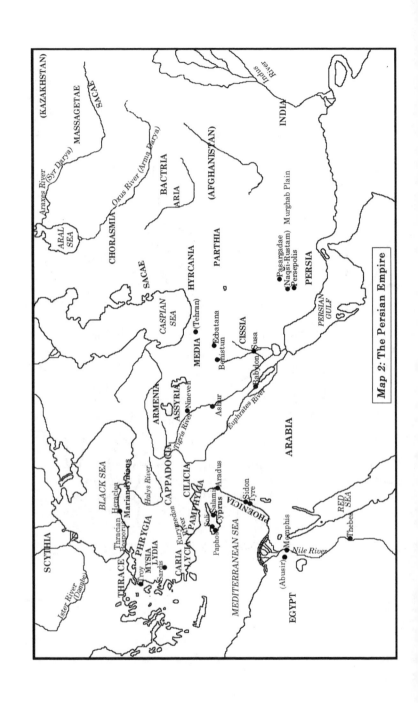

Map 2: **The Persian Empire**

The *Persians*, History, and Historical Drama

Presented at Athens in 472 BC, the *Persians* is the earliest surviving tragedy and the only extant tragedy based on recent events, the failure of the Persian king Xerxes' land and sea invasion of Greece in 480/79. The central interpretive problem of the play is whether it is a tragedy in the canonical sense – an enactment that can arouse sympathetic emotions such as pity and fear in the audience – or a depiction of Persian defeat and lament that celebrates Greek military and cultural superiority, inducing Schadenfreude at the spectacle of Persian pain.

This chapter is a preliminary to an interpretation of the play. It outlines the *Persians* and locates the play in its original performative context before briefly discussing Aeschylus' life and career. Then it sketches the conflict between the Greek city-states and the Persian empire for control of the Aegean and discusses poetic treatments of the Persian Wars before the *Persians*. The main point of this discussion is that although there were fundamental differences between the enemies Athens and Persia, there were also factors that could induce an Athenian audience to identify with the depiction of Salamis as a defeat and with the tragedy of a fallen empire.

This book discusses the *Persians* in sequence; but it may prove helpful for the reader to have a summary of the play in mind during this chapter.

The *Persians*

Parodos (choral entry song, 1-154): functions as a prologue. A chorus of Persian elders, caretakers of the kingdom in Xerxes' absence, fears the worst for the king and his army's homecoming (*nostos*): Asia's might has gone to Greece, but the chorus has no word of its fate. The elders catalogue the leaders and ethnic contingents that left 'to put the yoke of slavery on Greece' and describe the heightening anxiety and longing of parents and wives as time passes. Trying to assuage its fears, the chorus tells how the army marched across the Hellespont over bridges built for the invasion, 'putting a yoke on the neck of the sea'. The elders stress the ferocity of their godlike king, the invincibility of his 'divine flock', and Persia's divine dispensation of military supremacy on land. Xerxes' generation broke with this tradition by casting its gaze upon the sea. The chorus wonders what mortal can escape divine deceit and the nets of *Atê*, the spirit of destructive delusion, which seduces humans into their ruin. Anxious again, the elders imagine women performing antiphonal laments and tearing their robes at the news of defeat before resolving to sit in council to discuss the progress of the war.

First Episode, I (155-255). The Queen, Xerxes' mother and the late king Darius' wife, enters on a chariot. The elders fall to their knees and bow before her in a formal greeting. The Queen fears that Darius' divinely won prosperity and her son's life are in peril. Her fears are the result of last night's dream and this morning's bird omen – clear portents of defeat – which she describes. The chorus advises the Queen to sacrifice to the gods and to Darius, who appeared in her dream, to prevent the fulfilment of her visions and expresses confidence that all will turn out well. After an exchange about the aim of the invasion and the nature of Athens, a messenger runs on stage to announce the disaster: the ruin of Persia's prosperity and loss of the flower of its men in total defeat. Chorus and messenger lament the bad news (256-89), dividing the first and second parts of the episode.

First Episode, II (290-531). The Queen regains her voice and questions the messenger, who informs her that Xerxes survived but that a host of leaders, whom he lists, died ingloriously. Numbering the Persian fleet at more than three times the size of the Greek fleet, he recounts how Xerxes was tricked into believing the Greek fleet stationed on Salamis would flee at night, and blockaded the island to destroy it in flight. The

Greeks emerged at daybreak to fight and attacked Xerxes' fleet. Unable to manoeuvre, the Persian fleet was encircled and destroyed. The messenger then tells of the massacre of Xerxes' noblest warriors on an adjacent island. Xerxes, who watched from a conspicuous place, tore his robes at the disaster (a moment in his mother's dream) and ordered the army to flee. Finally, the messenger recounts the Persians' harrowing march from Greece to Thrace and announces the imminent return of a small remnant. After the messenger exits, the Queen recognizes the truth of her dream. Criticizing the elders, she nonetheless vows to make the sacrifices they earlier advised. Before she exits, the Queen orders the chorus to comfort Xerxes and escort him to the palace if he returns in her absence.

First Stasimon (532-97). Alone in the orchestra, the elders blame Zeus for the disaster and describe the luxuriant mourning of Persian women. The chorus sings a lament, alternately blaming Xerxes and ships for defeat and contrasting the deleterious young king with his benign father. Imagining sea creatures mauling Persian corpses and picturing the grief of elderly and childless parents, the elders foresee the dissolution of the Persian empire as a result of the naval defeat.

Second Episode, I (598-622): The Queen returns alone on foot, carrying ritual offerings. Humbled and frightened, she orders the chorus to raise Darius' ghost by singing a hymn while she pours offerings.

Hymn (623-80): The elders appeal to the gods of the underworld to release Darius' soul, praise Darius as a god for his wisdom and benevolence, and lament the death of Persia's youth. In an epode, they bewail the destruction of the fleet. The hymn divides the second episode into two parts.

Second Episode, II (681-842): Darius' ghost appears, but the chorus cannot bear to inform him of the disaster. He learns the news from the Queen. Darius recognizes that the disaster fulfils a prophecy and condemns his son's 'disease of mind' for treating the Hellespont as a 'slave in chains' and for seeking to 'dominate all the gods'. He then demonstrates that Xerxes' is the worst disaster in the history of the Persian kingship. In response to the elders' desire for vengeance, Darius orders them not to invade Greece. As proof, he prophesies impending defeat

13

for Persia's forces at Plataea as payment for looting statues and destroying Greek temples and altars. Darius advises the chorus to rehabilitate Xerxes and instructs the Queen to meet him with a new robe: he will return in rags. Darius returns to the underworld. The Queen exits, vowing to return with a new robe, but never returns.

Second Stasimon (852-907): The chorus praises Darius and enumerates the Aegean empire he conquered and ruled. The Persians have suffered a divinely inspired reversal of fortune: they lost these cities in naval fighting.

Kommos (908-1065): Xerxes returns alone in rags. The elders greet him with a lament for Asia's fall. King and chorus perform a ritual lament before Xerxes seizes control of the elders and orders them to mutilate themselves in mourning.

Exodos (1066-1077): Xerxes and the chorus lament in an epode as they exit to the palace.

Performance, playwright and producer

In fifth-century Athens all drama – tragedy, comedy, and satyr-play – was performed at festivals for Dionysus, god of wine, life-giving liquids, masks, and madness, who was worshipped particularly through dance.[1] The largest and most prestigious of these festivals was the City Dionysia.[2] Held at the onset of spring and celebrating the arrival of Dionysus to Athens from Eleutherae in Boeotia, the festival marked the advent of the sailing season and attracted visitors from all over the Greek-speaking world. The City Dionysia came to be associated with Athenian naval power, freedom, and empire.[3] The *Persians*, the earliest extant meditation on these subjects, has an affinity with the occasion of its performance.

Aeschylus presented four plays at the City Dionysia in 472: three tragedies, *Phineus*, *Persians*, *Glaucus of Potniae*, and a satyr-play, *Prometheus Fire-Kindler* (*Hypothesis* to the *Persians*). Only the *Persians* survives intact; we possess fragments from the other three. Aeschylus tended to present his dramatic vision in tetralogies, a continuous narrative in three tragedies, followed by a related satyr-play.[4] Aeschylus' dramaturgy mixed the concision of drama with the expansiveness of epic; his tragic

14

trilogies segued into burlesque and self-parody. While the *Persians* did not form a tetralogy with its companion plays, some argue that it shared unifying thematic links with them.[5] An attractive hypothesis, it is unconvincing on the evidence we possess.[6] As it stands, the *Persians* is both the sole surviving historical tragedy and the only self-contained tragedy in Aeschylus' extant *oeuvre*.

These four plays (not the *Persians* alone) won first prize in competition with two other tragedians.[7] Aeschylus was victorious thirteen times in his career, which spanned the years 499 to 456.[8] He was not an instant success in the theatre: he won his first victory in 484. The *Persians* is a work of his prime.[9]

The scion of an established and wealthy family, Aeschylus son of Euphorion hailed from Eleusis, renowned for the Mysteries of Demeter and Kore.[10] Like all Athenians of his generation, Aeschylus had first-hand experience of war. He is reputed to have fought in the defensive battles against the Persians on mainland Greece – Marathon (490), Salamis (480), and Plataea (479) – that form the spine of the *Persians* (*Life of Aeschylus* 4). Ion of Chios, a fifth-century poet and raconteur, claims that Aeschylus was present at Salamis (*FGrH* 392 F7).

Aeschylus died in Gela, Sicily in 456. The epitaph attributed to his grave makes no mention of his dramatic artistry but memorializes his infantry service at Marathon: 'the hallowed field of Marathon could tell of his celebrated valour and the deep-haired Mede who knows it'.[11] The biographies of the ancient Greek poets are notoriously untrustworthy.[12] The story of Aeschylus' death is a case in point: an eagle snatched up a turtle and tried to break it on his bald head, mistaking it for a rock (*Life of Aeschylus* 10).

The remains of Aeschylus' poetry (six plays of some 90, around 500 fragments, and the disputed *Prometheus Bound*), show that his style ranged from simple beauty to dense obscurity. Ancient critics noted his grandiloquent language and religious sensibility. Aeschylus depicted war as a crucible of personal and communal virtue; but he was equally inclined to treat warfare as boastful impiety and communal agony. His poetry combined aristocratic loftiness with democratic patriotism, religious majesty with an earthy aesthetic.

Aeschylus was a theatrical colossus: he composed the poetry, lyrics, and music for his plays; he choreographed the choral dances and may have designed the costumes.[13] He probably acted the leading parts, playing, for instance, the Messenger, Darius, and Xerxes in the *Persians*, while a male actor played the Queen, although the *Life of Aeschylus* reports that he used two professional actors (14-15).[14] Like all extant Aeschylean tragedies apart from the *Oresteia*, the *Persians* uses two speaking actors. Aristotle credits Aeschylus with the introduction of a second actor – before this tragedians used one (Aristotle *Poetics* 1449a15-19). Twelve Athenian citizens recruited for their talent played the chorus.

The chief magistrate of Athens, the Archon Eponymous (so-called because the year was named after him) assigned a producer (*chorêgos*) to each of the tragedians whose plays were selected for performance at the City Dionysia. The producer paid for the upkeep of the chorus while they learned their lines, lyrics, melodies, and dances. He also provided a venue for rehearsal and paid for the chorus' costumes; if the playwright won, he took the credit, fêted the chorus and actors, and erected a monument commemorating his victory.[15] The *Persians*' producer was a young man, Pericles son of Xanthippus.[16] Xanthippus had married into the most prominent family of Athens, the Alcmaeonidae ('the family of Alcmaeon').[17] Ostracized in 484, Xanthippus was recalled prior to the Persian invasion and elected general in 480/79. He spearheaded the Athenian counter-offensive against the Persians in 479/78.

Technically Pericles had no control over the plays he produced; the playwright was assigned to him. But he had personal motives for financing the *Persians*. The play's focus on Xerxes' bridges and cables (65-72, 112-13, 130-2, 719-26, 734-6, 745-51) would recall his father's generalship. The Athenians brought home the cables from Xerxes' bridges over the Hellespont under Xanthippus' command (Herodotus 9.121). Moreover, the maternal side of Pericles' family had been branded Persian supporters ('medizers') after the battle of Marathon in 490 (6.115, 121-31).[18] Pericles' involvement with the *Persians* might counter such charges; a victory would help launch his own political career. His ability to influence the drama, however, was limited. The *Persians* is silent about the battles at which Xanthippus was general, although it implies them (205-10, 876-903).

Pericles dominated Athenian democratic and imperialist politics in the generation after the *Persians*, leading Athens to the peak of its power and prosperity and embroiling the city in a war with Sparta and its allies. Given his involvement with the *Persians*, it is worth noting that Pericles would come to play Darius' role in his lifetime: the 'father' and exponent of empire as patrimony, whose prosperity and happiness would prove to be unsurpassable, and whose 'son', most notoriously his nephew and ward Alcibiades son of Clinias, would forget his commands, ruining the empire he consolidated, ornamented, and defended in a failed invasion of Syracuse in 415-13. The comedian Eupolis raised Pericles' ghost (and those of other Athenian 'fathers') in his comedy *Villages* just as Aeschylus raised Darius' ghost in the *Persians*.[19]

Persian empire and Greek freedom

That mainland Greeks could thwart the Persian empire in 480/79 was nothing short of a miracle. Under the successive rule of Cyrus son of Cambyses (559-530), Cambyses son of Cyrus (530-523), and Darius son of Hystaspes (522-486) the Persians had amassed the largest empire on the globe.[20]

While the Persians were building their empire, Athens was ruled by a native tyrannical family, which monopolized political power outside of law and custom. The founder of the line, Pisistratus, came to power in 560 and ruled intermittently until his death in 527, when his eldest son Hippias succeeded him.[21] In 514, the lovers Harmodius and Aristogiton murdered Hippias' brother Hipparchus in a botched plot to decapitate the ruling family and to vindicate their freedom and dignity as citizens – they aimed to kill Hippias.[22] Nevertheless, the Athenians remembered Hipparchus as 'tyrant', imagining the origins of their political order in this act of 'tyrant-slaying'.[23] The demos ('people') founded its power in the murder of a tyrant and distribution of his power to a free citizen body. The *Persians* is arguably a narrative of this type. The play depicts the Athe-

17

nian empire as an acquisition from a defeated tyrant, Xerxes. He inherited it from Darius, who won it by conquest (852-907).

The Pisistratidae were so deeply entrenched in Athenian society that the Athenians needed the military assistance of Sparta to expel them from Athens (Herodotus 5.62-5; 6.123). Aristocratic factions vied to fill the void. Athenian democracy was the fruit of this conflict. In 508, Clisthenes, an Alcmaeonid contending for power with a rival aristocrat, Isagoras, who was Archon Eponymous, appealed to ordinary citizens for support. These citizens voted to empower themselves to override the Archon Eponymous and institute a new tribal organization. The aim of this organization was to integrate the population and to weaken the local and clan affiliations that had fragmented Athens' territory, Attica, into viciously competitive groups.[24] Political power was distributed among the citizen body by a principle of numerical equality; the majority ruled. This principle of equality, *isonomia* (literally, 'equality of the law'), was antithetical to monarchy, in which a single household and family (*oikos*) monopolized political power.[25] Athens' collectivity and cohesiveness proved invaluable against Persia. The *Persians* recalls the triumph of this collective spirit over the desire of a monarch, Xerxes, to conquer and rule Athens and Greece.

Athens came into direct contact with the Persian empire principally because its oligarchic neighbours and Sparta were hostile to the city's nascent democracy. Surrounded by enemies, Athens sought an alliance with Persia *c.* 507/06 (Herodotus 5.73.1). Artaphrenes, Darius' paternal half-brother who administered Western Anatolia from Sardis in Lydia, demanded that Athens' envoys offer earth and water, symbols which opened a line of communication and acted as a promise to accede to the king's future demands.[26] The envoys made the offering on their own and faced charges when they returned to Athens (5.73.3). But it was too late to repudiate the gift. Athens was caught in the net of the Persian empire.

Exiles from the Greek world flocked to the Persians seeking restoration to their homelands as their agents. Exiled from Athens in 510, the tyrant Hippias petitioned Artaphrenes to return him to power *c.* 501/00 (Herodotus 5.96.1). Artaphrenes granted his plea and ordered the Athenians to restore him

(5.96.2). The Athenians rejected his ultimatum and 'decided to become openly hostile to the Persians' (ibid.). Their hostility soon became apparent. In 499, Greeks living under Persian rule in Western Anatolia revolted from Persia.[27] Starting in Miletus (5.28-38), the revolt spread from Byzantium to Cyprus (5.103-4). Our sole source, Herodotus, claims that the Persian-installed tyrant of Miletus, Histiaeus, and his nephew and son-in-law, Aristagoras, plotted to carve out a naval empire under the aegis of the Persian empire as compensation for salvaging Darius' invasion of Scythia (modern Ukraine) over a decade earlier (4.136-42; 7.10g, 52.1).[28] Darius' generals Megabazus and his son Megabates foiled their bid (5.23-36, 106.6; 6.2.1). Aristagoras renounced his tyranny and acted to depose Persian-backed tyrants 'in all Ionia' (5.37.2-38). The Milesian tyrants enlisted the support of ordinary citizens, who yearned for an egalitarian political order (*isonomia*), to ignite a full-scale revolt.

After failing to secure Sparta's aid, Aristagoras sought Athens' help (5.49-55.1). Appealing to their common ancestry as Ionians and piquing the demos' desire for the wealth of the Persian empire, Aristagoras induced the Athenians to join the revolt. They sent 20 shiploads of men to Miletus (5.97). Herodotus borrows from Homer to describe this fateful moment: 'these ships were the beginning of woes for both Greeks and barbarians' (5.97.3).[29]

The revolt started successfully. Athenians and Ionians captured the town of Sardis and set fire to a house. The fire spread through the cane and reed rooftops of the city and destroyed a temple of the Lydian great-mother goddess, Cybebe (5.100-2.1).[30] Soon afterwards, however, the Persians intercepted and killed many of the invaders at Ephesus (5.102.2-3). Athens abandoned the revolt (5.103).

By 494, the Persians had quelled the revolts and held Miletus under siege. A Persian navy manned by Phoenicians and Egyptians, among others, prepared to face a mainly Ionian navy off the island of Lade (6.6-13). Ruled by single families for over two generations, the Ionians lacked leadership. The fleet fled the scene of battle (6.14-16). The Persians undermined Miletus' fortifications and overwhelmed the city, enslaving women and children, and sacking and burning the temple and oracle of Apollo at Didyma (6.18-21). 'Miletus', Herodotus writes, 'was emptied of Milesians' (6.22.1). The image of Persia and Asia 'emptied of men' and 'emptied out' haunts the *Persians* (114-39, 548-9, 718, 730, 759-61). One of many ironic reversals of history in the play, it both recalls and reciprocates Persian atrocities against Ionians, including Athens, which was evacuated and sacked in 480/79.

From the Persian perspective, the burning of Cybebe's temple was an egregious breach of faith – the Athenians had given earth and water to Darius. Persian dignity required brutal and exact vengeance (Herodotus 5.102.1; 7.8b2-3, 11.2). Ionians were treated as a people who rejected the Great King, representative of the Persian god Ahuramazda on earth. Like other rebels, they worshipped 'demons' and their temples were destroyed.[31] The burning of Sardis offered the Persians an ironclad excuse for invading mainland Greece (Aristotle *Posterior Analytics* 94a36-b8).

In 493, the Persians attacked cities in Western Anatolia that had revolted. According to Herodotus, they collected the most handsome boys and made them eunuchs, sending them to the king along with the most beautiful girls before they burned their cities and temples (6.31.2-32). Over the next two years, the Persians regained the territories lost during the revolt and added others in the Aegean (6.31-45). One question remained: when would Persia punish Athens?

Historical tragedy as prophecy: Phrynichus' *Capture of Miletus*

Phrynichus' *Capture of Miletus*, the first tragedy of which we have any definite information, may have posed this very question.[32] The play's date is unknown, but the period 493-491 is most likely.[33] Not a word of it survives. Herodotus reports that during the performance of the play 'the theatre fell into tears and they fined him 1,000 drachmae for reminding them of their own woes (*oikeia kaka*) and ordered no one ever to perform this drama' (6.21.2).

Many interpret Herodotus' phrase 'their own woes' to mean

'the woes they caused' and argue that Phrynichus reproached Athens for abandoning the Ionian revolt. The architect of Athenian naval power, Themistocles, was Archon Eponymous in 493/92 and may have begun fortifying a more easily defensible harbour at Piraeus in anticipation of a Persian invasion.[34] Phrynichus, the argument goes, supported Themistocles.[35] The shame of his reproach angered the Athenians. Hence they fined him and banned the play.

It is impossible to determine Phrynichus' intentions in composing the play. We can only analyse the play's reception. Reminding the Athenians of 'their own woes' is unlikely to mean that Phrynichus reproached Athens for betraying Miletus. In Herodotus, the phrase 'one's own woes' refers to pain occasioned by the suffering of 'one's own people' (e.g. 1.45.2; 3.14.8-14). Phrynichus reminded the Athenians of 'their own woes' because he dramatized the trauma of 'their own people' – Ionians, Milesians, colonists, allies – forcing the audience to relive the pain of Miletus' fall.

The tragedy probably featured choral laments for Miletus' suffering.[36] The extant tragedy dealing with the capture of a city, Euripides' *Trojan Women*, laments the fall of Troy in a variety of registers.[37] The prologue establishes that the gods will punish the Greeks who destroyed Troy (Euripides *Trojan Women* 48-97). Cassandra foresees reciprocal vengeance against Agamemnon and his house (353-461; cf. 1100-17), predicts Odysseus' sufferings (431-44), and denies glory to the Greeks (375-405). The *Capture of Miletus* may have envisioned divine and human punishment of the Persians.

In ancient Greek culture, memory of the past is a warrant for knowledge of the future. Hesiod's poet has authority and inspiration from the Muses to sing 'what will be and was before' (*Theogony* 29-34; cf. 35-49; Homer *Iliad* 1.70). Aeschylus' Cassandra demonstrates her prophetic power by revealing the past (*Agamemnon* 1090-9). Thucydides offers his *History* to readers who will want to know the past and the future inferable from it, given the constancy of human nature (1.22.4). The *Capture of Miletus* was historical tragedy; but re-enactment of the event formulated a prophecy. While watching the *Capture of Miletus*, the spectators witnessed an image of Athens' impending destruction. The Athenians had every reason to consider themselves imminent targets of Persian reprisal. With the exception of Samos (Herodotus 6.25.2), the Persians emptied out, sacked, and burned the cities that had revolted, destroying their temples.

The *Capture of Miletus* marks a critical moment in the history of tragedy. Ancient theorists define the subject of tragedy as 'other people's sufferings' (*allotria pathê*).[38] Tragic practice conforms to this: spectators witness the sufferings of those distant in time, place, or affection. Such distance is required for pity as an emotion of tragic spectatorship. Pity requires the sufferer to be 'other' than the viewer and to be in some sense unworthy of suffering.[39] We pity in others what we fear for ourselves and our own.[40] Phrynichus' assault upon the sense of security required for the enjoyment of others' pains resulted in the institution of a boundary between self and other in tragic performance. Henceforth the subjects of tragedy were mythical figures remote in time and place or rarely, victims of the audience's violence as in Phrynichus' subsequent tragedy the *Phoenician Women* and Aeschylus' *Persians*. Historical drama risked alienating its spectators by dramatizing or implying events too painful for them to engage with emotionally and intellectually.[41] The *Persians* omits Herodotus' 'origin of woes for Greeks and barbarians' (5.97.3) and the burning of Cybebe's temple. The play stages 'someone else's suffering' (*allotrion pathos*) whose obverse is a Greek/Athenian victory.

If the *Capture of Miletus* contained two visions – impending Persian destruction of Athens and reciprocal punishment of the Persians – Phrynichus could hardly have imagined the deferral of both until a single moment, Xerxes' invasion of Athens in 480/79.

The empire strikes back: Marathon and Xerxes' invasion

In 490, Hippias directed a Persian/Greek fleet to Marathon, where some 9,000 Athenian and 1,000 Plataean hoplites met and defeated them (Herodotus 6.105-118).[42] The victory legitimated the Athenian democratic order at home and throughout

Greece. Athens alone faced the '46 peoples of the Persian empire' and prevailed in a kind of duel (9.27.5). In the *Persians*, Marathon is the precedent the battle of Salamis repeats on a larger scale.

When Xerxes succeeded Darius in 486, he inherited a plan to invade mainland Greece and to incorporate it into the Persian empire (Herodotus 7.1-4). According to Herodotus, Xerxes' sworn aims were to bridge the Hellespont, to capture and burn Athens as retribution for the burning of Cybebe's temple and sacred grove, and to avenge his father's defeat at Marathon (7.8b1-3; 8.102.3). He wanted to maintain the standard of conquest established by his predecessors (7.8a, 11.2) and intended to reinstate the Pisistratidae at Athens (7.6; 8.52.2). He contemplated bringing the Peloponnese under his power, holding an empire over Asia and Europe, and dreamed of uniting all lands under his rule: his empire would be differentiated only from the heavens (7.8g1-2; cf. 8.100.3, 101.2-3). In the *Persians*, Darius condemns Xerxes' acts as 'violent arrogance' (*hybris*); but the play includes his desire to avenge Darius' defeat at Marathon (473-7), to rule Europe and Asia (181-99), and to maintain Darius' standard of conquest (753-8). Interpreters of the *Persians* often stress the first explanation; but all three should be taken into account.

Herodotus calculates that Xerxes invaded Greece with 5,283,220 people, half of them military personnel (7.184-7.1).[43] A favourite Herodotean *topos* – which the *Persians* does not use – is that they drank rivers dry (e.g. 7.43.1). Such numbers are impossible, but the actual figures are elusive.[44] This exaggeration underwrites the Greek belief, central to the *Persians*, that a mere quantity of men was no match for the quality of free Greeks defending their land (7.101-4, 208-10). Xerxes' massive forces were a liability in the narrow battle-zones the Greeks devised for them (7.211.2; 8.16.2).

The Greeks considered Xerxes' invasion as much a pageant of power as a military operation. Placing himself at its centre, Xerxes assembled a moving catalogue of the peoples of his empire (Herodotus 7.21, 40-1, 61-100), marching it from Sardis to Greece in May 480. His fleet sailed in tandem with his army. Xerxes transformed nature to display his irresistible power. He had a canal cut behind Mount Athos to protect the fleet from storms that descended from the mountain and had damaged a Persian fleet in 492 (7.21-4, 37). He had two bridges built across the Hellespont. Constructed from 674 triremes and 50-oared galleys, the bridges spanned roughly 1.5 kilometres from Abydus on the Asian side to a promontory between Sestus and Madytus on the European side; men and animals crossed them (7.33-6). The *Persians* makes the 'yoking' of the Hellespont a symbol of Xerxes' 'violent arrogance' (*hybris*), and 'destructive delusion' (*atê*): his desire to rule an empire embracing two continents in violation of nature, divinity, and the freedom that is characteristic of the Greek *polis*.

Xerxes' army and navy broke through Greek defences at Thermopylae and Artemisium in late August 480. The *Persians* ignores these battles. We have a copy of an inscription of a decree proposed by Themistocles that mandates the evacuation of Athens: women and children were to go to Troezen, old men and property to Salamis; all others were to man the fleet at Artemisium. The decree's authenticity is debated.[45] Herodotus places the evacuation after Artemisium. According to him, the Athenians sent their children and dependents to Troezen, Aegina, and Salamis (8.41.1).

Xerxes' army carved a path of destruction from Euboea to Athens, looting and burning the land, homes, and temples of resisting communities; the people fled to the mountains and to safe regions (Herodotus 8.23, 32-9, 50.2). Entering an Attica 'emptied of men', the Persians destroyed fields and houses, demolished the city wall, damaged mines, destroyed public buildings, and besieged the Acropolis, which they looted. They set fire to sanctuaries, levelled altars, toppled temples, stole statues, and murdered suppliants (8.51-5, 65, 142.3; Thucydides 1.89.3; 2.16).[46]

In the following year, after Xerxes had left Greece, Xerxes' cousin and brother-in-law Mardonius forced a second evacuation, levelling anything still upright (9.13.2-3). Athenians rarely spoke of this in the fifth century; interpreters of the *Persians* often ignore it. Aeschylus keeps the memory of this atrocity alive in the *Persians*; his mythical tragedies project it onto others' suffering.[47] Readers consider the Persian Wars tragic only from the Persian perspective.[48] But in 472, they were still tragic from the Athenian perspective. Salamis was a victory predicated upon a defeat.

Xerxes accomplished his vow: he bridged the Hellespont, marched an army into Greece, burned Athens' temples, and sacked the city. The equivalence of the Great King's word and act was central to the ideology of his kingship. But Xerxes' vengeance would prove costly.

The empire strikes out:
Salamis, Plataea and Mycale

Athens was lost. The Peloponnesians on Salamis wanted to fight for their own land, retreating to the Isthmus of Corinth to face the Persian fleet (Herodotus 8.49, 70.2). Their generals ordered escape (8.56). Themistocles failed to convince an assembly of generals to mount a naval defence at Salamis (8.60a-b). Sensing that the moment for battle at Salamis was slipping away, Themistocles sent his slave Sicinnus to the Persian generals to report that he was on the king's side, that the Greeks were preparing to flee Salamis that night, and that Persian collaborators and resisters were more likely to fight a naval battle between themselves than to unite against Xerxes (8.75). The *Persians* names 'a Greek man from the army of the Athenians' who deceives Xerxes rather than his generals (355-71). Plutarch identifies Sicinnus as a Persian war captive who looked after Themistocles' sons (*Life of Themistocles* 12.3). Barry Strauss suggests that he was a Greek from Phrygia.[49] Historians have doubted this entire story.[50] Sicinnus was rewarded with wealth and citizenship at Thespiae in Boeotia (Herodotus 8.75.1). This suggests he played some role in the deception of the Persians. Aeschylus calls him Greek because of his citizenship or subsumes his identity under that of his master and the master-mind of the plot, Themistocles.

Based in Phalerum, the Persians decided to blockade the Greeks on Salamis and to crush them in flight. They spent the night occupying the island of Psyttalia (modern Lipsokoutali) in the middle of the passage between Attica and Salamis, blocking lanes of escape, and awaiting the Greek flight (Herodotus 8.76). The Greeks had no choice but to fight their way out (8.78-82). Maintaining good order, they cut through the disorderly Persian fleet, whose numbers were a lethal liability, driving it out of the water and slaughtering the Persians on Psyttalia (esp. 8.86, 95; 435-64). Not understanding the extent of the damage they had inflicted, the Greeks prepared for another battle (8.96.1, 108.1).

According to Herodotus, Xerxes feared that the Greeks would destroy the bridges over the Hellespont, trapping his forces in Europe (8.97). He therefore ordered the fleet to retreat the night after the battle (8.97, 107). In the *Persians*, Xerxes orders the land forces' immediate flight; the ships escape separately (468-70, 480-1). Herodotus claims that Xerxes left 300,000 troops under Mardonius' command to fight a decisive land battle and to attack the Peloponnese (8.100-3, 113; 9.32.2). Marching with the rest of his land forces to the Hellespont in 45 days (half the time of the march to Greece), Xerxes returned to Asia. The navy returned with the army and ferried it across the Hellespont; the bridges were down (8.115-20, 126; 130.1; 9.114.1). The *Persians* depicts the bridges as Xerxes' salvation (735-6) and returns him to Susa after Salamis. Herodotus keeps Xerxes in Sardis until the battle of Mycale in the summer of 479 (9.107.3), even though he also claims Persians lamented from the news of Salamis until Xerxes' return (8.99.2-100.1).

Mardonius unsuccessfully pressured Athens to join Persia (Herodotus 8.140-4; 9.3-4). Under intense prodding from Athens and Megara, Sparta finally sent an army and mobilized its allies to face Mardonius' army (9.6-11, 28-30), which was augmented with Greek conscripts (9.31-2). The armies massed on either side of the Asopus River in Boeotia. The decisive fighting at Plataea pit lightly armoured Persian cavalry and archers against heavily armoured Spartan hoplites (9.62.3). When Mardonius fell, the Persians fled (9.63). The rest of the army fell apart (9.68), escaping into a palisade fort built before the campaign (9.15, 65). The Greeks chased and killed them in flight; the Athenians besieged the fort and the Greeks continued the slaughter on a huge scale (9.68-70).

The defeat at Salamis destroyed the Persian fleet's fighting capacity and cancelled Persia's numerical advantage; Plataea slaughtered the Persian army and drove the remnant from Greece. A further Persian defeat at Mycale in Milesian territory caused Greeks in Western Anatolia and the islands to revolt from Persian rule (Herodotus 8.130-3; 9.90-106.1). The Greeks were now on the offensive.

Simonides: the *kosmos* of song and of virtue

The Greeks immediately celebrated their achievement. The poet Simonides of Ceos (*c.* 556-468) played a major role in the project. Most of the epigrams commemorating the Persian War dead were attributed to him. Many are later forgeries, but one theme stands out: the heroization of the war dead by compensating them with immortal glory (*kleos*).[51] The epigrams celebrate the eternal fame of Greeks who died for the freedom of Greece.[52]

Simonides composed poems on the battles of Artemisium and Salamis which probably predated the *Persians*.[53] The poem on Salamis glorified the naval victory and Themistocles' intelligence (Plutarch *Life of Themistocles* 15.2). The poem on Artemisium stressed the aid of the North Wind, Boreas, a kinsman by marriage of the mythical Athenian king Erechtheus. The Athenians claimed to have invoked Boreas to destroy the Persians moored on the coast of Magnesia in 480 and to wreck the Persian fleet off Mount Athos in 492 (Herodotus 7.188-92).[54] Unlike the *Persians*, these poems focused on named Greeks and Greece's magical and divine defence mechanisms.

Papyri from Egypt have yielded fragments of Simonides' *Plataea*, a poem on the battle written in elegiac couplets.[55] The date, place and occasion of the poem's first performance are debated.[56] The poem focuses on Sparta, describing itself as a remembrance '[of men who] warded off [the day of slavery] from Sparta [and Greece]' (fr. 11.24-6).[57] It attributes 'virtue' (*aretê*) and 'immortal glory among men' to the Spartans (fr. 11.27-8) and narrates the Spartan army's march to Plataea accompanied by the demigods Castor and Pollux and the hero Menelaus (fr. 11.29-31). 'Pausanias the son of divine Cleombrotus, best by far' (fr. 11.33-4) leads them. Unlike the *Persians*, the *Plataea* named historical Greeks. Spartan general of the Greek forces at Plataea, Pausanias was accused of trying to betray Greece to

Xerxes in 478/77. Either this story was not yet current when the *Plataea* was performed, or it did not affect his fame.[58]

The poem begins with a hymn to Achilles. Achilles and Pausanias are the named warriors through whom the unnamed Greeks retain their 'names', their *kleos*.[59] The poem renews the fame of the epic heroes by bestowing it upon soldiers who died at Plataea.[60] This performance is the antithesis of the *Persians*, which laments unburied Persian corpses, bewailing the ignominy of their deaths. The *Persians* implies *kleos* for the victors and assumes performances such as the *Plataea*; but heroization is not its function. The play does not recall the Greek dead.

Simonides bills himself as a new Homer, who conferred immortal glory on the Danaans for sacking Troy and returning home (fr. 11.13-18). While Simonides treated the defence at Plataea as a renewal of the fame of epic heroes, the Athenians were fighting a new Trojan War on the Hellespont and throughout the Aegean.[61]

A new Trojan War: from Sestus to Eion

In late 479, the Athenians and their newly won allies besieged Sestus, the centre of Persian rule on the Hellespont (Herodotus 9.114.2-118; cf. Thucydides 1.89.2). After the Persian governor Artayctes and his men escaped, the inhabitants opened the gates to the Athenians, who took control of the town (Herodotus 9.118). The Athenians hunted and captured Artayctes, returning him and his son to Sestus (9.119.2). Artayctes had persuaded Xerxes to give him the temple and sacred land of the Greek hero Protesilaus – the first Greek to die in the Trojan War (Homer *Iliad* 2.695-710) – to loot and desecrate as a warning against invading Asia (Herodotus 9.116.3). Encouraged by the citizens of Elaeus, an Athenian colony, Xanthippus nailed Artayctes to a plank and stoned his son to death before his eyes near where the Persians secured their bridges to Europe (9.120.4; cf. 7.33).[62] Artayctes' crucified body marked the boundary of Europe and warned the Persians against further invasion. It was a measure of Athens' implacable rage. Herodotus contrasts this event with the more restrained posture of the Spartan Pausanias, who refuses such reciprocal violence as 'characteristic of barbarians' (9.79.1; cf. 7.238). The

Athenians returned home with plunder from Mycale and the cables from Xerxes' bridges to dedicate to the gods (9.121), the first spoils and a banner under which a new Trojan War would be waged; and they symbolized Athens' hegemony in it.[63] Artayctes was the first Persian to die in this new Trojan War, just as the hero whose temple he violated, Protesilaus, had been the first Greek to die in Homer's Trojan War.

In the following spring, a Greek fleet and 'a number of other allies' assembled under Pausanias' leadership (Thucydides 1.94.1). Sailing from Cyprus to Byzantium, which they took by siege, the Greeks liberated Western Anatolia from Persian garrisons (Thucydides 1.94.2; Diodorus 11.44). Success divided the Greeks. The Athenians took the hegemony from the Spartans, who returned home with their allies (Thucydides 1.95). According to Thucydides, Pausanias' *hybris* toward the Ionians prompted them to beg the Athenians to replace him on the grounds of kinship: his leadership 'seemed more an imitation of tyranny than a generalship' (1.95.3).[64] According to Herodotus, the Athenians desired the naval hegemony against Xerxes but Sparta's allies rebuffed them; once Greece was secure and the counter-offensive began, 'they took it from the Spartans, offering Pausanias' *hybris* as a pretext' (8.3.2; cf. [Aristotle] *Constitution of the Athenians* 23.4).

The Persian withdrawal from the Aegean left a vacuum of power. The Greeks thought that Xerxes' desire was to rule 'all Greece' (Herodotus 7.157.1; cf. 138.1). The Greek leaders who vanquished him acquired this desire as a spoil of victory. Pausanias was the first victim of this syndrome: he 'had the desire to be tyrant of all Greece' (Herodotus 5.32; Thucydides 1.128.3). Trying to betray Greece to the Persians (Thucydides 1.128-30; cf. Herodotus 5.32), Pausanias wore the clothes, used the bodyguard, and ate the feasts of a Persian (Thucydides 1.130.1; Diodorus 11.44.5, 46.3). In the Greek imagination, the ideal reward for victory over the Great King was to become the Great King. Alexander the Great fulfilled this conflicted and long-standing desire after he defeated Darius III in 331/30.[65] The Greek response to the wealth and power of eastern monarchs was simultaneous aversion and desire.[66]

The transformation of Pausanias into a Persian tyrant is the founding myth of the Athenian empire. It justifies Athens' annexation of Persia's Aegean empire as an act of defeating Pausanias' *hybris*, which is the recrudescence of Xerxes' *hybris*, 'the desire to rule all Hellas'. It diverts attention from Athens' assessment of Persia's former subjects to pay an annual tribute of 460 silver talents.[67] Such an indemnity was as typically Persian as the stereotypes Pausanias allegedly enacted. The payment of tribute was a mark of subordination based upon force; it was a form of political slavery (Herodotus 1.6.2-3; 7.108.1; Aeschylus *Persians* 584-90).[68] A permanent indemnity for defeat or the admission of defeat deferred annihilation – what Homer termed 'the pitiless day' – the moment when an army destroys a community, enslaving its women and children and killing its men (Homer *Odyssey* 8.521-31; *Iliad* 9.590-6).[69] Such an arrangement was unprecedented in Greek relations.

Indemnification was the basis for the Athenian empire. Herodotus claims that many Ionians in the Persian fleet fought with valour 'to get gifts from the king' (8.10.3, 85.1), despite attempts to win them over to the Greek side or to attract Persian suspicion (8.19-22). The *Persians*' chorus asserts that Ionia provided 'the indefatigable strength of armoured men and allies of all sorts' (901-2). An Athenian envoy in Thucydides frankly expresses Athenian feeling toward the Ionians: 'They attacked us, their mother-city, with the Mede, and they did not have the heart, as we did, to destroy their property by abandoning their city. They were willing to endure their own slavery and to impose the same upon us' (6.82.4). Historians believe that this idea of the Ionians developed later; it is not attested until Thucydides' account of the Sicilian expedition.[70] But the Athenians are likely to have harboured this resentment while their city still reeked and smouldered from the Persian sack.[71] The Persians could not have mounted an invasion of such magnitude without men from Thrace, Western Anatolia, the Hellespont, Caria, and the islands to row their ships; they manned some 507 triremes (Herodotus 7.93-5, 185). After Salamis, Themistocles exacted indemnities from islands that provided rowers and ships to Xerxes' fleet, besieging Andros and extorting money from Paros and Carystus. Herodotus suggests that 'others gave and not these alone' (8.111-12).[72]

30

Themistocles sailed as far as Iasysus on Rhodes to exact penalties.[73] A decade earlier, Miltiades led 70 ships to extort 100
talents from Paros for lending a trireme to the Persian invasion
at Marathon (Herodotus 6.132-6; Herodotus explains this as a
private matter). Athens appropriated the rowers, tribute, and
ship-building capacity of Greeks formerly under Persian rule to
prevent another Persian invasion. The Greeks burned the
Ionian fleet after Mycale (9.106.1). To allow these cities to
possess ships which the Persians could use in another invasion
was too great a risk.

The purpose of Athens' empire, according to Thucydides,
'was to avenge themselves for what they had suffered by ravaging the land of the king' (1.96.1). But it was far easier to exact
compensation from Xerxes by diverting resources from subjects
whose compliance he could no longer compel (cf. 584-94). The
Athenian empire originated as a scheme for security, compensation, vengeance, and the exploitation of the resources of the
Aegean based upon naval dominance.[74] The 'allies' could no
better defend themselves against Athens in 478/77 than they
could at the height of the Athenian empire in 432. They had no
choice: they paid tribute either to Athens or to Persia.

The Athenians introduced ten 'treasurers of Greece' to handle the tribute and stored it on the island of Delos (Thucydides
1.96.2; cf. Diodorus 11.47.1). For this reason, scholars term this
phase of Athenian imperialism the 'Delian League'. The choice
of Delos fulfilled multiple objectives. The island was safe: the
Persians declared it sacrosanct in 490 (Herodotus 6.97). The
birthplace of Apollo and Artemis, Delos was an ancient centre
of Ionian worship and culture. Athens adopted Delian Apollo as
its patron against the Persians.[75] Athens had no standing temples to serve as focal point for the organization. Four treasuries
and a number of other monumental buildings sprouted on Delos
in the period 480-450.[76] By 454, the treasury was moved to
Athens and the Athenians began to dedicate one-sixtieth of the
tribute to their city goddess Athena.[77]

Athens dictated which cities paid tribute and which had
ships (Thucydides 1.96.1). City-states maintaining fleets instead of paying tribute were probably few: Samos, Chios,
Lesbos, Thasos, Naxos, and perhaps some others, such as Tenos

and Lemnos.[78] They had fought on the Greek side at Salamis or were enrolled in the Greek alliance after Mycale. These cities had the credibility to maintain a fleet: they risked Persian reprisal to fight on the Greek side. Thucydides claims that many allies initially maintained fleets, but they gradually lost the heart for war and chose to become tribute-paying subjects, forfeiting their own power while augmenting Athens' (1.99; cf. Plutarch *Life of Cimon* 11). This seems to be a self-justifying myth. Naxos, Thasos, Samos, and probably Tenos and Lemnos lost fleets from *c.* 465 to 440 (Thucydides 1.98.4, 100.2-101; 115.2-117); evidence for others is lacking. That their status slipped from ship-providers to tribute-payers confirms that tribute payment is a penalty. Thucydides, as Herodotus before him (6.11-32; 4.133-42) insists on the stereotype that the 'Ionian' chooses slavery over freedom.

Similar myth-making is apparent in Thucydides' claim that the allies were autonomous and conducted policy in assemblies in which each ally had an equal vote (1.97; 3.9-14; cf. 6.76.3-4; Diodorus 11.47.1).[79] There is no independent evidence for such assemblies and they are inherently unlikely. Even if they did exist, they did not prevent Athens from dominating the 'Delian League' in its own interests. As a general rule, tribute-payers do not get votes; and in any case, such political values played a distant second to Athens' security and compensation. The *Persians* does not call members of the Athenian empire 'free'. Their status is ambiguous: Cyrus and Darius conquered and ruled them; Xerxes lost them in naval fighting (770-1, 852-907).

The first league action in 476 aimed to secure and enrich Athens: the siege of Eion, a Persian stronghold on the Strymon River and westernmost point of Persian penetration in Europe at the time. Eion served as a supply depot on the land route from Asia to Greece (Herodotus 7.25.2, 113). The Athenians uprooted the Thracian population which supplied the fortress with food (Plutarch *Life of Cimon* 7.2), bringing its inhabitants to the brink of starvation. Taking control of Eion, the Athenians sold its population into slavery (Thucydides 1.98.1). Plutarch adds that they colonized the territory, which controlled silver and timber resources (Plutarch *Life of Cimon* 7.3, 8.2.). A scholium to Aeschines reports that this colonization effort ended in disaster.[80]

Athens' commemoration of Eion ignores the 'allies'. The city monopolized the glory of victory because it had a monopoly on power. The Athenians inscribed epigrams commemorating the siege on three herms, squared pillars representing phallic Hermes.[81] The first argues that Athenian hegemony enjoys Homeric validation (3-4). Since Homer depicted the Athenian Menestheus as a leader, 'all Athenians are leaders both in war and in manliness' (5-6; *Iliad* 2.553-4). What is true of a single Athenian in the distant past is true of all Athenians in the present; and if the epigram is a successful communication, it will remain true in the future, for the siege is a model for future generations to emulate (13-14). The epigrams are examples of the Athenian value of equality, which also governs the *Persians'* depiction of the Persian defeat: neither names a living Athenian. The name of the Athenians subsumes those of the generals. The demos, composed of equal and interchangeable members, wins the glory of victory and offers the epigrams as a 'wage' or 'reward' to its generals (11-12).

The epigrams herald the discovery of a new kind of siege, which brings 'burning hunger and chill Ares' to the enemy (8-10). They proclaim Athens' leadership of a new Trojan War and boast of surpassing the ten-year siege of Troy: Athens reduced the enemy to starvation. After Sestus, Byzantium, and Eion, Athens proclaims itself a siege power both as a mark of glory in the Greek tradition and as a reminder to the 'allies' of its source of power over them. Aeschylus' Persians similarly boast of their siege prowess (102-7, 858-79).

Phrynichus' *Phoenician Women* and Aeschylus' *Persians*

Around the time of the Eion campaign (476), Phrynichus presented a tragedy with the hero of Salamis, Themistocles, as producer; it was probably the *Phoenician Women*.[82] Basing its authority on Glaucus of Rhegium, a fifth- and fourth-century scholar who wrote on the plots of Aeschylus, the *Hypothesis* to the *Persians* claims that Aeschylus modelled his *Persians* on this play.[83] The *Hypothesis* relates that the *Phoenician Women* was set at Susa, like the *Persians*, but that the prologue featured a eunuch preparing the seats of Persia's imperial councillors and narrating Xerxes' defeat. At its outset, the *Phoenician Women* focused on the radical difference between the Persian empire and the Greek *polis* of citizen-warriors, symbolized by the eunuch.[84] The eunuch figures the lack of manliness that eastern despotism imposes on its subjects. The sole 'man' in his realm, the Great King mistrusts men.[85] Phrynichus exhibited Persia's inhuman practices; Aeschylus stages a ritual of greeting which implies that the Persian royal family was considered divine (150-8; cf. 588-90).

The *Phoenician Women* probably had two choruses: the imperial councillors and Phoenician women, who come from Sidon and Aradus to lament the deaths of their men (Phrynichus *TrGF* 1 F9). Presumably the councillors entered first; we do not know when the women entered, or whether they formed a semi-chorus or a separate chorus. The two choral groups would have allowed the distinct lyrical expression of private and public grief over the disaster, perhaps in counterpoint.

Phrynichus focused on the Phoenician naval defeat, spotlighting Athens' domination of the Aegean. Phoenicians formed the backbone of the Persian navy and faced the Athenians at Salamis (8.85.1; Diodorus 11.18.1); they play a minor role in the *Persians* (409-11, 963-6), whose catalogue lists only Egyptian sailors (35-40). Phrynichus' focus on Phoenicians might be related to the failure of his *Capture of Miletus*. The Phoenician navy was instrumental in Miletus' capture and in the ensuing violence against Greeks in Western Anatolia and the Aegean. His *Phoenician Women* might have stressed the reversal of Phoenician aggression at Salamis to vindicate his earlier drama.

Some suggest that the *Phoenician Women* introduced a second catastrophe, the defeat at Mycale.[86] If so, the chorus of imperial councillors would have lamented it. Phoenicians played no role in this land defeat (Herodotus 9.96.1); their women would not convincingly lament it. Accuracy is not required of historical drama. But errors tend to be tangential and to have dramatic force. The *Persians'* chorus of caretakers obviates such problems: a blow to any part of the empire is a blow to it.

That Themistocles produced the *Phoenician Women* has

tempted historians to see a parallel in the *Persians'* duo of Aeschylus and Pericles and to argue that the aim of both plays was to glorify Themistocles and to bolster his sagging political fortunes after Salamis.[87] As architect of Athenian naval power, general of the Athenian fleet at Salamis, and trickster who ensured the naval battle, Themistocles might hope to gain political capital by financing the *Phoenician Women*. However, he won little from it or from the *Persians* – he was ostracized sometime between 474/3 and 471/0 and later convicted of medism *in absentia*.[88] It is difficult to see how staging others' laments and explaining their sorrows could directly glorify a politician and general. The *Persians* depicts Salamis as a Persian defeat and a collective Greek victory, not as a general's victory. Any suggestion to the contrary would damage Themistocles more than help him.

Pour encourager les autres

The Athenian onslaught continued after Eion. In 475, they captured the island of Scyros, sold the native population into slavery, and colonized it (Thucydides 1.98.2; Plutarch *Life of Cimon* 8.3; Diodorus 11.60.2). Athens used this occasion to create another symbol of dominance. When the Spartans established hegemony in the Peloponnese, they marked the occasion by 'retrieving' the bones of Orestes from Tegea in Arcadia and 'returning' them to Sparta (Herodotus 1.66-8).[89] Cimon, who led the invasion of Scyros, 'discovered' the bones of Theseus on the island and 'returned' them to Athens.[90] The Athenians built a temple to house the bones, decorating it with images of Theseus as an agent of civilization, humanity, vengeance, and salvation.[91] Out of the ashes of the Persian sack, the Athenians refounded their *polis* as master of the Aegean.[92] Theseus, son of the mortal Aegeus, eponymous hero of the Aegean, and Poseidon, god of the sea, personified Athens' domination of the Aegean.[93]

Athens' sieges did not frighten all into submission; nor did the city differentiate between willing and forced collaboration with the Persians in exacting penalties. The Persians had forced Carystus, a town in southern Euboea, to join them after besieging it and destroying its crops in 490 (Herodotus 6.99.2). Eager to avoid trouble in 480, Carystus contributed one trireme to Xerxes' fleet (8.66.2). Themistocles extorted money from Carystus after Salamis and ravaged its land (8.121.1), but Carystus would not pay tribute without a fight, and Athens went to war with the town to force it into the empire (Thucydides 1.98.3).[94] Thucydides places this war between *c.* 475 and *c.* 465, after the capture of Scyros and before Athens crushed Naxos' revolt (1.98.3-4).[95] The date of Naxos' revolt is unknown, but according to Thucydides, the Athenians besieged the island and 'this was the first allied *polis* to be enslaved contrary to custom' (1.98.4). Naxos was the first ship-contributing *polis* to fall into tribute-paying status. The island joined the vast majority of Athens' 'allies'.

The Persians made an attempt to launch a fleet into the Aegean sometime between 469 and 466. Cimon, campaigning to force Carian cities into the empire, sailed with 200 triremes to the Eurymedon River in Pamphylia, where a Phoenician fleet awaited reinforcements with an infantry force.[96] The Athenians attacked the Phoenician ships in the mouth of the river, destroying the bulk of them and seizing the rest before routing the infantry and capturing a large cache of booty. Shortly afterwards, the Athenian fleet intercepted reinforcements coming from Cyprus and defeated them on the water. The Persians could no longer maintain a naval presence in the Aegean.

Athens 472

Xerxes' invasion refashioned the symbolic universe in which the Athenians lived. Mythical narratives gained new resonance as figurations of the invasion.[97] The trauma of 480/79 and subsequent victories united Athenians and became core elements of their communal identity. Athens' institutions expressed a civic form of life, were mechanisms of defence against Persia, and had enabled the city to take the leading role in the Aegean. Salamis transformed Athens' democracy. The entire citizen body faced the Persians at sea: all Athenians were the heroes of Salamis.[98] Their performance justified their political power at Athens and throughout Greece.[99] The basic values of

Athenian society – freedom, citizenship, free speech, equality, collectivity – had proved themselves superior literally under fire. Barbarian 'slavery', subjection to the Persian king, stratification based on birth and ethnic identity, and subordination to the desires of the royal *oikos* were now in the eyes of the Athenians irrefutably inferior to their own socio-political organization.

And yet both Athens and Persia relied upon numerical superiority for their power and required large amounts of money to maintain their domination. Both extorted money from communities as a contractual deferral of punitive siege. Indeed, Athenian imperialism was as old as the democracy, which planted colonies (cleruchies) in defeated communities such as Chalcis before the year 500 (Herodotus 5.77-8; cf. Salamis, ML² 14 = Fornara 44), providing land to citizens and establishing garrisons. By 472, Athens satisfied the criteria for empire: it permanently exploited Persia's former subjects by exacting tribute from them; it prosecuted yearly wars to increase or maintain its holdings; it sold defeated populations into slavery and/or took their land.[100] Athenian imperialism grew increasingly complex, self-conscious, and autocratic over time; the empire was nascent in 472.[101] By this time, however, Athens' naval power had become a means for indefinite expansion. This is a factor in assessing the play's depiction of Persia's disastrous naval imperialism, its fictionalization of the fall of Persia's empire, and the death of all Asians of military age. The defence at Salamis turned rapidly into aggressive imperialism. Though profitable, its dynamism could – and did – drive it to ruin in much the same way as Aeschylus imagines in the *Persians*.

Athens' ultimate form of control was the power to induce starvation. Athenian culture transformed this power into moral leadership; and tragedy was the pre-eminent voice of this leadership. Aeschylus' immediate aim in 472 was to win first prize in the tragic competition; but he also hoped to establish his drama as a voice of Athens' moral hegemony. He exhibited a tragedy which not only affirmed Athenian military power, but its justice, virtue, and wisdom by stressing the limits of human power in the cosmos and by depicting the fulfilment of insatiable imperialism in insatiable lament.

37

To return to our initial problem: does the *Persians* depict the disaster of Persia's empire as a spectacle to delight the victors, or does it fashion a negative example for the nascent Athenian empire? The following chapters will show how the play achieves both.

2

Fear

'The departed'

The chorus' first lines of the *Persians*, 'We are called the trusted of the Persians who departed for the land of Greece' (1-2) allude to the eunuch's first line of the *Phoenician Women*, 'these are ... of the Persians who went long ago'. The *Persians* uses the participle (*oichomenôn*), which means 'depart', 'be gone', or 'die' to indicate the Persians' absence.[1] The word conveys to the audience the feared reality that the forces have perished. The *Persians* plays on the meaning of this verb, repeating it in this ominous sense (13, 60, 178) until the messenger announces the catastrophe: 'the flower of the Persians is gone (*oichetai*), fallen in battle' (252). After that, the verb signifies the lamented Persian dead (546, 916).

This slight verbal shift signals Aeschylus' change of dramatic emphasis. Phrynichus' eunuch narrated Xerxes' defeat in the prologue; the remainder of the play lamented this *pathos* and perhaps introduced a new *pathos* to mourn. The *Persians*' dramatic conception differs. Aeschylus defers the *pathos* by exploring it as an object of fear. The dramatic characters experience, interpret, and seek to avert the realization of premonitions, a dream, a bird omen, and an historical precedent which represent Xerxes' defeat with increasing clarity and objectivity. In addition, Aeschylus pre-enacts the *pathos* as a particular version of a universal sequence of action, suffering, and emotional response: violent arrogance (*hybris*), destructive delusion (*atê*), and lament. Trying to alleviate their premonitions of disaster, the elders contribute to its fulfilment by symbolically enacting its causes and lamenting its outcome in the song and dance of the parodos.

Counting power:
the catalogue of the parodos

The elders enter reciting anapaests, expressing foreboding about Xerxes' and the army's homecoming (*nostos*). Xerxes mobilized his entire empire, but no one has arrived with news of the invasion (8-15). The chorus catalogues the leaders and the countless men who invaded – on horseback, ship, and on foot – to assuage its anxiety. Outlining the size of Persia's invading force, the elders depict the scale of Persia's *pathos*, which is also the reversal of their confidence in the power of material and numerical superiority. The catalogue is a balance sheet of Xerxes' power recited as a remedy against foreboding. The chorus displays the subconscious process by which countable resources – gold, men, materiel – produce the delusion of invulnerability, the prelude to enormous suffering.

Key terms are the adjective 'much' or 'many' (25, 46) and the prefix *poly-* ('much': 3, 9, 33, 45-6, 53).[2] Persia and its subject cities Sardis and Babylon are places of 'much gold' (3, 9, 45, 53). Numerical superiority is a source of confidence: Egyptian sailors defy counting (40); Lydia sends a 'crowd' (41-2); Babylon a mass of conscripts (53-4). In an exaggeration that rivals Herodotus', who counted 2,641,610 soldiers among Xerxes' forces (7.185.3), the chorus claims 'the entire might of Asia' (11) invaded Greece (cf. 57-8, 126-31). Persia's chieftains possess courage and the ability to inspire fear (26-9), but as the catalogue progresses, courage recedes; numbers of men and of chariots, useless in battle, become prominent (45-8). These are elements of a military pageant, an expensive display of power aimed at frightening the Greeks into submission. Such posturing – a kind of *hybris* – proves fatal to the Persians.[3]

The catalogue evokes a massive presence, making the absence of the men palpable. Its seventeen personal names create a Persian- and foreign-sounding atmosphere. Recalling the Homeric 'Catalogue of Ships', it endows the invasion with epic grandeur.[4] The leaders are not merely generals but 'chieftains of the Persians, kings subject to the Great King' (23-4), rulers (36-7), and 'captain kings' (44). The epic effect suggests the theme of a 'New Trojan War', which reflects upon Greeks

40

primarily through the Persians, who are depicted in Homeric terms.

The chorus lists five peoples of the empire: Persians (21-32), Egyptians (33-9), Lydians (41-8), Mysians (49-52), and Babylonians (52-5), adding the 'dagger-wielding people of all Asia' (56-9).[5] The Greeks of Western Anatolia are included under the Lydians (42). Apart from the Persians, this list omits fighting peoples of the empire – Medes, Sacae, Bactrians, and Indians (Herodotus 8.113). It is a small selection: Herodotus lists 46 invading peoples among Xerxes' land forces alone (7.61-80; cf. 9.27.5).

Including these particular peoples underscores the Persian confusion of wealth and military power. The chorus touts a 'crowd of delicate-living Lydians' (41), the first people to coin and use money and to engage in retail trade; the Greeks considered this lifestyle 'soft'.[6] The chorus' depiction of Mysians 'rushing to put the yoke of slavery on Hellas' (49-52) is nearly absurd: the Mysians were not a warlike people.[7] Indeed, the chorus lists peoples who paid the largest tributes, not those who contributed the most effective soldiers.[8] Babylon and Assyria together paid 1,000 talents and 500 castrated boys (Herodotus 3.92.1). Egypt was in a group that paid 700 talents in addition to grain and revenue from fish (3.91.2-3). Lydia and Mysia were in a district that paid 500 talents (3.90.1). The chorus exhibits the conflation of quantity and quality at the heart of tribute-collecting imperialism.[9] The relationship between imperial power and paying subjects is mutually enervating. Herodotus concludes his *Histories* with a parable about the tendency of empire to weaken its practitioners as they adopt the luxurious cultures of the peoples they conquer (9.122).

The catalogue is a dramatic fiction. The commanders the chorus assigns to a contingent did not actually lead it. Only five names in the catalogue – Artaphrenes (21), Megabates (22), Artembares (30), Arsames (36), and Ariomardus (37) – are borne by known Persians and kindred peoples; Artembares and Megabates were not involved in this invasion. Since transliteration from Persian into Greek was highly variable, other names may be approximations.[10]

Herodotus lists Mardonius and five other commanders of the

land forces. These include Xerxes' cousins, Tritantaechmes and Smerdomenes, and his full brother Masistes (7.82, 121.2). Another of Xerxes' full brothers, Achaemenes, his half-brother Ariabignes, who died at Salamis (8.89.1), and his second cousin, Megabazus son of Megabates, were among the commanders of the fleet (7.97, 236.1). The *Persians* names none of these men. The play shows no awareness that Xerxes' kin comprised the military command of the Persian empire. The *Persians* focuses on the triangle of father, mother, and son. The play presents Xerxes as a son and king, eliding his other kin relationships, including his marriage.[11]

Xerxes 'empties' Asia of its men, mobilizing his entire empire and losing it in defeat. The emotional correlate to Asia's emptiness is anxiety and longing for 'the flower' and 'youth' of men – in the land itself (61-2), among wives and parents (62-3, 132-9, 541-5; cf. 579-83), the city (511-12), and finally, between Xerxes and the chorus (955-1001). The chorus ends the catalogue on this ominous note.

'The wave of the sea is invincible': *hybris* and *atê*

The chorus concludes its procession into and around the orchestra and begins to sing in Ionic *a minore* metre – the cadence of the Persian voice in the play.[12] In the anapaestic prelude, Mysians rushed 'to put the yoke of slavery on Greece' (50). The elders now describe how the 'royal city-sacking army' crossed into Europe over the Hellespont, 'putting a yoke on the neck of the sea' (72). They depict Xerxes' army as an invincible force: a 'divine flock' (75), a 'great stream of men' which 'no one has the courage to keep out with strong defences' (87-9). In short, the chorus boasts, 'the army of the Persians is irresistible and its people is valorous at heart' (91-2). Energized by music and dance, the chorus sings of the transition from *hybris*, the arrogance of invulnerability, to *atê*, destructive delusion, as it narrates the Persian army's passage from Asia to Europe.[13] To enslave free peoples and sack their cities is *hybris*; to enslave the sea, divinity embodied in nature, is *atê*.

Xerxes is the focal point of the song. The 'impetuous

(*thourios*) leader of populous Asia' (73; cf. 718, 754), he bears a Homeric epithet of Ares (*Iliad* 5.30, 35, 355). His youthful, rash, and violent spirit does not so much desire battle as to terrify the Greeks into submission. A 'godlike man of a race born from gold' (79-80), Xerxes is also an earthborn monster, a chaotic rival to the gods of the sky. Like Typho, who has a hundred snake-heads, Xerxes has the darkly evil look of a 'murderous snake' and 'many hands and many sailors' (81-3).[14] He personifies his army as a chaotic force seeking to enslave Greece, 'yoking' the Hellespont and the continents it divides under his rule.

Xerxes appears 'driving an Assyrian chariot' (84). A prophecy which Herodotus reports the Delphic Oracle delivered to the Athenians contains a version of this phrase. Apollo warned the Athenians to 'flee to the ends of the earth' in the face of Xerxes' invasion, for 'Fire and sharp Ares will bring it down, driving an Assyrian-made chariot' (7.140.2). The *Persians'* use of the phrase 'driving an Assyrian chariot' suggests that this prophecy circulated sometime between 481/80, its date in Herodotus, and 473/72.[15]

'They learned to look to the sea'

The elders are supremely confident about Persian land power. They describe Persia's invincibility in wars that destroy city walls, feature cavalry battles, and drive populations from their homes as an ancient, divine dispensation (102-7). They fear that Xerxes' naval ambitions deviate from this tradition (108-13) and sense that Xerxes' desire to control the sea could be a divine trap.[16] The 'cunning-minded deceit of god' tempts mortals to their ruin (93-101).[17] The personification of this deceit, *Atê*, is like a hunting dog, enticing mortals into her cordoned-off zone and then trapping them in inescapable nets.

The keyword of this epode is 'mortal' (94, 99, 100). Whether Xerxes is a god, godlike, or mortal is a central ambiguity of the parodos. The chorus hopes that the ancient 'divinity' (*daimôn*) overseeing Persia's success in battle holds firm, and that Xerxes can prove his godhood through conquest (155-8). This hope is part and parcel of the *hybris* and *atê* that afflict not only Xerxes, but all Persia: the delusion that the king is 'divine'. The chorus is torn between Persian conventions and anxiety that the king is, after all, a mere mortal.

The elders' language betrays them. Xerxes yoked the neck of the sea (65-72), but referring to Persia's military force, the chorus declares 'the wave of the sea is invincible' (90). The moral/religious truth of the song and of the drama slips through the water imagery used to express Persian military supremacy: the sea is no man's slave.[18] In the naval battle at Salamis, the 'stream' of the Persian navy at first withstands the Greek attack, but then overwhelms itself in the narrows around the island (412-16) and 'a great sea of woes' breaks over the Persians and barbarian race (433-4). A similar, though more gruesome, inversion takes place with the idea of numerical superiority.

The parodos arouses memories of a *pathos* that is parallel to the one unfolding in the drama: the evacuation and sack of Athens. The chorus' description of the 'city-sacking army of the king' (65-6), its depiction of Xerxes 'driving an Assyrian chariot' (84), its portrayal of the Persian army as a unstoppable force (87-92), and its affirmation of Persia's divine dispensation to penetrate city walls and 'drive out cities' (102-7) may seem to be boasts, but they were realized in Xerxes' invasion, and are calculated to revive the audience's emotions of that experience. Although the *Persians* focuses on 'someone else's suffering', the play does not entirely forget Athens' 'own suffering'.

Moreover, the parodos frames the antithesis between the Persian past and present, natural and learned behaviour, land and naval power, in a way that resonates with Athenian history.[19] Athens became a naval power only in the decade before the play. For Thucydides, the Athenians became a 'naval people' in response to Xerxes' invasion (1.18.2). Herodotus pushes the time back slightly in the 480s, when Athens and Aegina were at war (7.144.2). After two generations of Athenian naval supremacy, the Syracusan Hermocrates roused his men to battle in 413 by asserting that Athenian control of the sea was neither 'ancestral' nor 'timeless'. The Athenians were more land-lubbers than the Syracusans: 'they were forced to become a naval people by the Medes' (Thucydides 7.21.3).[20]

'My heart is torn with fear': the harvest of tears

Shifting to lyric trochaic metre (lecythia), the chorus returns to the keynote of fear (114-19),[21] imagining that the women of Susa will lament in a city 'emptied of men' (*kenandron*, 119) and that the women of Cissia will shout *oa!*, a Persian exclamation of woe, and tear their linen robes in response (120-5). The elders raise the audience's expectation that choruses of women may perform laments in the drama, an expectation aroused perhaps by the choruses (or semi-choruses) of the *Phoenician Women*. But the elders themselves perform a series of laments: in tandem with a speaking actor (256-89), solo (548-83), and in concert with a singing actor, Xerxes (932-1077). The chorus describes women's laments (133-9, 537-45), but it will shout *oa!* and other exclamations of grief (570, 573, 578, 581).

The chorus' description of its fear, 'my heart wearing a black tunic, is torn with fear' (114-15) introduces the focal verbal and visual image of the drama – the tearing of clothes in grief, sorrow, and shame.[22] The image originates in the chorus' heart as a seal of sincerity, an interior sensation which the drama will gradually externalize as a grievous spectacle for the audience to witness. The Greek word 'tunic' (*chitôn*) was a loan-word from Phoenicia. The Greeks borrowed other words meaning 'linen' from the East. Linen is the material of Xerxes' bridge cables, the chest protection of eastern warriors, ships' sails and tackle, robes, veils, and the Ionian tunic.[23] Linen cables hold the hull of a trireme together like a 'girdle'.[24] Linen is the fabric that is torn in this play about the shattering of a fleet, the hacking to pieces of men, and the self-mutilating lament it causes in Persia.

The final strophic/antistrophic pair, sung in the play's metre of lament, lyric iambic, summarizes the parodos. It establishes an inverse relationship between Xerxes' 'yoking' of Asia and Europe to put the 'yoke of slavery' on Greece and the marriage 'yoke'.[25] The bridges enabled Xerxes to 'empty Asia', leading soldiers and horsemen into battle 'like a swarm of bees' (126-9). In response to the emptiness, Persian wives 'fill their beds with tears' (133-4), and 'each and every Persian woman ... is left yoked alone with longing for her husband' (135-9). The Queen's dream will play on the yokes of empire and marriage. The image of the yoke figures the *hybris* and *atê* of imperialism. It represents the desire to enslave and exploit through conquest which transgresses fundamental boundaries. The shattering of this yoke destroys the manpower of Asia, its *hêbê* ('vital youth'), the capacity of Persia to reproduce itself through marriage and inheritance, and Persia's 'happiness in prosperity' (*olbos*), causing insatiable lament in Persia.

Hybris, atê, lament

The structure of the parodos is that of the tragedy: *hybris* (65-107), *atê* (93-101, 108-13), and lament (114-25). Spellbound by the gleam of gold, the fearsome appearance of men and materiel, and the 'divinity' of their king, the elders hymn the *hybris* of Persian imperialism.[26] They do not use the word *hybris* – like another key idea of the play, freedom (*eleutheria*), whose root appears only three times (twice at 403, 593), *hybris* occurs just twice in the play (808, 821). The elders are not conscious of their state of mind and do not see the invasion as *hybris*; rather, they intuitively grasp that the invasion entails *atê* (93-101), which implies *hybris*. The elders recreate the invasion as a spectacle of invincibility to alleviate their fear, singing and dancing the sequence of action by which an empire strives beyond its limits and laments its losses.[27] Darius will make this pattern explicit (821-2). Prior to this, the drama presents it as a recurrent pattern for the audience to contemplate.

The parodos establishes the terms for the reversal of Persia's imperialism. Countless numbers of sailors, ships, chariots, horsemen, and archers will be reduced to nothing; their pains and corpses will defy counting (429-32). Rather than inspire fear (27, 48), they will experience it in the face of the Greek fleet (386-93). The Persians, 'an invincible wave of the sea' will become sea-tossed corpses crashing against the shores of Salamis (274-7, 302-30, 419-21, 962-6, 974-7). Their armada will become fragments of wood, used to club and slice them like fish (408-28). Their chieftain-kings and captain-kings (23-4, 44) will be butchered like meat (441-64). Wealth expended to enslave the Hellespont and Greece will destroy Persia's happiness in prosperity (249-52) and purchase the luxuriant lament of Persian wives (537-45). The yoke will be shattered; the empire will crumble (181-99, 584-94, 852-907). And finally, 'the godlike man of a race born from gold' and shepherd of 'a divine herd', Xerxes, will appear in rags as a fallen mortal to re-enact and bewail his disaster (73-80, 181-99, 832-51, 908-1037).

'At the tomb of Darius'?

The elders return to reciting anapaests, exhorting themselves to consider the progress of the war 'sitting at/in this ancient building' (140-3). The word translated 'building' (*stegos*) is ambiguous: it could mean a roofed structure or a containing vessel such as an urn or a tomb. The *Hypothesis* to the *Persians* sets the play at Darius' tomb. The most economical hypothesis concerning the play's setting integrates this roofed structure and Darius' tomb, making it either adjacent to or coextensive with it.[28] The difficult problem is whether the tomb and the *stegos* are the same structure.[29] Some believe the epithet 'ancient' (*archaion*) applied to the *stegos* cannot apply to Darius' tomb, since he died in 486, six years before the dramatic date of the play (but fourteen years before its performance).[30] If the chorus' fear of Darius can be 'old' (*archaios*, 694-6) and 'ancient' (*palaion*, 703), however, then perhaps anything associated with him might be considered 'old', or 'reverend'. Darius is the 'ancient ruler' (657-8; cf. 856) even though, from the perspective of the play, his rule ended only six years ago. The epithet *archaios* need not rule out a reference to Darius' tomb. The simplest solution is to posit a temporary wooden structure (*skênê*) as a combined tomb/council chamber. It remains possible that the *skênê* represents a council chamber and Darius' tomb is a separate feature of the stage space, though as we shall see, this complicates the staging of Darius' arrival. One thing is certain: the *skênê* does not represent the royal palace, as it does it in the *Agamemnon* and *Libation Bearers*.[31] The palace is off stage in the *Persians* (159-60, 228-30, 524-31, 832-4, 849-50, 1038, 1068, 1076-7).

Others think that the *stegos* is an imagined council chamber.[32] The chorus' reference to 'this ancient building' cues the audience to imagine its existence; it is not physically present.

Moreover, the argument goes, the theatre had no temporary wooden building (*skênê*) to function as a backdrop to the acting space until Aeschylus' *Oresteia* of 458.[33] But why would the chorus say 'sitting in/at this (*tod'*) ancient building' unless a building were there?[34] 'Let us take good and deep-counselling thought' (141-3) suffices to convey the intention to deliberate. As it is, the chorus' words only indicate an intention to sit and deliberate. They do not enter the building to sit in council; the Queen's entrance interrupts them.

The council chamber/tomb remains before the eyes of the audience throughout the play: this is where all the stage action takes place. There is no need to posit changes of scene in the *Persians*, as actually happens in Aeschylus' *Eumenides*, where the scene changes from the Delphic Oracle to the Athenian Acropolis and Areopagus at the base of the Acropolis.[35]

The bow and the spear: a clash of cultures

The elders want to consider the question 'whether the draw of the bow is the winner or the might of spear-tipped lance has won' (147-9). Since they have no information for such a council, some have viewed this motivation as a result of Aeschylus' imitation of the *Phoenician Women*, which opened with a council scene.[36] Aeschylus alludes to Phrynichus' drama; but he makes something different of the council scene. The elders deliberate at the wrong time; the Queen's entrance interrupts them before they begin. Such mistiming is characteristic of the *Persians*' staging. Moreover, the chorus expects a confrontation of land forces – bow and spear – but a naval battle is decisive.

Throughout the parodos, the chorus stressed Persia's bowmen (26, 30, 55, 85-6). The spear and the bow are metonyms which simplify the national characters of Greeks and barbarians. They symbolize the quality and courage of free men and the quantity and cowardice of Persian subjects (cf. Herodotus 7.226). Archers fight from afar, hesitant to risk their lives in battle, but eager to kill. This defines the Greek view of barbarian warfare; Salamis and Psyttalia will exemplify it. Greek hoplites, by contrast, fight face-to-face, protected by bronze armour.[37] They value their persons – which are their own and not a master's – but risk their lives as the price of inflicting death. When he brings news of the disaster, the messenger declares 'many missiles all mixed together came futilely from Asia to the land of Zeus, the land of Greece' (268-71). They were useless in the naval battle (278-9). In the *kommos*, Xerxes exhibits his nearly empty quiver: multitudes of arrows, men, and money are ineffective against valorous Greeks (1019-25).

This antithesis does not tell the full story. Athenians wield the bow at Psyttalia (459-61); the Mysian leaders Tharybis and Mardon are 'anvils of the spear' (51-2; cf. 320-1). Darius 'acquired great wealth for his children with the point of a spear' (754-5).[38] Dadaces falls from his ship under the blow of a spear (304-5), but the conspicuous spear in the *Persians* is that of Spartan hoplites – the 'Dorian spear' – which lurks menacingly in the future of the drama (816-17). The bow and the spear symbolize a cultural difference between Greeks and Persians.

'A light like the eyes of the gods': conquest, wealth and *olbos*

The Queen's entrance sets a pattern for the play's stage action. Each entry interrupts an action, defers an exit, or displaces another entry.[39] The mistiming of the play's staging is symptomatic of Persia's misfortune. The Persians are unable to act at the right time or in the right measure. In Homer, effective performance in the proper sequence and at the appropriate time is termed 'in order' (*kata kosmon*).[40] The staging of the play visualizes the Persian failure to act *kata kosmon*. The concept becomes increasingly important as the Persian forces display good order (*kosmos*) at the wrong time and dissolve into disorderly (*akosmos*) flight in the heat of battle (374, 422, 470, 481). The play will pivot on an attempt to provide Xerxes with a new royal robe (*kosmos*, 833, 849) to replace symbolically the loss of his 'array (*kosmos*) of men' and empire (920). The narrative and staging of the play treat the lack of *kosmos* in the full sense of the word as endemic to the Persians.

The Queen enters on a chariot, a visible correlate to the verbal image of Xerxes on an Assyrian chariot (81-6). 'A light equal to the eyes of the gods' (150), she arrives from her palace, 'furnished in gold' (159). Xerxes, by contrast, has the dark look of a snake on his chariot (81-2). It is difficult to tell when she began to enter.[41] She is aware that the chorus sang 'my heart is torn with fear' (160; 114-15), and may be visible to the audience at this point. In an ideal staging, the audience would see her chariot as the chorus describes Xerxes on his chariot. An 'ornament of super-rich luxury' ([Aeschylus] *Prometheus Bound* 465-6), the chariot is a symbol of *hybris* – military posturing which threatens conquest and the dispossession of the vanquished (41-8, 81-107, 181-99; cf. Aeschylus *Agamemnon* 750-974). It represents visually the theme of this scene: the expenditure of wealth to achieve conquest as a condition for 'happiness in prosperity' (*olbos*). The parodos and this scene juxtapose two sides of Persian culture: violent acts of enslavement and city-sacking and bedazzled servitude to the royal *oikos*.

The elders state their intention to bow in obeisance and address the Queen in a formal greeting (151-4). For the Greeks, *proskynêsis*, a Persian social ritual by which inferiors bow from their knees to greet superiors, defined Persia as a slave society.[42] Since all mortals were inferior to the Persian king, *proskynêsis* was required in his presence (Herodotus 7.136.1; Plutarch *Life of Themistocles* 27). The Greeks reserved this gesture for gods – hence their belief that the Persian king was considered divine.[43] Greeting the Queen as wife and mother of a god – unless Xerxes fails – the chorus sees the invasion as a test of Xerxes' divinity (155-8). The *Persians* positions Xerxes at three thresholds: a youth on the verge of manhood, a son trying to emulate and avenge his father, and a mortal seeking divinity.

The chorus addresses the Queen in trochaic tetrameters. Aristotle describes this metre as characteristic of primitive drama, whose poetry was more danceable and suitable to satyrplay (*Poetics* 1449a21-23).[44] Its use here indicates emotional excitement as the chorus bows before the Queen. The Queen responds in the same metre to indicate her emotional distress (her language is barely coherent). She establishes sympathy with the chorus (161). The chorus depicted Xerxes' invasion from multiple perspectives – the Persian tradition of land conquest, the wives and mothers of Persian soldiers, the earth of

Asia, the cosmos in which gods maintain supremacy over mortals through deceit. The Queen offers a single perspective, that of the royal *oikos*.[45]

The Queen expresses her fear as a proverb 'that "great Wealth (*Ploutos*) lifting a cloud of dust from the ground, overturn with its foot the prosperous happiness" (*olbos*) Darius won not without one of the gods' (161-4). This proverb is not otherwise attested and its meaning is debated.[46] Its obscurity arises from a mixture of metaphors: Wealth is an army raising a cloud of dust and a figure which overturns *olbos* 'with its foot'.[47] Groeneboom suggests that *Ploutos* is a horse driving a chariot containing *olbos*, which is overturned.[48] This fits the visual meaning of the chariot on the stage. Though it can be specifically connected to horsemen and chariots, a cloud of dust is an index of an army on the move, as smoke is an index of fire.[49] The Queen fears that Xerxes' expenditure of wealth in a failed bid to conquer Greece will subvert the *olbos* Darius acquired by divine favour.

Olbos is a central concept of the *Persians*. The tragedy dramatizes Persia's loss of *olbos* in a failed invasion. *Olbos* is a quality of *ploutos* connoting happiness in prosperity, divine favour, good fortune, good repute, and the capacity to transmit these to the next generation. In Homer *ploutos* and *olbos* are sometimes paired, but *olbos* appears in contexts in which a wealthy man wins honour from his people, makes a good marriage, has fine sons, and perpetuates his legacy.[50]

Olbos is notoriously impermanent. One way of dealing with its instability is to claim that it bears no relation to a person's moral worth: 'Zeus gives *olbos* to mortals, both to the good and to the bad, however he wishes to each' (*Odyssey* 6.186-9).[51] Another is to seek moral-religious explanations for its possession or lack (Hesiod *Works and Days* 280-5).[52] That *olbos* is a permanent attribute of the dead is a central tenet of the Eleusinian Mysteries (Homeric *Hymn to Demeter* 480-2). In his confrontation of Solon and Croesus, Herodotus depicts this idea as essential to the ideology of the Greek *polis* in contrast to that of eastern despotism, which conflates *olbos* with such temporary goods as wealth and power (1.30-3).[53]

The Queen is in a double bind. She realizes that 'when wealth lacks manhood (*anandrôn*)' it fails to command the masses' fear and respect; it is not honourable (166).[54] The Queen reveals later in the drama that Xerxes invaded Greece for this reason. He endured taunts that Darius' conquests provided wealth for his children, but that he failed to add to his paternal *olbos* because of 'lack of manliness' (*anandria*, 753-8). At the same time, she understands that it is impossible to realize social and political power without a sufficient quantity of wealth: 'for those who lack wealth the light does not shine to the extent of their strength' (167). Xerxes' chariot and serpentine gaze and the Queen's chariot and divine radiance converge at this point. They are the origin and final product of a process of conquest, dispossession of others' wealth, and legitimation of that wealth as power and blessedness (*olbos*).[55] Wealth derived from conquest has the 'honour' (*timê*) required for its realization as socio-political power; but it must be reinvested to renew and extend that power. Conquest, wealth, and *olbos* form a potentially endless cycle. The Queen worries that Xerxes' defeat may end it.

The real object of the Queen's fear is the untimely death of her son, whom she calls the 'eye', the source of her household's light and life, its best and most vital part, the metaphorical root or bud from which a family reproduces itself.[56] The *Persians* treats Xerxes as a youth with no children, the only son of Darius and the Queen (Darius has other sons, presumably by other women, 717, 754). Xerxes is the 'eye of the house', which the Queen glosses as 'the presence of the master' (168-9).[57] If Xerxes dies, the royal *oikos* will be unable to replicate itself.[58] The master (*despotês*) will be absent; the *oikos* will be blinded, fall into darkness, die.[59] This is the ultimate tragedy in the Greek universe; but it will not befall the Persian royal *oikos*. The 'eye' of the house will survive, but only at the cost of Xerxes' 'eye', the best and most trusted segment of his kingdom (441-4, 955-1001).

That the 'eye' of the house is its source of light and life becomes clear after the messenger announces Xerxes' survival (299). The Queen rejoices in the news as a great 'light' and a 'bright day after a black night' for the royal household (300-1). While the light of the royal *oikos* shines, 'murky grief' (535-6) and a 'Stygian mist' (669-70) descend on Persia. The light emanating from the wealth of the royal house, personified by the 'eye of the house', Xerxes, is the 'evil eye': the gaze that causes blight, death, and barrenness.[60] Xerxes' malevolent, dark-blue look (81-2) also emanates from his 'dark-eyed ships' (559) – the hulls of triremes were decorated with marble circles, painted as eyes.[61] Both will be averted at Salamis by Greek ships and by the light of the sun. The white horses carrying the chariot of the day into the sky will shine upon the Greek defence against Xerxes' Assyrian chariot (386-7).

The land of the Ionians

Changing to iambic trimeter, the main spoken metre of drama, the Queen confides that she has experienced many dreams 'from the time my son raised an army and departed, wanting to sack the land of the Ionians' (177-8). The *Persians* exploits its depiction of Persian speech to create solidarity among Ionians. Near Eastern peoples called all Greeks 'Ionians'; Persians called them and their land *Yaunâ*.[62] But accuracy is not the principle governing the use of ethnic terms in the drama. The Persians call themselves, their land, race, language, and army 'barbarian(s)', the Greek word for non-Greeks.[63] Persians in the play distinguish between Ionian and Dorian (183, 816), but sometimes fail to distinguish themselves from the Medes, a different Iranian people with whom the Greeks conflated them (236, 791).[64] Darius, a Persian, traces the origins of his kingship to an eponymous ancestor of the Medes, Medus (765).

When the Queen refers to the 'land of the Ionians', she speaks in a non-Greek way; but a reference to ethnic Ionians is irrepressible.[65] The lyrical portions of the play which attribute responsibility to 'Greeks' for the Persian defeat at Salamis exclusively use the term 'Ionian(s)' (560-4, 950-4, 1011-13, 1025). The play underwrites Ionian naval supremacy even as it implicitly remembers a history of Ionian pain and considers the liabilities of naval supremacy: Cyrus' conquest of Ionia (770-1), the sufferings of city-states involved in the Ionian revolt (852-907), the sack of Athens (807-14), and the disaster of Xerxes' naval imperialism. The play's use of Ionic *a minore* metre and its high incidence of Ionic forms suggest a tragic intersection between the 'delicately living Ionians', whose cities and temples the Persians destroyed, and 'Ionian Ares', the Athenian sailors who 'cut', 'reaped', and 'harvested' the Persians (950-4), just as the Persians destroyed Athens' land and city.[66] To be called 'Ionian' is to be addressed as a Persian subject. Herodotus thought that 'The rest of the Ionians and the Athenians flee the name, because they do not want to be called Ionians and even now many of them seem to me to be ashamed by the name' (1.143.2-3; cf. 4.142). In the *Persians*, the name of the Ionians unites pride of victory and lament for a history of pain.

The yoke shattered: the Queen's dream

The Queen asks the chorus to advise her on a remedy for a dream she had last night and a bird omen she witnessed this morning, calling on the 'trusted old men' to be her advisors; they readily agree (170-5). The elders are indeed 'called the trusted' as they claim in the parodos (2, 171). They suppress their premonitions of disaster to hearten the Queen. In cultures that lack freedom, the function of interpretation and speech is to gratify the sovereign. When the elders imagine the fall of the Persian empire as a result of the king's loss of dominating force, the people speak freely (584-94). Herodotus develops this aspect of Persian despotism: the risk of free speech to Xerxes is decapitation.[67] The *Persians* is milder. The wisdom of frightening the Queen at this stage is debatable; and the Queen expects frankness from the chorus (520).

The Queen dreamed of two large and beautiful women, both well dressed, one in Persian, the other in Dorian clothing – the Ionian tunic is similar to the Persian (181-5).[68] Most take the women to represent Greece and Persia, but some consider them personifications of Europe and Asia, while others think they represent mainland and eastern Greeks.[69] Greece and Persia are the central referents: they wear Dorian and Persian clothing, are 'sisters of the same race', and fight one another; Greece (not Europe) shatters Xerxes' yoke at Salamis. The women are 'sisters of the same race' (185-6) through Perseus, son of Danae fathered by Zeus in a golden shower. Perseus' son Perses is the eponymous ancestor of the Persians. Persians express this view in the play (79-80, 145-6); the historical Persians adopted this myth as propaganda.[70] The Queen tempers Persian foreignness, making conflict with Greece conform to an expectation of tragedy – violence among kin (Aristotle *Poetics* 1453b15-26).[71] That she terms the struggle between the two women 'internecine strife' or 'civil war' (*stasis*) reinforces the bond between the peoples (188-9). The difference between them is cultural and behavioural: they wear different clothing; they have been allotted different lands (186-7). One is proud to bear the yoke; the other will not endure it (192-6).

When Xerxes learns of their *stasis*, he tries to control and mollify them: putting a yoke upon their necks, he fastens them to his chariot (189-92). The woman in Persian clothing proudly obeys; the other bucks, tears the harness to pieces, shakes off the bit, and shatters the yoke through the middle (192-6). Xerxes falls and his father stands beside him, pitying him (197-8). When Xerxes sees his father, he tears his robes (198-9).

The dream figures Xerxes' invasion of Greece as an act of civilization – taming a wild horse and healing internal strife. From the Greek perspective, it is an act of enslavement, an attempt to exploit their lives and labours and to deprive them of their humanity. In the *Prometheus Bound*, Prometheus boasts 'I was the first to yoke wild beasts ... as slaves ... so that they might be successors of mortal bodies' greatest toils' (462-5). The Greeks will not endure this exploitation. Indomitable, they shatter Xerxes' yoke of slavery.

The Queen's dream elides any sense of geographical, historical, or religious transgression that made the chorus anxious. It is a mother's dream, the vision of a son's perverse marriage, an attempt to marry two women simultaneously.[72] The chorus indicated this dimension of Xerxes' 'yoke' across the Hellespont in the parodos – it left Persian wives 'yoked alone' (126-39). A tale Herodotus tells transfers Xerxes' yoking of two continents to his desire for two women – his brother's wife and daughter. Xerxes desired his brother's wife, so he married his son Darius to his brother's daughter hoping to get her mother – a kind of double marriage that goes awry, for Xerxes falls in love with his son's wife. Xerxes' wife finds out and mutilates his brother's wife, blaming her for Xerxes' love-affair with Darius' wife. Xerxes ultimately has to have his brother killed (9.108-13).[73]

The Queen's prophetic dream prefigures events in the dramatic narrative in a different register. In the dream, Xerxes tears his robes as a response to his father's pity: he laments his failure in his father's eyes (197-9). In the messenger's narrative, Xerxes tears his clothes out of grief at the depth of the disaster he witnesses (465-8). Nor does the dream envision events as they will be staged in the play. Like the chorus' vision of two female choruses in antiphonal lament (114-25), the Queen's dream contains an element the drama leaves unfulfilled. Darius shows little pity for his son. He censures his aims and actions as a 'disease of the mind' (744-51), a defiance of his commands (782-3), and the worst disaster in Persian history (759-64, 784-6). Darius envisions Xerxes' return in rags (832-8), ordering the chorus to educate him (829-31) and the Queen to palliate his grief and shame (832-8, 845-51). To this extent, he shows pity. In the staged play, the chorus substitutes for the father in the dream, instilling shame in Xerxes (913-6, 932-4) and pitying him (1030-2).

The bird omen

After her dream, the Queen tries to make apotropaic sacrifice of a *pelanos*, a porridge-like substance consisting of honey, oil, and meal (200-4). A *pelanos* can be burned and offered to the gods of the sky or poured to the gods of the earth.[74] Hoping to communicate with the gods above, the Queen is unable to make the offering. A bird omen pre-empts it: a hawk chases an eagle to the altar of Apollo, plucking the eagle's head with its talons; the eagle cowers, allowing the hawk to maul it (205-10). The omen defers the Queen's *pelanos*-offering until after news of defeat, when it is directed to the gods of the underworld to release Darius' soul (524-6, 606-21). The final *pelanos*-offering of the drama, the blood of Persian warriors at Plataea, is a payment for the Persian destruction of Greek temples, altars, and looting of statues (807-20).

The omen represents Xerxes' flight from Greece and his inability to defend himself from counter-aggression. Herodotus reports that an omen appeared to Xerxes as he crossed the Hellespont: a horse gave birth to a hare. The omen symbolized the entire invasion: 'Xerxes was destined to drive an army upon Greece with the greatest pride, pomp, and circumstance, but later running for his life, he was destined to arrive at the same place' (7.57.1). The *Persians'* omen figures the difference between Xerxes as depicted in the parodos – the hybristic and god-like leader of a 'divine herd' – and in the *kommos*, a defeated king in rags leading a self-mutilating lament.

The Greeks considered the eagle emblematic of the Persian empire.[75] The hawk or falcon, sometimes associated with Apollo, mauls the eagle at Apollo's altar. One of Apollo's names, Phoebus, has a sound similar to the word for fear, *phobos*. The two words create a jingle in the Queen's description (206). But more than sound-play is involved. Pythian Apollo received tithes from the spoils of all the Greek victories over the Persians.[76] And Athens organized its empire around Delian Apollo. The omen has a meaning beyond the drama, symbolizing Delian Apollo's 'ravaging' the Persian eagle just as the Athenians sought vengeance 'by ravaging the land of the king' (Thucydides 1.96.1). The omen refers specifically to Xerxes' flight from Greece, but it also figures the counter-offensive after Mycale: Xerxes 'cowered' while Athens annexed his Aegean empire.

The Queen's dream is a *mise en abyme* – a part of a work of art which depicts the whole in miniature.[77] It depicts the essence of the narrative and plays on possibilities for its dramatic enactment. The omen figures Xerxes' flight and homecoming but also leads beyond the work of art to the work of empire.

Isonomia and accountability

The Queen informs the chorus that Xerxes' success would make him a 'man to be admired', but failure and survival mean 'he rules this land just the same – he is not accountable to the *polis*' (211-14). Xerxes will monopolize the glory of victory and become a god, but he is unaccountable for defeat (Herodotus 8.102-3). Herodotus associates *isonomia* with four practices: referral of decisions to an assembly of citizens, majority rule, selection of offices by lot, and accountability for office-holders (3.80.6). The

Persians implicates Persia's lack of *isonomia* in the tragedy. One man – Xerxes – rules Asia as his household slaves; he survives and remains king, while all men of military age in his empire perish because of his violent arrogance (*hybris*) and delusions of divinity (*atê*). Darius will explain that Zeus punishes humans for 'excessively arrogant intentions' (827-8), and Xerxes will have to account for the men he abandoned in Greece (908-1007). But the final lament of the play dramatizes the Queen's meaning: Xerxes takes control of the elders and scores his defeat, shame, and sorrow onto their bodies. In this regard, Persia is antithetical to Athens, where successful leaders faced the wrath of the demos for failures real or imagined.[78] The Athenians had to recall Xanthippus and Aristides from ostracism to lead them against the Persians; they ostracized Themistocles either before or within two years after the *Persians*.

Returning to trochaic tetrameters, the elders prescribe apotropaic and propitiatory sacrifices to the gods (215-19) and liquid offerings to the Earth, to the dead, and to Darius to bring success to light but to keep disaster in the darkness (219-23). The chorus adopts an optimistic tone (224-5), delighting the Queen: she views the chorus' advice as a good omen 'for my child and my house' (226-7), ignoring the chorus' reference to 'the city and all your nearest and dearest' (219). The prospect of a ritual solution briefly relieves the Queen and chorus of their premonition and anxiety.

Cue for disaster: Marathon

Before the Queen exits, she asks the chorus about the aims of the invasion and nature of Athens (230-45). Queen and chorus conduct a dialogue in single lines of verse, stichomythia ('talking in lines'), which often builds toward a climax. The Queen establishes herself in the role she will play in the next half of the episode: questioner. Her questions conclude with a mention of the last bad omen for the invasion, the defeat of Darius' 'large and beautiful army' (244) at Marathon, the messenger's cue to arrive and announce the disaster at Salamis. Often considered an excuse to praise Athens, the scene is akin to the 'Teichoscopia' in *Iliad* 3.139-244: a non-Greek adversary comes to

know the Athenians, who stand for the Greeks, later than our
sense of narrative logic permits. Even so, the timing of this
scene is out-of-kilter, as are the chorus' council and the Queen's
apotropaic sacrifices.

The Queen asks about Athens' location (230-1). The chorus'
answer, 'far away at the settings of the waning sun' (232)
locates Athens in the gloom of Hades, a place of darkness and
death, setting up the images of corpses littering the sea and
shore around Salamis. Athens will be a land of death for the
Persians. Since Greeks imagined their opposition to Persians in
terms of sun and moon, the description of Athens' location may
seem favourable to the Persians. In Herodotus, just after
Xerxes leaves Sardis for the Hellespont, there is a solar eclipse.
His *magi* interpret it as a favourable omen: it predicts the
'abandonment' (eclipse) of the Greek city-states, since the sun
was the Greeks' predictor and the moon the Persians' (7.37.2-
3).[79] The perishing sun may prefigure the defeat of the Greeks
from the Persian perspective.

Such confidence may explain the Queen's next question –
why Xerxes 'desires' to capture Athens (223). The verb 'capture'
applies to animals and suggests the Persian practice of forming
human dragnets to 'hunt' the people of a *polis* (Herodotus
6.31).[80] The image of the invasion as a hunt dovetails with the
chorus' earlier worry that Xerxes may be unable to escape the
hunting nets of *Atê* (93-101). The Great King, who depicted
himself as a hunter, will be caught in the nets of a superior
hunter – who turns out to be a fisherman.[81]

The chorus' answer, 'all Greece would become the king's
subject' if Xerxes captures Athens (233-4), expresses an Atheno-
centric view of the invasion. Athens is a synecdoche for Greece.
Herodotus describes Xerxes' invasion as nominally directed at
Athens but aimed at subjugating 'all Greece' (7.138.1). Athens
is the key to the Persian conquest. The city 'held the balance' in
the war: whichever side it joined was likely to win (7.139.5).
Herodotus believes the Athenians deserve the title 'saviours of
Greece' (ibid.).[82]

Given the Persian stress on countable objects, it would be
surprising if the Queen did not ask about quantities of men and
money. The chorus answers the Queen's question about the size

of Athens' army (235) in terms of its quality (236), but this description and a reminder of the quantity of 'woes' Athens' army inflicted at Marathon make no impression on her. The Queen's question about whether Athens has 'sufficient wealth for its homes' (237), reinforces her fixation on the *oikos* as opposed to the *polis* and differentiates the private value of Persia's wealth from the public value of Athens'. According to tradition, Themistocles persuaded the Athenians to use a surplus from their silver mines to build a fleet of triremes in the period 483-480 rather than distribute ten drachmae to each male citizen as first planned (Herodotus 7.144.1-2; cf. Thucydides 1.14.3; [Aristotle] *Constitution of the Athenians* 22.7). Athens' silver is collective wealth, the material embodiment of shared values and interests; Persian gold is private, luxury wealth, expended to buy Xerxes' immortality.[83] Athens' 'fount of silver, a treasure trove of the soil', contrasts with Persian gold and tribute extorted by force (238, 584-90) and suggests Xerxes' imperialist greed: he desired Athens' 'fount of silver' but discovered 'a fount of woes for his nearest and dearest' (743).

Recalling the description of the Persian army as a 'divine herd' (73), the Queen asks, with reference to the Athenians, 'what shepherd is set over them and who is master (*despotês*) over the army'? (241). The chorus' answer, 'they are called neither the slaves nor the subjects of any man' (242), concentrates the thrust of the scene, the despotic grip of the royal *oikos* on Persia and the consequent inability of Persians to hold the king accountable and to live as free men and citizens. The Greeks live and fight with no master above them to monopolize the material and symbolic rewards of their lives and labours. They fight because they have a stake in the battle: their families, heritage, glory, honour, profit, freedom (402-5; cf. Herodotus 5.78; Hippocrates, *Airs, Waters, Places* 16, 23). The Persians, by contrast, fight as slaves of the Great King (Herodotus 7.135.3), who takes credit for victory, but diverts responsibility for defeat onto others (8.102). For this reason, henchmen must drive his soldiers into battle under the whip (7.56.1, 103.4, 223.3; Xenophon *Anabasis* 3.4.26).[84]

That warriors would remain to face the enemy without compulsion confounds the Queen (243). The chorus reminds her that the Athenians destroyed Darius' 'great and beautiful army' (244). The second reference to Marathon disturbs her: 'you say terrible things for the parents of those who are gone to consider' (245). With these words, the chorus announces the arrival of the messenger, whose 'Persian running' indicates 'he brings some clear outcome, good or bad to hear' (246-9).[85]

3

Pathos

'A multitude of woes'

The messenger announces the *pathos* as a realization of the chorus' and Queen's fears. The 'flower' (*anthos*) of Persian men which the chorus ominously described as 'departed' (60) is now 'departed, fallen in battle' (252). Persia's *olbos* is ruined in a 'single blow' (251-2; 163-4). The defeat is total: 'the entire army of the barbarians has been destroyed' (255). The swiftness and completeness of the reversal belie the five generations of conquest that built the Persian empire (759-86).[1] If any narrative prior to Thucydides' account of the Athenian invasion of Sicily in 415-413 (7.61-87) makes palpable the catastrophic reversal and total defeat of an imperialist invasion, it is the messenger-speech of the *Persians*. The point of the messenger's gruesome detail is not so much 'to revel in the destruction of the Persians', as to recall the merciless and divinely sanctioned violence that defenders of their homeland inflict on invaders, and to stress the multiplier-effect distance from one's own land exerts on a failed invasion.[2] Invaders aim to 'enslave' a community and subject it to unspeakable degradation. Defenders therefore fight without restraint, righteously slaughtering them; survivors must abandon their dead. The *pathos* of the *Persians* is a story of interlocking military disaster and glorious defence, both a memory of the Greeks' 'day of freedom' and an exemplum of an invasion gone disastrously wrong.

The messenger decries his role as the first to announce the catastrophe, but declares it 'necessary to unfold the entire suffering' (*pathos*, 253-5). The metaphor derives from papyrus rolls, which were unfolded to read.[3] According to Herodotus, amanuenses accompanied Xerxes to record the peoples of his invading force and the name, patronymic, city-state, and captain of sailors who excelled at Salamis (7.100.1; 8.90.4). The *Persians'* messenger lists details – names, military titles, and national origins – as if derived from written records. Around the time of the *Persians*, the Athenians began to inscribe lists of their war dead by tribe, including military title or function, and, if non-Athenians, place of origin, to preserve their names and 'immortal glory'.[4] Persian deaths, however, are not glorious: they are a 'disgrace to the Persians' (332). Invading Greece with men and resources beyond count, Xerxes draws down 'a multitude of pains' (477) and 'a multitude of woes' (429) upon his people: 'never on a single day has a multitude of so great a number of men died' (431-2). Ten days would not suffice for the messenger to tell the entire tale (429-30).[5]

'How I lament when I remember Athens'

The chorus laments in response to the messenger's announcement, performing the role it envisioned for Persian women (114-25). For Herodotus, news of the naval defeat interrupts Persian celebration over the capture of Athens (8.99). The Persians break into 'boundless lament' and 'tear their tunics' (8.99). Xerxes' arrival stops their lament, which they perform out of fear for him rather than for grief over the ships (8.99.2-100.1). Herodotus corrects the *Persians*, which stages its most intense lament at Xerxes' homecoming and stresses Persia's anguish over ships (548-64, 678-80, 950-4, 1008-37, 1074-5). In the initial lament of the *Persians*, neither the messenger nor the chorus mentions Xerxes. At the moment of *pathos*, Aeschylus' Persians are members of a *polis* rather than slaves of a king. This continues until Xerxes re-establishes control in the *kommos*.

Chorus and messenger perform an epirrhematic lament which divides the first episode into two 'acts'.[6] The messenger speaks in iambic trimeters; the chorus sings in lyric iambics. They respond to one another, building on each others' words, and growing in sympathy as the exchange develops. They first register the shock of total defeat (256-61).[7] As is the convention, the messenger affirms that he was an eye-witness (266-7). Dramatic convention and extra-dramatic reality merge if Aeschylus played the role of messenger: he was witness to the disaster.

The second strophe and antistrophe focus on Persia's deluded numerical superiority and lack of order. The chorus bewails the ineffectiveness of 'the many arrows all mixed together' that went to Greece (268-71). The messenger describes the carnage in terms of Persian numbers (*plêthos*): the corpses of the men Xerxes emptied from Persia fill (*plêthousi*) the shores of Salamis (272-3; cf. 419-21), just as Persian wives filled their empty beds with tears in longing for their husbands (133-4). The principle of reciprocity, action balanced and redeemed by suffering, operates both at the level of verbal imagery and as a law of cosmic order in the play. The chorus seeks to impose ritual order on the horrific spectacle by imagining Persian corpses in a sea-tossed funeral procession (274-7).[8]

The pair focuses on the causes of the catastrophe. The chorus implicates the gods (280-3), while the messenger singles out Salamis and Athens: 'O name of Salamis, greatest object of hatred to my ears. Alas, how I lament when I remember Athens' (284-5). The chorus elaborates the messenger's lament, declaring Athens 'detested' to its enemies and recalling how 'it made many Persian women bereft of children and of husbands' (286-9). The lament, like the stichomythia prior to the messenger's entrance, concludes on an Athenian note, merging past and present, Marathon and Salamis, in a single moment of Persian pain. The Persians confront the audience with their anguish and hatred. Does the audience reciprocate this hatred?[9] Does it surmount enmity and feel pride that the 'name of Salamis' – 'divine Salamis' according to the Delphic Oracle (Herodotus 7.141.4) – conveys such intense animosity to the Persians? Does the Persian memory of Athens induce the audience to remember Persia, both for the *pathos* it inflicted on them, and because Xerxes' disastrous invasion of Greece is the product of delusions that are the vulnerability of human nature?[10] This is the riddle of the *Persians*.

3. Pathos

Counting the dead who count:
the messenger's catalogue

The Queen speaks in iambic trimeters, explaining her silence during the lament: she was 'struck out of her senses' (*ekpeplêgmenê*, 290-1). The play explores the sympathetic relationship among the 'blow' (*plêgê*) endured by the fleet, the 'blow' to Persia's happiness in prosperity (251), and the 'blow' both inflict on the Persians, giving it visual expression in the dance of the *kommos*, as Xerxes and the chorus recreate the 'blow' dealt to Persia (1008-15, 1046-55). The Queen's body registers Persia's pain in the play, reflecting the shock, grief, and humbling effect of the defeat.

Picking up the messenger's image of a papyrus roll, the Queen orders him to unfold 'the entire disaster (*pathos*)', even though he laments (294-5). Returning to the role of questioner, she tries to shape the narrative according to her demands for knowledge. The most important matter for her is whether Xerxes survived the catastrophe. She tactfully pursues this line of inquiry (296-8). The messenger understands her question and answers that 'Xerxes himself lives and looks upon the light' (299). The Queen's fears about the 'eye of the house' are assuaged (300-1; 168-9). The royal *oikos* will not endure the darkness that descends in the absence of a male heir.

The Queen cannot exercise complete control over the narrative. The messenger rapidly lists the leaders who died at Salamis, giving name, ethnic, title, and a description of the unburied corpse or manner of death (302-30). The messenger offers a selection; a full account of Persian 'sufferings' is impossible (329-30).

The chorus' list of Xerxes' military leaders (21-59) is now a list of the dead. The five names repeated from the chorus' catalogue – Artembares (30, 302), Arsames (36, 308), Arcteus (44, 312), Ariomardus (37, 321), and Tharybis (51, 323) – create continuity.[11] Thirteen new names give a sense of overwhelming losses, as do deaths of men from peoples not named in the parodos, such as Bactrians (306, 318) and Cilicians (326-8). As in the chorus' catalogue, accuracy is not the aim. It is unlikely that Bactrians died or were 'wiped out' at Salamis (732).[12]

Indeed, the messenger's catalogue is not entirely consistent with the chorus'. Tharybis commands Mysian infantry in the parodos (51-2), but the messenger's Tharybis hails from elsewhere and commands 250 ships (323-5). Likewise Ariomardus: a leader of Egyptian Thebes in the parodos, his death 'gives grief to Sardis' (321-2) as if he were Lydian.

Elaborating the epirrhematic lament, the messenger offers vignettes of unburied corpses crashing against the shores of Salamis (303, 307, 309-10). How does an invading navy retrieve its dead in alien and hostile territory? This is a problem inherent in naval power: abandoning the dead is the price of defeat. In their public funerals, which featured one bier for the cremated remains of each tribe, the Athenians provided an eleventh bier for the 'invisible' dead (Thucydides 2.34.3), those whose corpses were irretrievable.

These descriptions advance a further theme: Athens is a hard land which produces 'hard' men.[13] Artembares' corpse strikes the 'rugged' coast of Salamis (303; cf. 963-6); others 'knock up against the mighty land' (308-10). Artabes' corpse is 'a resident alien of the hard earth' (319).

A single leader, the Cilician Syennesis, whom Herodotus lists among the most celebrated non-generals of the Persian forces (7.98), fought courageously and 'died gloriously' (326-8). He is the exception. The messenger catalogues Persian ignominy. The Queen's reaction makes this explicit (331-2).

The deceit of a Greek man and the envy of the gods: *hybris* and *atê*

The Queen assumes that the Greeks had a numerical advantage if they challenged the Persians to battle (333-6). According to the messenger, whose assertion that he knows the Persian tally well may declare Aeschylus' presence, the Persians had 1,000 triremes, of which 207 were built for speed, while the Greeks had 300 triremes, and only ten built for speed (339-43).[14] Herodotus numbers the Persian fleet at 1,207 ships (7.89.1, 184.1) and the Greek fleet at 380 ships (8.11.3, 82). If numbers were decisive, the messenger declares, the barbarian fleet would have won (337-8). On this fateful day, the Persian fleet sank under its size and weight (345-6).[15] Persia's excessive numerical superiority was self-defeating.

Without prompting, the messenger declares that 'the gods saved the goddess Pallas' city' (347) – Athens. Readers have tried to explain why the play refers only here to Athena.[16] The city's salvation could not be attributed to civic gods. They proverbially abandoned a captured city (Aeschylus *Seven against Thebes*, 216-18).[17] Athena evacuated the city before the Persians sacked it (Herodotus 8.41.2-3; Plutarch *Life of Themistocles* 10.1).

The Queen interprets the messenger's declaration to mean that Athens remains un-sacked (348). The messenger's reply, 'a defence (*herkos*) composed of men is secure' (349), responds to the chorus' boast in the parodos that it is impossible to keep out the Persians 'with mighty defences (*herkesin*)' (87-9).[18] The *Persians* omits the 'wooden wall' which the Delphic Oracle prophesied Zeus 'grants to Tritogenia (sc. Athena) alone to be un-sacked' (Herodotus 7.141.3), and which Themistocles interpreted as the Athenian fleet (7.143). Nor does the messenger equate Athens' fleet and the *polis*, as Herodotus' Themistocles does (8.61). A *polis* consists of territory, a city wall, buildings, institutions, cults and rituals, narratives, male citizens and their dependents. It is also a communal spirit and ethos. The Persians ransacked and burned the material of the *polis*, but they did not impose political rule. They destroyed things, not people or institutions. The Athenian idea that persons are more valuable than immoveable property was born at this moment (Thucydides 1.143.5 attributes it to Pericles). The messenger's reply defines the *polis* in non-material and unquantifiable terms. This is antithetical to the Persian mindset, which conceives of reality (and power) materially and quantitatively.

The Queen now suspects that Xerxes, 'exulting in his number of ships', started the battle (350-2). Xerxes' excess of men and materiel was intended to induce submission without a fight. Herodotus makes this explicit (7.8g3, 101.2, 146-7, 210, 212; 8.6.2, 10.1). In the *Persians*, when 'a Greek man from the army of the Athenians' tells Xerxes that the Greeks will escape under cover of darkness (355-60), he lures him into arraying his massive fleet in the narrows around Salamis (363-70), turning his numerical advantage into a liability. At this moment,

Xerxes' *hybris* – his confidence that numerical superiority alone will attain victory – turns to *atê*, disastrous delusion.

Greek/Athenian 'cunning-intelligence' (*mêtis*), the capacity to victimize the physically stronger through deceit and disguise and to dominate by mastering the opportunities of the moment, is the catalyst for this transformation.[19] 'Trickery' (*dolos*) is a fundamental element of *mêtis*. Divine powers, envious of a mortal seeking divinity, also conspire against Xerxes: 'a spirit of vengeance or evil divinity' (354), 'the cunning-minded (*dolomêtis*) deceit of god' (93), and 'the envy of the gods' (361-2), abet 'the Greek man' in luring Xerxes into disaster. So the rich and powerful in general and Xerxes in particular come to ruin in the Greek imagination.[20]

Xerxes compounds his blindness with cruelty, threatening his admirals with decapitation if the Greeks escape (369-71).[21] Yet his fleet responds with good order and an obedient spirit (374-6). When night falls, every sailor is 'lord of the oar' and every marine 'master of his arms' (378-9). The ships sail to their stations, staying at oar throughout the night (380-3).[22]

Herodotus stresses division in the Greek ranks; the *Persians* omits it. Nor does the play indicate that the 'Greek man' was a slave or name Themistocles. Rather, the messenger focuses on the drama of Xerxes' deception and the process by which the Persians recognize that the Greeks are resolved to fight rather than to flee, reversing their expectation and frustrating their aims. The night is the time of Xerxes' delusion (357, 364-5, 377-83). Daylight illuminates the truth and heralds the appearance of the Greek fleet to fight 'with confident courage' (384-94).

'O sons of the Hellenes, go, free your fatherland': Salamis

The barbarians were orderly when they thought the enemy would flee. This is a Greek stereotype of the barbarian: brutal when he senses he can kill without risk (cf. the archer), cowardly when he faces an army in rank.[23] Hearing the Greek battle song but unable to see the Greek fleet – an Aeschylean formula for fear – they experience blinding terror.[24] The song, a paean, was sung after the battle sacrifice and prior to the blare of the trumpet; if women were present, they shrieked in response to it.[25] In the *Persians*, the paean resounds shrilly off the rocks; its echo substitutes for the shriek of women and causes the barbarians to lose their wits (388-92). In Herodotus, Xerxes' uncle Artabanus warns him that envious gods 'strike fear' into massive armies, allowing them to be 'destroyed unworthily' by smaller forces (7.10e). This is how the naval disaster unfolds in the *Persians* (but not in Herodotus).

A trumpet blare signals the Greek attack. The messenger uses synaesthetic imagery to describe its effect: it 'set their whole side ablaze with its blare' (395). The appearance of the Greek fleet is a cosmic event, like the rising of the sun. The sun 'sets the earth ablaze with its beams' (364; cf. 504) as the trumpet sets the Greeks ablaze; like the day, 'brilliant to the sight' (387) the fleet appears 'conspicuous to the sight' (398). The messenger describes the rhythmic beat of the Greeks' oars, which sound out the depths of the sea and threaten the 'depth' of the impending Persian disaster (465, 712). Then he describes the appearance of the Greek fleet, the right flank followed by the rest of the line. He emphasizes the good order (*kosmos*) and discipline of the Greeks (396-401). In the *Persians*, the appearance of the Greek fleet is itself an epiphany, obviating the divine signs and epiphanies found in the later tradition.[26]

The rising sun heralds the Greeks' 'day of freedom'. A Homeric phrase, 'day of freedom' appears in negative contexts in the *Iliad*: warriors 'strip' it from the females of the defeated (6.455; 16.831; 20.193). After Xerxes' invasion, the 'day of freedom' appears in positive contexts.[27] Though not called the 'day of freedom' in the *Persians*, the day of the battle of Salamis appears on a chariot driven by white horses (386-7) to defeat Xerxes, who desires to enslave Greece by yoking it to his chariot (189-92). Freedom (*eleutheria*) is itself a kind of life-giving light which enables a community to flourish, grow to fullness, and reproduce itself, both physically and through *kleos*.[28]

Herodotus' Themistocles delivers a battle exhortation to the marines before they embark upon their ships. Listing good and bad qualities 'in the nature and constitution of men' he adjures the men to chose the better over the worse (8.83.1-2). In the

Persians, there is no general's speech. Rather, the entire fleet speaks with a single voice as it rows into battle (402-5):

> O sons of the Hellenes, go, free your fatherland, free your
> children and wives and the seats of your fathers' gods and
> the graves of your ancestors. Now is the contest for everything!

Although the root of the word appears only three times in the *Persians*, freedom is a keyword of the play; it is the stakes of the Persian Wars for the Greeks, who fight for socio-political life and light, to protect their families and to live within the laws and customs of their fathers and their gods. The Greeks fight to prevent a 'master' from exploiting their lives and labours by imposing a surrogate ruler upon them, extorting tribute, and demanding troops and ships. For a *polis* to wear the 'yoke of slavery' is its death. Reduced to ash, its wealth pillaged, its men slaughtered, its women and children carried off into slavery, the *polis* is deracinated.[29] The paradox of Salamis is that Athens suffered the 'yoke of slavery', but its people and institutions emerged unscathed and empowered. This is reflected in the Queen's dream: the woman who represents Greece shatters the yoke only after it has been placed on her neck (189-96).

The battle exhortation applies more strictly to the Athenians than to the other Greeks in the fleet. At the time of its utterance, the Persians occupied and were destroying their fatherland, the seats of their gods, and the graves of their ancestors; their wives and children were deposited in Troezen, on Aegina, and on Salamis. The loss, destruction, and recovery of their *polis* lent the Athenians an authoritative voice on what constitutes a *polis* and on what it meant to be Greek (see esp. Herodotus 8.144). The messenger's account of Salamis is but one example of the Athenian capacity to articulate the values of Greek culture to a Panhellenic audience.

The messenger's first answer to the Queen's question about the beginning of the battle stressed divine agency: 'a spirit of vengeance or malicious divinity appearing from somewhere' induced Xerxes to array his fleet in the narrows (353-4). His second answer involves human agency: 'a Greek ship started the ramming, and shattered the entire high stern of a Phoenician ship' (409-11). According to Herodotus, the Greek ships were backing water and running aground, but Aminias of Pallene launched his ship and rammed an enemy vessel. He could not extricate his ship, and other Greek ships coming to his aid joined the fray (8.84.1). The Athenians were arrayed against the Phoenicians at Salamis (8.85.1; Diodorus 11.18.1). They would have taken the messenger's narrative of the ramming of a Phoenician vessel as their action.

In the beginning, the 'flow' or 'flood' of the Persian navy holds firm against the Greek attack (412-13; Diodorus 11.18.4). In the end, its sheer size defeats it. Persian ships mass in a narrow space and are unable to manoeuvre; they strike each other, shearing off each other's oars (413-16). Herodotus says that Persian ships stationed in the rear tried to move to the front ranks to impress Xerxes, but crashed into ships fleeing from the front (8.89.2). In the *Persians*, Greek ships 'not unskilfully' encircle the tangled mass of Persian ships, striking and upending them (417-19). The sea disappears beneath the wreckage of ships and carnage of men (419-20). The shores and rocks jutting up from the sea's surface catch corpses from the choppy seas (421). The Persian ships flee in disarray (*akosmôs*), reversing their orderly advance to await the Greek flight (422-3; 374-83).

It was a Greek commonplace that barbarians could not swim.[30] The inability to swim (*nein*) signalled a lack of mental capacity (*noein*). Unlike Herodotus, the *Persians* does not stress this lack.[31] Rather, the play depicts the barbarians as slaughtered while seeking the safety of land. The Greeks 'keep striking them, keep slicing them in half with fragments of oars and shattered bits of wreckage like tuna or a haul of fish' (424-6; cf. 974-7) – a manifestation of their 'cunning intelligence' (*mêtis*).[32] The slaughter at Salamis realizes the image of Xerxes' *atê* in an unexpected way – his men are caught in fishing rather than in hunting nets (93-101).[33] So long as the sun shines, the Persians suffer horrors and their wailing holds the sea, 'until the dark eye of the night takes it away' (426-8). The transition from day to night, crucial to the Persians' deluded hope for victory, finally ends their torment.

The messenger quantifies the debacle: 'never on a single day has a multitude (*plêthos*) of so great a number of men died' (431-2). The Queen, silent during the long narrative, uses the appropriate metaphor to describe the defeat: 'a great sea of sufferings has burst forth upon the Persians and the entire barbarian race' (433-4). The sea defies quantification, human control, and the imperialist urge. Xerxes sought to put a yoke on its neck, to unite Europe and Asia physically and politically under a yoke of slavery. The battle of Salamis shattered that yoke as it shattered Xerxes' fleet.

Psyttalia: quantity vs. value

The messenger tells of a disaster after Salamis that 'counterbalanced the scale twice as much' (436-7) as Salamis. He does not name the place of the disaster, Psyttalia, or its agents, the Athenians.[34] The defeat at Psyttalia recapitulates the Greek/barbarian distinction of quality to quantity within the Persian ranks. The value of the Persian nobility slaughtered on the island is twice that of the largest number of corpses ever produced on a single day.[35]

The messenger says that Xerxes sent the force to the island to save Persians and to kill Greeks emerging from wrecked ships (450-3; cf. Herodotus 8.76.2-3).[36] He stresses Xerxes' cruelty: these Greeks would be 'easy to kill' (450-2). Psyttalia reaffirms Xerxes' flawed knowledge of the future and his disastrous moral/intellectual blindness (454; cf. 373).

Athenians gird their bodies in 'finely crafted bronze' and leap from their ships after the naval victory, encircling the Persians on the island (454-9). Herodotus places the attack during the mêlée of the naval battle (8.95). Surrounded and immobilized, Aeschylus' Persians are struck by stones and arrows, and finally butchered like meat (457-64).[37] Their deaths complement those of the sailors, who are encircled, clubbed, caught, and filleted like tuna (424-6). The barbarian invaders fall below slaves in the chain of being: they are killed and prepared as food.

Aeschylus and Herodotus agree that every Persian sent to the island was slaughtered (464; 8.95).[38] For Aeschylus, Psyttalia annihilates the Persian nobility (441-4). The stratification of Persian society contrasts with Athenian equality – all citizens belong equally to the *polis* and merit equal material and symbolic rewards for their labour. The Psyttalia episode devel-

ops this theme. Athenian lower-class stone-throwers and archers encircle and immobilize the Persian nobility;
middle/upper-class hoplites hack them to pieces (457-64). Athens' early depictions of democracy as a moral force project class
solidarity. The Athenians memorialized their first hoplite victory *c.* 506 over the wealthy 'knights' (*hippobotai*) of Chalcis,
whose land they seized and settled, and Boeotians, whom they
ransomed, with a bronze statue of a four-horse chariot, emblem
of horse-loving aristocrats (Herodotus 5.77-8). An epigram at
the base of the statue proclaims that Athenian hoplites 'extin-
guished' the fiery gleam of their adversaries' *hybris*, 'breaking'
them in battle (5.77.4). *Hybris* is deviant behaviour induced by
wealth, youth, and status.[39] Athens represented its uses of
military force as moral action against such *hybris*.

Psyttalia glorifies Athenian light-armed troops and hoplites
for their role in the defeat of the Persians. Herodotus uses the
battle more particularly to praise the achievement of Aristides
and Athens' hoplites, who had been stationed on Salamis but
did not row in the fleet (8.76.3, 95).[40] Aeschylus' hoplites may
have rowed, served as marines, or been spectators on Salamis
– it is impossible to tell.[41] Aeschylus invokes the Athenian
hoplite tradition by associating Psyttalia with the god Pan
(447-9), who was worshipped at Athens after Marathon
(6.105.2-3).[42] Yet it is mistaken to read the episode as an
attempt to honour Aristides and Athenian hoplites at the ex-
pense of Themistocles and the navy.[43] Psyttalia complements
and duplicates the naval victory as a victory on land – where
the Persians were allegedly invincible.[44]

Athenian hoplites and light-armed troops inflict twice as
much harm on the Persians as the sailors do. Psyttalia exaggerates the infantry's role; but it also foregrounds the agony of
Persia's nobility.[45] The audience might take this as a horrifying
dimension of war in general.[46] It might also view the slaughter
of the Persian nobility a function of naval invasion. The destruction of Athens' best citizens was associated with the conduct of
naval imperialism.[47] The Queen blames the navy, composed of
lower-class non-Persians, for the defeat of the upper-class Persian infantry (728). The play's ominous treatment of the word
and concept of *plêthos*, 'number', may also address Athenian

concerns about the conduct of democracy and imperialism. In Athenian political and legal discourse, the word *plêthos* refers to the ruling majority.[48] The *Persians* depicts the investment of a *plêthos* of men and ships in a sea-borne invasion as a formula for a *plêthos* of woes. Unlike later treatments of Salamis, the *Persians* is silent about the size of the Athenian navy, which comprised nearly two-thirds of the Greek fleet (e.g. Thucydides 1.74.1). The play stresses Persia's catastrophic numerical superiority, but this is also a feature of naval warfare for the audience to consider.

The flight from Salamis to Thrace

Xerxes is a spectator and a spectacle at the battle, occupying a conspicuous seat (465-8).[49] According to Herodotus, his gaze impelled his sailors to fight with greater zeal at Salamis than they had fought at Artemisium during his absence (8.86). In the *Persians*, he sees the 'depth of woes', and imitates the shattering of his fleet and wailing of his sailors, 'tearing his robes and wailing shrilly' (465-8). Rapidly relaying orders to his infantry to flee, 'he went in disorderly flight' (469-70).

At this moment, Xerxes realizes his mother's dream. Darius' pity in the dream seems to be a function of Xerxes' similarity to him: both suffered defeat at Athens. The Queen treats their defeats as parallel, returning the episode to the cue for its beginning, the battle of Marathon. Xerxes' attempt to avenge his father's defeat turned out to be 'bitter': he was not content with Persian deaths at Marathon (473-7). Salamis repeats the earlier Persian defeat on a larger scale; it renews the glory of Athenian valour against Persian aggression. 'Celebrated Athens' (473), the defender of Greek freedom, foiled Xerxes' attempt to avenge his father's defeat at Marathon.

The messenger-scene follows a recurrent pattern. The Queen requests specific information; the messenger answers her question, but adds a cascade of lamentable news. The Queen now asks for the location of the surviving ships (478-9). The messenger replies that the ships' captains 'set sail ... in no well-ordered (*ouk eukosmon*) flight' (480-1). Then he launches into an account of the land forces' march home.

Describing the Persian route home, the messenger catalogues Greek territories which collaborated with the Persians
(482-3; Herodotus 7.132.1; 8.31; 9.31.5). The king of Macedonia,
Alexander I, was a medizing Greek, though Herodotus depicts
him as a clever double-dealer.[50] In Boeotia, the heart of Greek
collaboration, the Persians die of thirst and from a condition
that has dropped out of the text (482-4). Phocis resisted at first,
and the Persians sacked their towns, but at the battle of
Plataea 1,000 Phocians fought on the Persian side. Their name
was not inscribed on the 'Serpent Column' commemorating the
31 *poleis* that 'fought the war' against the Persians.[51] The cities
of Thessaly, where the Persians wintered in 480/79 (Herodotus
8.113, 129.3), welcomed the Persian army on its homeward
march, but 'the most died here of thirst and hunger' (488-91).
Medizing Greek *poleis* were deadly to the retreating Persians.

The *Persians* suggests that the land of Greece itself harmed
the Persians, irrespective of individual cities' actions. In this
way, the play introduces the theme of poverty as preserving
Greek freedom. Darius reiterates this point: Greek soil cannot
support a large invading army (792-4).[52] Poverty was second
nature to the Greeks, who imported 'virtue/courage' (*aretê*) to
combat poverty and despotism with wisdom and law (Herodotus 7.102.1; cf. Aristophanes *Wealth* 557-64). The collective and
law-governed nature of Greek societies stems from their poverty and contrasts with the vast surplus and unchallenged
power of the Persian king.

Edonian territory in Thrace was a hot-spot of Greco-Persian
conflict. Darius rewarded Histiaeus of Miletus with a colony at
Myrcinus, which controlled timber, precious metals, and manpower; Megabazus thwarted this plan (Herodotus 5.11.2, 23-4;
124.2; 7.112; cf. Thucydides 4.108.1). The climax of the narrative of retreat takes place here at the Strymon River, which
divides Macedonia from Thrace (495-7). When the river freezes
during an unseasonably cold night, the Persian remnant thinks
it has achieved miraculous salvation. Even those who 'thought
the gods of no account' heap prayers upon them, and 'bow in
obeisance to Earth and Heaven' (497-9). Those who began to
cross before the sun melted the ice made it to the other side; but
as afternoon wore on, the sun melted the ice (500-5), and the

Persians 'fell upon one another'; the quickest to die were luckiest (506-7). Salvation turns to disaster: the men lethally crowd one another in the river, just as Persian ships crowded one another at Salamis, and sink to their deaths. Night is the time when events delude the Persians into thinking their hopes will be achieved; the sun illuminates the truth and destroys them. The Persians' treatment of the river's freezing as proof of the gods' existence and their prayers and prostration before the earth and sky rather than before the king ironically highlight the deadly consequences of the delusion that Xerxes is divine.[53]

Salamis and Psyttalia required human agency. The disaster at the Strymon is divine deception unmediated by mortals. The formation of a bridge of ice across the Strymon re-enacts and reciprocates Xerxes' bridging of the Hellespont.[54] Darius describes Xerxes' attempt to bind 'the sacred flowing Hellespont' as a 'disease of the mind' (745-50). To stop the flow of the Hellespont is a crime against the cosmos – matter, time, change, differentiation – turning water into land. The mysterious forces of nature exact vengeance for Xerxes' deformation of the landscape to link the continents, fashion symbols of power, unite Europe and Asia under his rule, and achieve transition from mortality to divinity. Herodotus and Simonides in his *Artemisium* treat natural phenomena as Greek defence mechanisms against the Persians.[55] In Aeschylus, the cosmic order vindicates itself. Greek soil and the Strymon River punish the Persians with the two worst forms of death, starvation and drowning (Homer *Odyssey* 12.340-51).

Xerxes ordered a bridge constructed over the Strymon which the invading force used (Herodotus 7.24, 114.1); the retreating Persians probably crossed it (8.115, 126). An alternative tradition, which Herodotus rejects, suggests that the Persians encountered difficulty here. Xerxes marched as far as the Strymon but did not cross it. He sailed from Eion to the Hellespont (8.118-20). It is possible that the narrative in the *Persians* derives from such a tradition, but it is more likely a moralizing fiction.

The Persians controlled the Strymon until the Athenians captured Eion in 476. According to a commentator to Aeschines'

On the False Embassy, Thracians slaughtered Athenian colonists there.[56] A parallel Athenian disaster may lie below the surface of this narrative. The Strymon forms a significant and ominous boundary between Greece and Thrace. It belongs neither to Greeks nor to Persians.

Xerxes' arrival?

The messenger concludes the longest series of speeches delivered by a single character in extant tragedy by preparing the Queen, chorus, and audience for the arrival of a small Persian remnant (cf. Herodotus 8.115.1) and for the lament of the *polis* (508-12). The messenger's final words assert the truth of his narrative and reiterate that it was a selection of the Persians' 'god-inflicted' woes (513-14). As the messenger exits, the chorus bewails the divinity who brought 'hard suffering', 'leaping with both your feet upon the entire race of Persians' (515-16; cf. 911-12). The *daimôn* trampled the Persians, who trampled the Hellespont, the Strymon, Greece, and Athens.[57]

The Queen recognizes that the disaster fulfils her dream, and rebukes the elders for their interpretation (518-20). Even so, she resolves to perform the rites they earlier advised. Though too late, they may somehow improve the Persians' prospects (521-6). She is also concerned that the chorus remain faithful advisors in the aftermath of the disaster (527-8).

The Queen now considers Xerxes' arrival. Assuming the role she will play in the next episode – chorus leader – she orders the chorus to 'console him and send him into the house' if he returns so that he does not multiply his woes (529-31). Xerxes' homecoming does not happen when first expected. The Queen's return pre-empts it; Darius arrives from Hades before Xerxes returns from a figural Hades, Athens. This 'false preparation' has prompted much discussion.[58] But it is a red herring. The deferral of Xerxes' entrance is part of an ensemble of pre-empted, delayed, and unexpected stage events. The chorus' deliberations are too late; the Queen's entrance interrupts them. The bird omen pre-empts the Queen's apotropaic rites; the messenger's entrance defers the Queen's exit and renders apotropaic rites gratuitous. The Queen's concern is for her son.

Before exiting, she arranges for the chorus to soothe him and escort him to the palace.[59] This is deferred until the end of the play; but it does not happen on the Queen's terms. Xerxes will return in rags to multiply his woes by re-enacting the Persians' suffering in lament. And he will regain control of the chorus and command the elders to escort him to the palace (1038-77).

From Salamis to the end of empire: lament

Alone in the orchestra, the chorus performs the first stasimon. An anapaestic prelude restates the narrative as a lament. The chorus ceases to speak vaguely of 'divinity' or 'god' as the cause of Persian suffering and blames 'Zeus the king' for destroying 'the army of the boastful and multitudinous Persians' and for obscuring Persia in mists of 'gloomy lament' (532-6). Darkness – the matrix of Xerxes' hopes at Salamis and Persian joy at the Strymon – now settles on Persia, obscuring the gleam of its wealth, power, and *hybris* under mists of tears. The elders describe women's tender hands rending their veils, their breasts drenched with tears in grief (537-40). They focus on 'delicately lamenting' brides who long to see their 'newlywed husbands' (*artizugia*, 'recent yoking', 541-2). The word recalls Xerxes' 'yoke' on the Hellespont as a perverse marriage and hints at the theme of a new Trojan War. Protesilaus was a newlywed, leaving a half-built house and a bride tearing her cheeks in mourning (Homer *Iliad* 2.695-710).

The messenger stated that the *polis* would lament 'longing for the dearest youth (*hêbê*) of the land' (511-12). The word *hêbê* designates men of military age. More generally, *hêbê* is a state of physical and sexual maturity, a benchmark or 'measure' of human life, when the body reaches its peak of vigour and desirability.[60] It is the time when men become warriors and fathers and women are ready for marriage and child-bearing.[61] *Hêbê* is the object of two kinds of lament: for its evanescence, as youth yields to old age, and for its loss in battle.[62] Persian women combine these: longing for 'exquisitely cushioned marriage beds, the pleasure of luxuriant youth (*hêbê*)' (542-4), they mourn their husbands' deaths in battle as the loss of their own *hêbê*.[63]

78

The chorus eroticizes Persian women in lament. The keyword for their delicate luxury is *habros*, which forms such compounds as 'luxuriant in lament' (135) and 'delicately lamenting' (541; cf. 543).[64] Persia's feminine luxury is the obverse of its imperialism, as the Queen's entrance displayed. The desire for wealth and empire has no point of satisfaction. Xerxes' expenditure of wealth to conquer Greece purchases female laments that are superlatively 'unsatisfiable' (545). Lament is the final act of imperialist luxuriance in the *Persians*.

Recalling the first line of the play, the elders decide to honour the fate of 'the departed' (546-7; cf. 1, 60, 178, 252). They sing a lament in lyric iambic metre. Describing the land of Asia as 'emptied out' and grieving (548-9; cf. 119), they reduce the dramatic narrative to its essence and punctuate it with exclamations of anguish. The story has a single subject: Xerxes. He led, destroyed (or lost), and foolishly managed the battle at sea (550-4). The chorus reiterates the messenger's stress on Xerxes' moral/intellectual failure (361-2, 373, 454).

The chorus blames Xerxes' yearning for naval empire, contrasting his calamitous desire with Darius' benign leadership of archer-citizens (555-7). The chorus made a similar distinction in the parodos (102-13). Darius wielded power within the limits of the Persian tradition. Xerxes tried to control the sea. The antistrophe identifies the disaster as specific to naval imperialism (558-63). Ships replace Xerxes as the subject which led and destroyed/lost, sharing blame with the reckless young king. Both Xerxes and ships have a malignant 'dark-blue' look (559; 81-2) and bear an equivalent emotional charge in this lament.

The disaster of the Persians' learning 'to cast their gaze upon the hallowed field of the sea' (108-13) has multiple, contradictory meanings. It reinforces Athens' naval supremacy in the Aegean. That the chorus uses the term 'Ionians' for 'Greeks' here (563) and subsequently in its laments (950-4, 1011-13, 1025) instead of 'Greeks', as the messenger does, signals this tendency of the drama. But it also expresses a general warning against naval imperialism and associates it with the violation of sacred space.[65] To defend one's homeland against a barbarian invader as Athens did at Salamis differs from launching fleets as a siege power – the Athenian modus operandi after Salamis. 'Others' pains' – even when inflicted by the audience – are the sole source of tragic wisdom. History assumes the form of myth in tragedy because what is alien somehow becomes one's own and the particular gains a general resonance.[66]

Persian laments for the disaster thus sound the perils of naval power, which was notoriously impermanent, and associated with greed, invasion, and the destabilization of tradition.[67] In a period of three decades, Ionians, Phoenicians, and Athenians dominated the Aegean. Their stories are cautionary tales. The first Greek naval imperialist, Polycrates of Samos (ruled *c.* 540 to 522) ended up crucified and decapitated, enticed to his death by what he thought were chests of gold (Herodotus 3.122-5). The Milesian tyrants' bid for naval empire ended in disaster – Histiaeus too was decapitated (6.30). Herodotus laments the ships Athens sent to Miletus as 'the beginning of woes for both Greeks and barbarians' (5.97.3). Phrynichus' *Phoenician Women* bewailed the end of Phoenician naval power.

Ships enabled the Persians to prosecute a large-scale invasion which risked and incurred total defeat. They would similarly seduce the Athenians. The fourth-century orator Isocrates exaggerates when he lists the Athenian loss of 200 ships in Egypt in 454, 150 ships in Cyprus, 10,000 hoplites in Drabescus in 464, 40,000 men and 140 ships in Sicily in 413.[68] 'Who could count', he realistically adds, 'ships lost by tens and fives and more, and men dying by the 1,000 and 2,000'? (*On the Peace* 8.86-7). Naval power was expensive and unsustainable without tribute-collecting imperialism; it expended human lives more prodigiously than land power. Even a modest fleet of 60 triremes gambled some 12,000 lives, more than Athens risked at either Marathon or Plataea. Thucydides' Pericles asserts, 'know that the city has the greatest reputation for not yielding to disasters and for expending the most lives and efforts in war' (2.64.3). The *Persians* depicts such carnage as a Persian problem; and unlike Pericles' Athenians, Aeschylus' Persians yield to unbridled lament after the disaster. Such laments are radically other, it is true; but they are inescapably human, and linked specifically to naval imperialism. As Athenian deaths in war escalated, the tragic theatre became an outlet for the expression of communal grief, misrecognized as 'others' woes'.

The chorus' lament ends where the messenger's narrative did, with Xerxes' escape through Thrace (564-7). Modulating to lyric dactylic metre, the elders go beyond the messenger's speech. Their vision borders on fantasy and prophecy. Uttering the exclamations of woe they feared the city would hear in the parodos (114-19), they direct themselves to lament the Persians' 'heaven-sent woes' (571-5) and imagine Persian corpses 'horribly mangled' by fish, 'the voiceless children of the undefiled one' (576-8). This kenning expresses the Greek idea that the sea is immune to religious pollution and that to perish at sea is a kind of nothingness, to enter the food chain and to disappear without a trace.[69] The messenger described Persians caught, killed, and prepared as food (424-6, 462-4). The chorus completes his vision: fish devour the Persians, a moment Herodotus also includes in his *Histories* (6.44.3). Returning to a keynote of the anapaestic prelude, the chorus mourns for Persian households, which 'stripped of its man grieves', and tells of 'elderly, childless parents lamenting heaven-sent woes' (579-83).

The return to the prelude of the ode signals a new beginning. The chorus becomes prophetic: Persia's Asian empire will crumble because of defeat at Salamis. Subjects will no longer tolerate Persian rule, pay tribute under 'despotic necessity', or be ruled and bow down before the king (584-90). The elders performed *proskynêsis* before the Queen; but they will not bow before the Queen or Xerxes after the defeat. The rest of the empire will follow. Free speech figures the fall of empire: 'the people has been set loose to speak freely, for the yoke of power has been loosened' (591-4). The image of the yoke is a vehicle for telling the story of the play: Xerxes yoked the Hellespont (65-72, 721-30, 744-51) and sought to put the 'yoke' of slavery on Greece (50, 190-2). Salamis shattered the yoke of Persian slavery, destroying the 'yoke' of Persian marriages and removing the 'yoke' of silence from the people. The failed attempt to conquer mainland Greece threatens the Persian empire at its heart.[70] We will see result of this when the elders speak freely to Xerxes upon his return (918-1001).

Persian power and grandeur lie on the bloody fields of Ajax's island, Salamis (595-7). These last words of the lament echo a Greek memorial for the dead at Salamis: 'but now the island of Salamis holds us' (*FGE* 'Simonides' XI). The Persian *pathos* ends where it began, on the 'island of Ajax' (307, 368), separated from Attica at its narrowest point by a fraction over a kilometre. Homer designated Ajax 'the bulwark (*herkos*) of the Achaeans' (*Iliad* 3.229; 6.5; 7.211), the word for Athens' defenders in the *Persians* (349). Ajax is an apt hero for the battle. The defender who wears a gigantic shield, he is unable to withstand the Trojan onslaught by himself. He withdraws, enabling Hector and the Trojans to set fire to the Achaean ships (Homer *Iliad* 16.101-24). So too the Athenians withdrew and the Persians set fire to Athens.

Remembering the victory at Salamis from the perspective of the Persian disaster allows the Athenians to celebrate the greatest victory in their history and to lament their greatest defeat. To understand the Persian, and by implication, the Athenian, *pathos*, the play raises the ghost of Darius. But he bears little resemblance to the historical Darius. Is Darius a figment of the barbarian imagination or a mask for the play-wright's own message? This is the question the next two chapters will attempt to answer.

A Tragedy of Succession

'Everything is full of fear'

The Queen enters embodying the abjection of Asia and its hope for the propitiation of the gods responsible for the disaster. As in her first entrance, she is afraid. Now, however, she sees the world through the filter of her reversal of fortune. For those who suffer 'a wave of woes', she says, 'everything is likely to cause fear' (599-600). By contrast, those who enjoy continuous good fortune 'trust that the same wind of fortune will always blow' (601-2). The Queen locates herself among the former: 'everything is full of fear' (603). Depicting the human condition as a perilous voyage contingent upon invisible powers, the Queen again formulates the appropriate response to the Persian maritime disaster (cf. 433-4). Her appreciation of the mutability of fortune and expectation of further misfortune differ markedly from the chorus' expression of invincibility in the parodos.[1]

The Queen's physical appearance attests to Persia's reversal of fortune. She first entered on a chariot and was the object of the chorus' *proskynêsis* and formal address (150-8). Now she enters unannounced; her chariot and 'finery' are gone (607-8).[2] The Queen sees, hears, and feels a spectacle of inner pain. Visions of divine hostility and menacing sounds – like the Greek paean that terrified the Persian fleet – assault her (604-5; cf. 388-92). Astonishment (*ekplêxis*) caused by suffering 'strikes out' her senses (606; cf. 290-1). The Queen's body and mind register the 'blow' to Persia's *olbos* delivered at Salamis (251-2).

The Queen proposed to return with a *pelanos* as a gift to the earth and the dead (521-6). Now she arrives carrying ingredients that may qualify as *pelanos*, but lack meal, the staple of this porridge-like substance: milk, honey, spring water, wine, olive oil, and flowers.[3] The Queen endows these objects with magical properties by naming them in kennings (611-18).[4] These kennings turn simple produce into remedies for disaster, prefiguring the intended effect of Darius' appearance, a 'cure for woes' (631-2). The 'unyoked cow' (literally, 'pure') is innocent of Xerxes' transgressive 'yoke'.[5] The 'blossom-working bee' is a foil for the invading army, which was compared to 'a swarm of bees' (128-9). The garlands recall and reverse the loss of 'the flower of the Persians' (59-62, 250-2, 925-7), who remain unburied, never to return to the earth, the mother who bore and laments them.[6] Food and drink offerings counter Persian deaths by thirst and starvation (482-4, 490-1).

The kennings also allude to Athens' destruction and rebirth from Persian fire. The 'wild mother' (614) suggests the 'mountain mother' Cybebe, whose temple at Sardis the Athenians and Ionians burned.[7] The description of the olive as 'forever teeming with life in its leaves' (616-17) may refer to a tradition that Xerxes sent Athenians to sacrifice on the Acropolis after he burned it. They reported that the olive which Athena produced to win patronage of Athens, though burned, had shot up overnight (Herodotus 8.55). This olive symbolized the free community of Athens and its capacity to reproduce itself from the original autochthonous line (Euripides *Ion* 1433-6; cf. *Trojan Women* 799-803). The Queen figures the restorative power of her offerings in a riddling language which hints at the Persian and Athenian *pathos* and their capacities for regeneration.[8]

The dominant trope of these riddles is personification. The life-giving mother and the pure virgin, Demeter and Kore, are present in the language. The pair is also prominent in the fourth-century comedian Antiphanes' parody of such kennings (*Aphrodisius*, fr. 55.3, 9 [K-A]), which includes three of these items: 'streams of the buzzing bee' (honey, 7), 'sweat of Bromius' fount' (wine, 12), and 'dewy drops of the nymphs' (spring water, 13).

The Queen's offerings are foils for the chariot, a symbol of wealth won by conquest and dispossession of the vanquished; they suggest *olbos* derived from the earth. In its religious form, *olbos* is a relation to the earth: those who are 'blessed' (*olbioi*) are favoured by Gaea, Demeter, and Kore.[9] The derivation of *olbos* from conquest is at the heart of the Persian disaster. The second episode returns to the earth and the dead father buried in it as a remedy. This act of remediation has special resonance for the Athenians, whose land and ancestral tombs were destroyed in 480/79.[10]

The raising of Darius' ghost comes as a surprise. The Queen withholds the purpose of her offerings until the end of her speech. She enters carrying 'propitiatory libations to the father of the child, soothing to the dead' (609-10). After her kennings, she orders the chorus to invoke 'the divinity (*daimôn*) Darius' with hymns while she pours 'these honours to the gods of the lower world' (619-22). The kennings transform propitiatory offerings to the dead into ingredients of a necromantic rite. They also signal a change in the Queen's dramatic role. A seeker of advice and questioner in the first episode, the Queen assumes the role of chorus leader, commanding the chorus' performance and determining the stage action.[11] Aristotle theorized tragedy's origin from 'the chorus leaders of the dithyramb' (*Poetics* 1449a9-14); an actor in the role of chorus leader is essential to Aeschylean drama. This is the position of power, authority, and risk; the chorus leader acts as a director on stage. In the *Persians*, the role evolves as it passes from the messenger, to the Queen, to Darius, and finally to Xerxes himself, who regains despotic control of the kingdom as a leader of choral lament.[12]

Before our eyes, the Queen and the chorus raise Darius from the dead. Necromancy is a nocturnal rite *par excellence*; conducted in daylight by dramatic necessity, it nevertheless stages the inversion of day/night, light/darkness that was integral to the messenger's narrative.[13]

Darius' tomb

The elders accept their role in an anapaestic prelude, which covers movement into position at Darius' tomb to perform the rites and sing the hymn (623-32). Precisely how the tomb was represented and where it was located within the theatrical space are unknown. The most ingenious theory is that of Nicholas Hammond, who argues that a rock outcrop on the eastern edge of the orchestra, which was removed sometime between 463 and 458, functioned as an elevated acting space and was outfitted to serve as Darius' tomb in the *Persians*.[14] A.W. Pickard-Cambridge and Oliver Taplin also locate the tomb on the side of the orchestra (though not on the outcrop).[15] Peter Arnott believes that an altar on an elevated stage functioned as Darius' tomb.[16] It is difficult to see how the ghost-raising was staged if this was the arrangement, since the altar would not have been large enough to conceal Darius or his movement into position for the scene.[17] David Wiles asserts that 'In performance terms the climax of the play demands use of the strongest point' and argues that the tomb was located at the altar in the centre of the orchestra, the *thymelê*; but this gives Darius an anti-climactic entrance 'as a disembodied spirit ... to the orchestra from the terrace behind'.[18] Positing a *skênê* as both a tomb and council chamber is the most elegant hypothesis, though it is by no means certain. It has the advantage of making the tomb the visual focus of the theatrical space and of offering a mechanism for concealing Darius' body and screening his emergence to the top of the structure. But basic uncertainties about the theatre in 472 – whether it featured a *skênê*, whether an acting space was elevated above the dancing space (*orchêstra*) – make any hypothesis tenuous.

The power of lament: the chorus' hymn

Addressing the divinities responsible for releasing the dead to the world of the living, the elders explain their demand for Darius' return: 'if he knows some further cure of our woes, he alone of mortals might speak their fulfilment' (627-32). The chorus classifies Darius as a mortal; that he is dead in Hades and must return confirms it (688-93).[19] References to his divinity are part of the ideology of Persian kingship and the rhetoric of the disaster. Darius lived 'a fortunate life like a god among the Persians' (711). 'Surpassing all mortals in *olbos*' (709), he embodies the *olbos* Xerxes' invasion ruined and which plays an ambiguous role in the etiology of the disaster.

The hymn is rhythmically varied, but the first line, containing four Ionic *a minore* metra, establishes its cadence, which grows increasingly Ionic before concluding with an iambic and dactylic epode.[20] The metre of *hybris* and *atê* in the parodos, Ionic *a minore* now conveys the magical power of Persian language and sorrow to awaken the dead; it is the rhythm of Persia's reversal of fortune, pain, loss, and longing. It has the power to communicate across the gulf that separates living and dead, Greek and Persian, evoking joint Persian/Ionian suffering.[21]

The elders seek to establish communication with Darius, asking 'the blessed godlike king' if he can hear them. Dolefulness and variations of pitch and volume are required for the living to reach the dead. An exotic quality helps: the chorus describes its utterances as 'barbarian' (634-9).[22] The antistrophe beseeches chthonic powers to grant Darius' release. Amplifying their praise, the elders call Darius 'god of the Persians born in Susa', unique among those buried in Persian soil (640-6).

Making heavy use of anaphora, the second strophe elaborates the hymn's opening. The elders proclaim love for Darius, his tomb, and his character, before directly appealing to Hades to escort 'the divine master Darian' to the living (647-51). 'Darian' approximates Darius' Persian name, enhancing the exotic sound of the hymn and intensifying the personal bond between chorus and king. The antistrophe reiterates the desire for Darius' return in terms of his difference from Xerxes (652-6). Darius' prudent and successful leadership contrasts with Xerxes' destructive maritime ambitions (cf. 555-7).

A doleful exclamation, *êe*, follows Darius' name at the end of the second strophe and concludes the antistrophe (651, 656). The concluding refrain of the third strophic/antistrophic pair punctuates the command for the 'harmless father Darian' to arrive with the exclamation '*oi*' (663-4, 671-2).[23] In the first stasimon the exclamations *popoi* and *totoi* followed 'Xerxes' and 'ships' (550-1, 560-1); similar cries punctuated the chorus' lament for the dead who would never return (568-81). In this hymn, the chorus attaches the pain of the disaster to Darius' name to compel his presence.

The hymn reaches its incantatory peak in the third strophe/antistrophe. The chorus repeatedly calls upon Darius to arrive and appear, invoking him with the exotic title '*ballên*, ancient *ballên*' (657-8), either a Phrygian royal title or a title derived from a Babylonian word for royal decree, *palû*, the source of the Phoenician honorific Ba'al.[24] The chorus defines expectations for Darius' visual appearance, commanding him to appear on his funeral mound's or tomb's 'highest pinnacle' wearing the Persian 'crocus-dyed slipper' and revealing the 'tip of your royal tiara' (659-61), the hat which only the Persian king could wear upright.[25] Darius' ornate and intact royal costume will contrast with Xerxes' rags.[26] The elders state their reason for commanding Darius' presence: to hear 'strange and new woes' (665). Ironically reducing the difference between the place where Darius is and the place where they order him to appear, the chorus describes Persia as a kind of Hades: 'the mist of the Styx hovers, for now the entire youth of our land has perished' (669-70).

The text of the epode is corrupt, but the chorus reminds Darius of lavish laments for him at his death. His appearance will repay this favour. As Marathon was the cue for the messenger's arrival, Salamis is the cue for Darius'. The elders end the hymn on the keynote of the naval defeat: 'for all the triremes in this land have perished; the ships are no ships, no ships' (673-80). The loss of the fleet is the painful blow to Persia. Again, this stress highlights the Athenian achievement even as it underscores the evanescence of naval power.

When Darius emerges from Hades, he tells the elders that the Queen's libations made him afraid (684-5) and that their wailing 'with soul-attracting laments, invoked me pitiably' (686-8). The hymn arouses the canonical emotions of tragic performance, pity and fear; song, music, and movement work a kind of magic.[27] The Queen's dream focalized pity for Xerxes through Darius (198). In the staged drama, Darius pities the *polis* rather than his son, engaging the audience's emotions with the *polis* as the victim of disaster. Performing a lament which 'leads souls' from Hades, the *Persians* lures a ghost to the world of the living and a Greek audience into a Persian tragedy.

Darius' entrance

The staging of Darius' arrival is impossible to determine. Oliver Taplin suggests that he may emerge through an underground passage.[28] Mae Smethurst conjectures that he arises from behind a moveable prop representing his tomb.[29] Others suggest that he surmounts an object such as a mound or rock decorated as a tomb.[30] Some have used vase painting to support their positions, but these paintings do not inspire confidence as precise renditions of a moment in a tragedy.[31] A wooden structure is a simpler and more economical theatrical device than an underground passage or a specialized prop. Depicted as a god, Darius may have appeared on top of a *skênê* which represented his tomb; the later theatre would stage this arrival as a *deus ex machina*.[32]

Premonition, dream, omen, oracle: the fulfilment of tragedy

Darius' emergence into the light extends the scope of the drama backwards and forwards in time, from the origin of the Persian/Median kingship six generations earlier to three generations after the Persian defeat at Plataea. The stichomythia between the Queen and Darius articulates the tragedy as a fulfilment of the chorus' premonition, the Queen's dream and bird omen, the precedent of Marathon, and prophecies known to Darius (703-43). Darius condemns his son (744-52), places his disaster in the context of the history of the Persian kingship (759-86), and prophesies defeat at Plataea (800-20). Finally, he describes the tragedy as the sequence of *hybris*, *atê* and lament, naming Zeus as the god who punished Xerxes for his 'overweening ambitions' (821-8), and attempts to remedy the disaster, ordering the chorus to educate Xerxes and the Queen to provide him with a new *kosmos* (829-38).

The *Persians* is constructed from repeated patterns.[33] Darius' ghost arrives as the Queen did in the first episode – spectacularly but fearfully to seek information from the elders (681-2; cf. 170-2). Aware of lament in Persia – wailing, breast-beating, scoring of the earth – he does not know, as he asks in plaintive alliteration, 'what pain pains the *polis*'? (682).[34] Darius knows the past and future, but he is ignorant of the present. The first part of this episode is his recognition scene: he learns that the Persian disaster fulfils prophecies which he thought would be realized in the distant future (739-41).

The chorus' response to Darius' question repeats and intensifies the spectacle of fear and reverence at the Queen's first entrance. In three anaphoric and rhyming lines, the elders express their inability to look at or to address Darius because of their 'old fear' of him (694-6). Darius responds in trochaic tetrameters, signalling his impatience as he pleads with the chorus to tell him the news (697-9). Awe-struck, the elders are unable to deliver bad news to their beloved king (700-2).

Darius appeals to his 'noble wife' to stop her lament and to tell him something 'clear' (703-6). He uses maxims to coax her into divulging the news (706-8). Darius' sympathetic awareness shows that he is ready for bad news. Treating land and sea as separate spheres, however, he is unprepared for Xerxes' act – bridging the Hellespont – transforming sea into land and incurring disaster on both land and sea.

The Queen, as the messenger before her, bluntly states the catastrophe: 'the empire of the Persians has been nearly destroyed (literally, 'sacked')' (714). The *Persians* recalls Athens' sack (65-72, 81-107, 177-8, 807-12) but turns the tables on the Persians, representing their defeat as a metaphorical 'sack' of their empire.[35] The reversal instantiates the principle of 'action' (*drama*) and 'suffering' (*pathos*): the Persian sackers are sacked. That the Greek word for Persians, *Persai*, is the aorist infinitive of the verb 'to sack', enhances the idea.[36] The Queen pairs the 'sack' of the Persian empire with Xerxes' 'emptying out the entire plain of the mainland' (718), developing Persia's *pathos* as the analogue and antithesis of Athens'.

The Queen defines the military disaster and object of lament: 'the navy, being defeated, destroyed the infantry' (728). Such a relationship between the Persian fleet and army became conventional wisdom. In Herodotus, Queen Artemisia of Halicarnassus advises Xerxes not to risk a naval battle at Salamis. Greek sailors, she contends, 'are better than your men at sea as men are better than women' (8.68a1).[37] Xerxes already holds Athens; to fight a naval battle for it would be superfluous. She advises the king to march to the Peloponnese (8.68a2-b2). Quoting Aeschylus' Queen, she concludes, 'I fear that the fleet, being defeated, will destroy the land army too' (8.68g1). Herodotus considers Artemisia's advice sound (7.99.3); modern historians have been less enthusiastic.[38] The *Persians* locates the vulnerability of Xerxes' invasion in the navy. Herodotus and Thucydides follow suit (Herodotus 7.139; Thucydides 1.73.4-74.1). Explaining Xerxes' defeat in these terms justifies Athens' title as 'saviours of Greece' (Herodotus 7.139.5); but it also identifies the navy as the enabling factor in a total defeat which jeopardizes the socially superior land forces.

Darius' lack of concern for Xerxes and his own *oikos* is conspicuous; he does not know which of his sons led the invasion (717). The Queen steers the discussion toward Xerxes, informing him that, as one of few survivors, he crossed the bridge 'yoking the two lands' to safety (734-6). Herodotus insists that the bridges were down (8.117.1). The *Persians* treats the bridges both as Xerxes' destructive madness and as his means of salvation.

Xerxes' salvation triggers Darius' recollection of prophecies of the disaster. He thought time would delay their fulfilment (740-1), but it came in an unpredictable instant (739-40).[39] Darius blames Xerxes for accelerating their realization: he attracted divine assistance (742). The dialogue isolates Xerxes' yoking of the Hellespont as an act of madness, the moment when 'divinity' abetted his *hybris* and caused him to lose his senses (719-25). The play stresses interplay between man and god in realizing the catastrophe; now, however, the Greeks are hardly in the picture. The gods' role in abetting Xerxes predominates.[40]

The *Persians* does not specify the source or content of these prophecies. Some conjecture that the *Phineus* (a prophet, in some accounts, blinded by the gods), which preceded the *Persians*, contained them.[41] These prophecies seem to have a dual message. They portend the 'sack' and 'evacuation' of the Persian empire (714, 718) and the king's 'salvation' (735-8).[42] In this regard, they are parallel and opposed to the two prophecies Herodotus claims the Delphic Oracle delivered to the Athenians before Xerxes reached the city. Both prophesied the sack of Athens, but the second hinted at Athens' salvation through evacuation and naval battle at 'divine Salamis' (7.141.3). The surviving Athenian collective is analogous and antithetical to the surviving individual Xerxes.

The *Persians* gradually depicts the Persian *pathos* on the model of Athens': evacuation, sack, salvation, fulfilment of a double prophecy. The bridge over the Hellespont is Xerxes' destructive delusion and means of salvation; the Athenian fleet enables the sack of Athens and the salvation of the Athenians as a *polis*. Such echoes develop the Persian *pathos* as reciprocal vengeance for the trauma they inflicted on Athens. They instantiate the play's major theme, that action (*drama*) necessitates reciprocal suffering (*pathos*) that is no less violent and painful. The Persian *pathos* – the loss of a fleet, all men of military age, the nobility, and with them, *olbos* and empire – compensates for the Athenian *pathos*. At the same time, the symmetry and opposition between Persia's and Athens' *pathos* also enables the audience to experience an effect crucial to tragedy: to realize the self in the pain of the other.[43]

'A disease of the mind'

For Darius, Xerxes' ignorance, youthful audacity, and defiance of his commands are the cause of the disaster (744, 782-3). Darius condemns Xerxes, accusing him of hoping 'to hold the sacred flowing Hellespont in bonds like a slave' (745-6), changing the shape of the Hellespont (747), and making a path for his great army 'by throwing hammer-beaten shackles' on the Hellespont (747-8). Darius' charge is not that Xerxes tried to enslave a free people, or that he challenged superior Greek sailors to a naval battle, as we might expect if the *Persians* aimed simply to celebrate Greek superiority. Rather, he excoriates his son for trying to dominate all the gods, singling out Poseidon, god of sea (749-51).[44] Darius calls this his son's 'disease of the mind' (750-1). In Aeschylus' *Eumenides*, the Erinyes declare that '*olbos* ... comes from the health of the mind' (535-7). The *Persians* demonstrates the converse: Xerxes' 'disease of the mind' ruins Persia's *olbos*.

Herodotus relates that Xerxes, enraged after a storm destroyed his first bridges, ordered the Hellespont punished. He imposed 300 lashes upon it and cast a pair of shackles into its depths, fettering and stigmatizing his errant slave (7.35). Themistocles berates Xerxes for this as well as for destroying Athens' temples, citing these acts as proof that mortals were not responsible for Xerxes' defeat: 'gods and heroes, whose envy prevented one unholy and transgressive man from being king of Europe and Asia, accomplished this' (Herodotus 8.109.3). This is the thrust of Darius' condemnation in the *Persians*. Xerxes sought to dominate 'all the gods'. Zeus punished his presumption (827-8).

Most scholars rule out reference to Xerxes' punishment of the Hellespont in the *Persians*.[45] Yet how 'hammer-beaten shackles' (747) can refer to Xerxes' bridges, boats lashed together with Phoenician white linen and Egyptian papyrus, anchored, and winched taut, is difficult to see (Herodotus 7.33-6; cf. 8.20).[46] The solution is that 'shackles' are a metaphor for the bridges. Not only did they 'yoke' the continents, they 'chained' the sacred water demarcating them.[47] Xerxes' crime is expecting 'to hold the sacred flowing Hellespont like a slave in chains', turning ever-flowing water into inert land, and marching an army over it (745-8).

A tragedy of succession

Darius fears that his wealth, which he treats as its essential value – the labour (*ponos*) he expended to acquire it – will be pillaged in the aftermath of Xerxes' defeat (751-2). His fear dovetails with the omen of the hawk mauling the eagle (205-10) and with the chorus' vision of the end of tribute (584-90). Darius is a materialist. The Athenians defined their empire as immortal glory (*kleos*) – symbolic rather than financial capital.[48] They expressed the value of empire as the risk and expenditure of life and effort (*ponos*) that earned *kleos*, gratitude (*charis*), and expressed their virtue and excellence (*aretê*) as a community.[49] Viewing imperialism from a Persian perspective, the *Persians* demystifies it as a kind of *hybris* aimed at the accumulation of money and power and the appearance of 'blessedness' (*olbos*) derived from dispossessing others.

According to Herodotus, 'the Persians say Darius was a merchant, Cambyses a despot, and Cyrus a father' (3.89.3). Darius established fixed tribute assessments from 20 districts, essentially to fund an augmented navy (Herodotus 3.89-96).[50] Xerxes' defeat annuls Darius' labour and undermines the empire's economic foundations, which enable its dynamism and growth. Tribute supports conquest, which generates additional wealth, enabling conquest to be funded on an increasing scale. The Queen referred to this process (161-7): she feared that wealth embodied in an invading army might subvert the quality of wealth that gives it non-economic value, *olbos*. Yet she also realized that wealth without the imprimatur of conquest does not command respect.

Darius does not implicate Persian imperialism in Xerxes' disaster. The Queen makes this connection. She depicts the disaster as a tragedy of succession. Xerxes sought to avenge his father (473-7) and to attain his standard of conquest and enrichment. She insists that Xerxes 'learned these things associating with bad men', who ridiculed him for failing to measure up to his father: Darius 'acquired wealth (*ploutos*) by the point of the spear', but Xerxes 'wielded the spear in the house because of lack of manliness (*anandria*) and did not increase his paternal *olbos*'.[51] Responding to these reproaches, Xerxes planned the invasion of Greece (753-8). Readers dismiss this as a mother's excuse for a son who can do no wrong.[52] Herodotus, however, found this position plausible. Xerxes' uncle Artabanus tells him on the eve of the invasion of Greece that he has achieved a measure of wisdom, but that 'the company of bad men trips you up'. Such men, he claims, urge an invasion that 'increases *hybris*'. They neglect the wisdom 'that says instructing the soul always to seek to have more than it has is wrong' (7.16a).

The constant yearning to acquire more is the heart and soul of ancient imperialism; Darius condemns it (825-6). The *Persians* shows that it is endemic to empire. How does the son of a father who surpassed all mortals in *olbos* (709-11) increase his inherited *olbos*? The *Persians* locates Xerxes in a no-win situation between avenging his father's failure at Marathon and surpassing his success. Aeschylus' trilogies tend to explore the workings of an inherited curse (e.g. *Oedipus Trilogy, Oresteia*).[53] In the *Persians*, the blessing of superlative paternal *olbos* becomes an inherited curse. Xerxes must prove his fitness for kingship by conquest; this is how Darius and Persia's kings acquire *olbos*. Aeschylus' Queen understands this. Herodotus' Atossa voices this view of Persian kingship and empire: imperial power cannot be idle. It must be employed to add 'peoples' and 'power' to itself (3.134.1). This is especially fitting for a young king who is 'master of much wealth': he must demonstrate his virtue 'so that even the Persians will know that they are ruled by a man' (3.134.2).

The tragedy focuses on the imperative for a son, and indeed, for a younger generation, to attain the standard of their fathers. This is encoded in the Queen's dream: Xerxes tears his robes not because he falls, but because he sees his father pitying him (197-9). In Herodotus, Persian 'tradition' (*nomos*) mandates Xerxes' invasion of Greece: from the time Persia took the hegemony from the Medes, Persian kings pursued an uninterrupted path of conquest. Following the god who led them, the Persians acquired numerous peoples under Cyrus, Cambyses, and Darius (7.8a). Herodotus' Xerxes locates himself in this tradition and measures his worth according to it. In the *Persians*, Darius places Xerxes in this tradition and finds him wanting (759-86).[54]

The *Persians* envisions that once empire becomes patrimony, it assumes a life of its own. It cannot be lost, squandered, or alienated; it must be increased. It is a possession of the past, present, and future simultaneously: the present generation holds it, but it belongs to the fathers who acquired it and must be bequeathed to sons as a larger legacy. At some point, the problem arises: how can the heirs of an empire ensure that they do not fall below the standard of their forebears, who acquired and augmented the empire by expending their lives and labour (*ponos*)?[55] The *Persians*, Herodotus' *Histories*, and Thucydides' *History* offer similar answers: by calamitous overextension of their power and resources in an act of invasion intended to emulate the greatness of the fathers and to increase their legacy.[56] Empire is configured to realize itself as a tragedy of succession. A blessing, empire eventually turns into a curse because it has no point of satiation. *Hybris* and insatiability (*koros*) are embedded in it, inevitably producing *atê* and lament.[57] For Herodotus, Thucydides, and Xenophon, the story of an empire is a tragedy which ends in lament. They followed Aeschylus' *Persians*.

In this perspective, Xerxes is a tragic figure trapped between 'lack of manliness' (*anandria*), failing to measure up to his father, and *hybris*, surpassing his accomplishments.[58] Critics have noted that the *Persians* does not feature a debate or fateful moment of choice.[59] The tragedy of the *Persians* is not a matter of choice, but of necessity. Herodotus' narrative of Xerxes' invasion features a similar lack of choice. At first Xerxes does not want to invade Greece; he is preoccupied with Egypt (7.5). Under the influence of Mardonius and Greek exiles, he announces his intention to invade, but then changes his mind, deciding to follow Artabanus' advice (7.5-13). A 'large and handsome man', however, appears to Xerxes in two dreams, threatening him with a rapid and humbling fall from power if he fails to invade (7.12-14). Xerxes persuades Artabanus to wear his clothes, sit on his throne, and sleep in his bed as a test of the dream's divinity (7.15-17). The dream visits Artabanus and threatens him with punishment if he 'deters what must happen' and is on the verge of burning out his eyes with hot irons when he awakes and accedes to the invasion, interpreting the dream to mean that the gods are sending ruin to the Greeks (7.17-18). Xerxes has a third dream – a clear omen of failure – which the *magi* misinterpret as sign that 'all men will be his slaves' (7.19), abetting the delusion implanted by the gods.

The *Persians*' producer Pericles went on to become the greatest Athenian exponent of empire as patrimony (Thucydides 1.144.4; 2.36, 62.3). The generation that succeeded him sought to rival and surpass their fathers (Thucydides 6.17.7, 18.6-7), crippling the empire after total defeat in a sea-borne invasion of Syracuse.[60] Pericles adjured the Athenians never to fall short of the standard set by their fathers and to preserve their empire at all costs. The strategy he adopted against Sparta and its allies was essentially to re-enact Salamis – to sacrifice homes and land to the invading Peloponnesians (but not the city, which was fortified and connected to the ports at Piraeus by long walls) and to protect their 'liquid' assets, their tribute and fleet.[61] One basis for this strategy was the idea that Athens was an island (Thucydides 1.143.5; [Xenophon] *Constitution of the Athenians* 2.13-16; cf. Herodotus 1.174). Although the long walls were not completed until 456, this mode of thinking dates to directly after the Persian Wars (Thucydides 1.93).

According to Thucydides, Pericles first told the Athenians that they not only ruled 'allies', but were 'most supreme over the entire sea' in 430/29 (2.62.1-2). A permanent, tribute-collecting naval empire, however, is predicated upon such a belief. In Thucydides' narrative of the final battle in the harbour of Syracuse, Athenian generals reproach admirals of retreating ships with the question, 'Are they retreating because they think enemy land more their own now than the sea, acquired through no little pain'? (7.70.8). The Athenians came to view the sea as property over which they exercised authority. Aeschylus attributes such a delusion to the Persians.

Few would deny that Athenians of Pericles' generation conducted the empire in a manner comparable to the Persians.[62] How does this fact relate to the *Persians*? Most analysts consider it a coincidence, asserting that Athenian imperialism was too rudimentary in 472 or denying that the play has a visionary quality.[63] By this time, however, Athenians applied the figure of 'the Mede' to their own citizens. If we accept the restoration of an ostrakon from the agora, somebody called Aristides 'the brother of Datis' (the Mede who led the Persians at Marathon) to exclude him from the citizen body.[64] After the battle of Salamis, Callias son of Cratias was tagged 'the Mede' or 'from the Medes' on nearly 20 ostraka and sketched as a Persian archer on one.[65] Aeschylus' choice to dress himself and other Athenians as Persians to re-enact their defeat and loss of empire at a time when Athens was forming its own empire should be seen as a function of ambivalence towards the city's new role as both leader of an anti-Persian alliance and heir to the Persians in the Aegean. The *Persians* dramatizes a fictionalized fall of the Persian empire to demonstrate how empire collapses through overextension and to avert such an outcome for Athens' imperialism.

Fathers and sons: a history of Persian imperialism

Darius ceases to speak in trochaic tetrameters and shifts to iambic trimeters (759), marking the end of his recognition scene. Juxtaposing the present with the origins of Zeus-bestowed monarchy over all Asia, Darius characterizes Xerxes' disaster as the worst in Persian history, describing it as the complete 'emptying out' of Susa and 'always to be remembered' (759-64). Darius' denunciation refines the analogy and polarity between the Persian and Athenian *pathos*. For the Athenians, Salamis was 'always to be remembered', because it produced 'immortal glory.'[66] As the complete 'emptying out' of Athens, however, it was also the worst catastrophe in Athens' history.[67] The *Persians* reproduces the complexity of Salamis by transposing a version of the Athenian *pathos* to Susa. From this distance, the Persian perspective focalizes Greek liberation, grief for its costs, and the vulnerability of naval imperialism.

Darius describes the first king Medus as *hêgemôn stratou*, 'leader of the army' (765).[68] The principle of hegemony in Athenian society was also military. Citizens with the most political power were generals, elected for yearly, renewable terms. Sons tended to follow their fathers in the office.[69] Military success legitimated the power of the demos as a whole; the demos was a collective *hêgemôn stratou* of its empire.

Herodotus relates that the Persian kings hailed from the clan of Achaemenes, a sub-group of the tribe Pasargadae, which had the highest status in Persian society (1.125.3). The historical Cyrus and Darius derived their entitlement to rule from Achaemenes.[70] In the *Persians*, the Persian kingship begins with Medus, eponymous ancestor of the Medes, a different Iranian people. This was a typical Greek conflation. Epigrams commemorating the defence against the Persians declare victory over 'the Mede'.[71] They also distinguish Medes from Persians or claim to have vanquished the Persians.[72] The Greek word for collaborating with the Persians is *mêdismos*, 'taking the side of the Mede'. To the Greek ear, 'Mede' connoted the barbarian invader.[73]

Herodotus narrates a succession of Median kings – Deioces, Phraortes, Cyaxares, and Astyages, who lost the kingship to his half-Persian grandson, Cyrus son of Cambyses (1.95-130; cf. 1.75.1).[74] Herodotus stresses the dual nature of Cyrus' rise to power – he 'liberated' the Persians and 'enslaved' the Medes.[75] Aeschylus depicts the kingship of Asia as continuously Median/Persian; a figure such as Astyages does not fit his conception of royal history. Similarly, he treats kingship and empire as originating together. He therefore omits a king corresponding to Deioces. Herodotus uses Deioces, the first Median king, to exemplify the incompatibility of kingship and equality and the inverse relationship between political order (*eunomia*) and political freedom (1.95-101).[76]

Aeschylus' Medus approximates to Phraortes, who began the conquest of the Near East (Herodotus 1.102). The next king corresponds to his son, Cyaxares, who consolidated rule over the peoples on the eastern side of the Halys River (1.103.1-2). He defeated the Assyrians, sacking Ashur in 614 and capturing Nineveh in 612. According to Herodotus, Cyaxares avenged his father, who had died trying to take Nineveh (1.103.2). Darius describes him as completing his father's work (766). Herodotus refers to a tradition of praise for Cyaxares (1.103.1). Darius praises Medus' son for his self-control – 'the rudder of his mind controlled his spirit' (767). Metaphors from seafaring figure in praise which frames Xerxes' blameworthy naval ambitions (550-63).

In Darius' catalogue, Cyrus is the second father in the sequence of named fathers and anonymous sons. He is the 'third' from Medus; his relationship to Medus' son is unexplained. His epithet *eudaimôn* ('blessed', 'having a good *daimôn*', 768) aligns him with Darius but contrasts him with Xerxes, whose *daimôn* is malicious and shifts course on him (158, 942-3), deluding (472-3), trampling (515-16, 911-12), and cutting down the Persians (920-1). As Darius will explain, Xerxes 'despised his present *daimôn*' (825-6). A function of a person's moral choices, *daimôn* is connected with character. As the philosopher Heraclitus proclaims, 'a man's character is *daimôn*' (fr. 119 D-K). In the *Persians*, however, character is more a function of outcomes than of choices.

Cyrus 'conquered all Ionia by force' (768-71). The presumption is that the Ionians resisted but lost. Herodotus' narrative of the Persian conquest of Ionia contains a similar premise (1.169.1; 7.51.1). Defence is always praiseworthy; invasion is praiseworthy only if it succeeds. Divine favour and virtue are entailments of this success. Thus 'God did not hate' Cyrus, 'because he was well-intentioned and intelligent' (*euphrôn*,

772). Cyrus' success recalls Xerxes' failure: he 'directed everything foolishly' (*dysphronôs*, 553-4). Enslaving the Hellespont and seeking to dominate 'all the gods' (745-50), he was not 'in his right mind' (725); he suffered from a 'disease of the mind' (750-1).

The tyrant's son is a degenerate figure. Reared with an entitlement to do as he pleases and the power to satisfy any desire, his pleasure is to realize transgressive desires and his life unfolds as a series of destructive crimes. In the tradition Herodotus followed, Cyrus' son Cambyses exemplifies this stage.[77] In the *Persians*, however, Cambyses is the dutiful fourth king to 'govern the army' (773). The *Persians* does not treat succession as degeneration.[78] The early history of the Persian kingship features two pairs of named fathers and anonymous sons. Medus' son is an exemplary son-king; Cyrus is the paradigmatic father-king (cf. Herodotus 3.89.3, quoted above). Xerxes is antithetical to both. He is the only named son and the only son to fail his father.

The fifth king Mardus prefigures Xerxes' place in the drama. Both are disgraces to their fatherland and kingship (774-5, 932-4) and victims of 'trickery' (*dolos*, 361-2, 775-7). The *Persians* does not specify Mardus' disgrace. In Herodotus, Mardus bears the name Smerdis. He is a pretender of the wrong ethnic group and caste, a Mede and a *magus*. His name is the same as Cambyses' brother – whom Cambyses had assassinated – Smerdis (3.30), and he physically resembles him (3.61.2). In the Behistun Inscription, Darius names this pretender Gaumata, a *magus* who takes the name and identity of Cambyses' murdered brother, named Bardiya, and rules in his place.[79] In Herodotus, the struggle to remove the pretender Smerdis is part of the larger conflict between Medes and Persians for domination (3.65, 73). In the Behistun Inscription, Darius declares that he restored the kingship to its rightful clan.[80]

Mardus' reign explains how Darius gained the kingship, restored its legitimacy, and re-established succession between father and son. A member of the group of friends who murdered the pretender, Darius attained the kinship by lot (779; cf. Herodotus 3.80-6). Recent scholars have been inclined to include line 778, 'sixth was Maraphis, seventh Artaphrenes' in the text.[81] Edith Hall claims that Maraphis' and Artaphrenes' kingship has 'psychological impact' and 'implies an unstable and bloody barbarian court, susceptible to vicious intrigues and serial coups'.[82] Such an impression is difficult to derive from this line and inconsistent with the rest of the catalogue, which is a model of stable succession. Wherever it is found – Darius' Behistun Inscription, Herodotus' *Histories*, Ctesias' *Persian History* – the story of the vanquished pretender explains how Darius became king of Persia. Including line 778 makes it explain how Maraphis and Artaphrenes became kings. The best explanation is that this line belongs to a list of conspirators, 'the men bound by friendship and kinship, whose business this was' (777) and was mistakenly added after the fifth king.[83]

Condemning father and condemning audience

The *Persians* presents Persian history as the succession of fathers and sons in a society geared toward military conquest. Fathers are self-made and named; except for Xerxes, sons are dutiful and anonymous. Darius concludes that in the history of the Persian kingship, Xerxes harmed his *polis* more than any other king (784-6). Darius' catalogue implies that Xerxes alone was responsible for the debacle. Darius thus counters the Queen's insinuation that his *olbos* proved to be his son's problem. Youthful impetuosity impelled Xerxes beyond the boundaries of sense; he forgot his father's commands (782-3), striving beyond the limit, and incurring Zeus' punishment (827-8). Darius authorizes earlier blame of Xerxes (361-2, 373, 454, 548-57) and absolves Persian culture, kingship, and empire from responsibility, diverting sole responsibility upon Xerxes. This is a problem for those who consider the play an indictment of barbarian kingship and empire.[84] According to Darius, Persian kings have been self-controlled, moderate, blessed, and beloved of the gods.

Darius' catalogue is inconsistent with the depiction of Persian imperialism in the rest of the play. The elders speak of the Persian empire as an invincible city-sacking force, enslaving men and nature alike (65-107), forcing subjects in Asia to pay tribute and bow before the king, and stifling their freedom of speech (584-94). They consider divinity a reward for Xerxes' success (157-8) and treat Darius as a divinity (150-8, 640-56). Darius' history of the Persian empire is a story of continuous expansion. But what are its limits? This is the problem of empire: the only way of finding its limits is by transgressing them.

Most readers emphasize Darius' assertion that 'Zeus bestowed this honour: for one man to be chieftain of all flock-nurturing Asia, holding the governing sceptre' (762-4), and argue that Xerxes' transgression was his attempt to extend Persian rule to Europe.[85] The matter cannot be so simple. Athens' empire includes Asia (898-902). Aeschylus' audience knew that Darius extended the Persian empire into Europe; the *Persians* describes Darius as conquering and ruling an empire in Europe (858-79): 'so many cities as he captured not crossing the passage of the Halys River or stirring from his hearth' (865-7). Does the play distance Darius from the Persian debacle because he used surrogates to conquer? This is a superficial and unsatisfactory distinction.

Darius condemns his son for actions he himself committed. Darius bridged the continents, hiring Mandrocles of Samos to link them across the Thracian Bosporus to invade Scythia.[86] The invasion was a matter of record: Herodotus reports that Darius erected inscriptions recording the act and that Mandrocles dedicated a painting of Darius leading his army across the bridge in the temple of Hera on Samos (4.88). Aeschylus allows a hint of Darius' transgression to slip through – Darius calls the Hellespont the Bosporus when castigating his son (723, 746). In the second half of this episode, Darius will condemn all Persians for destroying temples and altars and looting statues (800-31); the historical Darius inaugurated these atrocities. Historically, the king who condemns his son and people shares their guilt.

This is important. On the one hand, the audience can suspend belief and accept Darius' condemnation of Xerxes as the playwright's message. Readers of the play often equate Darius' and Aeschylus' perspectives.[87] On the other, the audience can see that Darius' history of Persia's kinship and imperialism, featuring pairs of named fathers and anonymous sons, seeks to deny a tragedy of succession. At the same time, Darius allows the audience to see the growth of Persia's empire to the point of his son's disastrous overextension.

Darius focalizes multiple perspectives. This scene features him in the role of condemning father; but Darius is also the pitying father of the Queen's dream. Darius' perspectives guide the audience between the poles of pity based on shared experience and condemnation from a position of moral and intellectual superiority. Xerxes can be a scapegoat for Persia's imperialist *hybris*; he can be an object of pity for his place in the succession of kings and in the history of Persian expansion.

To complete the episode, Darius prophesies future disaster at Plataea, explaining it as a function of general laws. The Darius-episode juxtaposes past, present, and future in an intelligible pattern. It constitutes the synoptic moment of the drama, enabling beginning and end, action and suffering, individual and group responsibility, Persian and Greek to be understood together.

5

The Synoptic Moment

The *Persians* extracts usable knowledge from the Persian disaster. When the chorus breaks its silence to ask Darius how the Persians can act in their best interest, Darius rules out a large-scale invasion to avenge their losses, 'for the land itself is their ally' (787-92).[1] Ancient historians continued the tradition. Herodotus stresses that enemy land is insidious for invaders: it lures them in until it starves them (7.49). For Thucydides, it is axiomatic that long-distance invasions rarely succeed, both because invaded peoples unite in defence and because of problems of provisioning (6.33.5).

The chorus suggests sending an elite force to Greece, but Darius unexpectedly reveals that such a force currently in Greece will not return (795-7) and prophesies its defeat at Plataea (800-20). Darius' catalogue of Persian kings stressed Xerxes' sole culpability. For the balance of the episode, however, the Persians share Xerxes' guilt and punishment.[2] Discussion of Salamis focused on Xerxes' transgression against gods embodied in nature. The defeat at Plataea punishes Persian crimes against gods embodied in culture – the destruction of temples and altars and the looting of statues. For this, not only Xerxes, but all Persians are responsible. The transition from individual to group responsibility at the point of desecrating temples elaborates Persian *hybris*; but it also furthers the symmetry between the Persian and Athenian *pathos*. As the narrative envisions events in the future outside the drama, it also arrives at an origin in the past: the burning of Cybebe's temple.

Darius was the subject of the original *pathos*, the attack on Sardis. He is also the author of Persia's retributive *drama*: Xerxes fulfilled his vow to punish Athens (Herodotus 5.105).[3]

Darius articulates the principle that explains both Persia's and Athens' *pathos*: desecration of temples, altars, and statues entails the guilt and punishment of entire communities, not merely their perpetrators.

The synoptic moment of the *Persians*

The Darius-scene permits the audience to understand the tragedy from its beginning, Zeus' bestowal of the ruling sceptre on 'one man to be chieftain of flock-nurturing Asia' and 'leader of the army' (*hêgemôn stratou*, 762-5) to its end, the mounds of Persian bones that for three generations 'will signal without a voice to the eyes of mortals that it is not right for a mortal to think beyond his nature' (818-20). This trajectory implies that political/military hegemony is configured to exceed the boundaries of mortal nature and moral sense. If empire is patrimony that must be augmented each generation through conquest, a point of disastrous transgression is foreseeable.

In the *Poetics*, Aristotle argues that the parts and whole of a dramatic plot should be comprehensible in relation to one another (1450b34-1451a15). The beauty of a plot consists in its arrangement and magnitude. If it is too extensive, it cannot be comprehended all at once or as a whole in relation to its parts. Too short a plot yields little meaningful information. Aristotle advises that parts of a plot be 'easily seen together' (*eusynoptos*). His definition of such a magnitude is that 'beginning (*archê*) and end (*telos*) be capable of being seen together' (1459b19-20).

The presentation of a synoptic moment – a speech, ode, or episode that articulates the beginning and end of the narrative, allowing the audience to comprehend the action as a whole – while also deferring its *telos* – is characteristic of Aeschylus' dramaturgy. The Cassandra-scene in the *Agamemnon*, which defers and predicts Agamemnon's murder and foresees Orestes' vengeance, placing both in the context of the 'original crime' of the House of Atreus, the feast of Thyestes, is the best example of this moment (*Agamemnon* 1035-330; cf. *Seven against Thebes* 720-91). Tragic action in Aeschylean drama unfolds over generations; the magnitude of this action sometimes requires characters with special knowledge to make its meaning intelligible. Darius performs this role in the *Persians*. His final speech articulates two principles of the dramatic narrative: that violent action (*drama*) entails reciprocal suffering (*pathos*, 813-4) and that *hybris*, flowering into *atê*, produces a harvest of lament (821-2). The first explains the defeat at Plataea outside of the drama; the second explains the final episode in the drama, the *kommos*, which stages a harvest of tears. Readers often consider the Darius-episode the transcendent climax of the play.[4] But it also possible to see it as deferring the climax – Xerxes' homecoming and lament for his defeat – and providing the context for its reception.

Reciprocity: *drama* and *pathos*

Darius foretells Persian defeat at Plataea as a reciprocal payment for '*hybris* and godless intentions' (807-8), the looting of divine statues and destruction of temples and altars in Greece (809-12). The 'height of sufferings' awaiting the Persians at Plataea will be 'payment' (*apoina*) for these transgressive aims and actions. *Pathos* will redeem *drama*: action and reaction, aggression and suffering, crime and punishment will balance one another, but only at a minimum.[5] The Persians suffer and will suffer more than the harm they inflicted (813-14). This is a basic principle of Aeschylean narrative.[6] If Darius describes Persian punishment for the desecration of Greek temples as building a 'temple of Woe' whose foundations are yet to be finished (814-15), the verbal imagery itself reciprocates the crime.[7] Persian suffering is a metaphorical 'temple of Woe' which compensates for the temples they toppled.

Darius' condemnation of Persian looting and destruction of Greek sacred property is another of the drama's surprises. The Queen and chorus do not anticipate it.[8] Pericles Georges argues that as barbarians Persians do not realize that they are atrocities.[9] But Darius does; and in Aeschylus' *Agamemnon* the herald declares the destruction of Trojan temples a glorious act (524-37). Barbarians do not have a monopoly on such violence in myth or history.

'The most beautiful victory of all we know': monument and sacrifice

Darius figures the battle at Plataea as a kind of perverted sacrificial ritual (816-17).[10] A *pelanos* is a bloodless offering; the final *pelanos*-offering of the tragedy will be a blood-payment for the '*hybris* and godless intentions' (807-8) that bloodless offerings could not avert or remedy (201-11; 524-6, 609-22).

The Athenians do not avenge the destruction of their temples. Darius credits the Spartans and their allies, the 'Dorian spear', with exacting this vengeance (817).[11] Readers tend to undervalue the role of Plataea in the *Persians*.[12] Certainly the play stresses Athenian/Ionian naval power as dealing Persia the decisive blow; Salamis is sole object of Persian lament. But unlike the navy, the 'Dorian spear' vindicates the moral-religious order, imposing justice and long-term meaning on events. Plataea is a redemptive sacrifice that produces a monument – the mounds of bones – as a warning to mortals. Pietro Pucci observes that 'sacrifice is the violent ritual through which men achieve a remedy … establish order in chaos, compensate for losses and ruins'.[13] This is the function of Plataea in the *Persians*. It distances the audience from its own vindication and makes it spectators of the laws of the cosmos. In the struggle which the Persians depict as a battle between the bow and spear, the Spartans wield the spear.

Herodotus calls Pausanias' victory at Plataea 'the most beautiful victory of all we know' (9.64.1). He too depicts Plataea as a payment, though he makes the payees the Spartans. Mardonius' death at Plataea fulfils Delphi's demand for recompense for King Leonidas' death (8.114; 9.64.1). Leonidas' death, in turn, spared Sparta from Athens' fate, for Delphi prophesied that Sparta would either lament a dead king or be sacked (7.220.3-4). The Persian dead compensate for the deaths of Leonidas and the Spartans at Thermopylae (9.79.2).

Like Aeschylus, Herodotus represents Plataea as a massive killing field. Of the alleged 260,000 Persians at Plataea, Herodotus claims that barely 3,000 survived (9.70.5; cf. 9.43.2). Both stress that the Persian dead remained unburied. The Plataeans allowed the corpses to rot and then heaped their bones into a massive mound (9.83.2).

Look to the end: *hybris*, *atê* and lament

Darius elaborates the meaning of these bones: 'for *hybris*, when it comes to full flower, produces the fruit of *atê*, from which it reaps a harvest of complete lament' (821-2). The Greeks conceived of *hybris* as excessive and fruitless potency.[14] When applied to plants, it means that they grow prodigious flowers and wood, but bear no fruit.[15] *Hybris* is a self-defeating and unsustainable performance: it appears as exuberance and power, but reaps a harvest of death and tears. Herodotus quotes a Delphic Oracle which prophesies that after the Persians sack Athens, 'divine Justice will extinguish mighty *Koros*, son of *Hybris*' (8.77.1; cf. Pindar *Olympian Ode* 13.9-10). Violent arrogance and insatiability feed off one another.[16] The image of luxuriant growth for arrogant, violent, and chaotic behaviour interlocks with the play's themes of wealth (*ploutos*), confidence in numerical superiority (*plêthos*), and happiness in prosperity (*olbos*).[17] Luxuriant growth underlies the metaphor of the 'flower' (*anthos*: 59-62; cf. 252, 922-7) and 'native youth' (*hêbê*) of Asia and Persia (922-7; cf. 511-12, 541-5).

Hybris is the essence of Persian imperialism.[18] *Atê* and lament are its fulfilment. The sequence of *hybris*, *atê* and lament has recurred throughout the play. The chorus enacted it in the parodos; the messenger's narrative of Salamis and Psyttalia implied these terms; the drama staged this pattern from the parodos to the lament of the first stasimon. Darius identifies this pattern as the beginning, middle, and end of Xerxes' invasion of Greece. Thus he solves a kind of puzzle encoded in the drama. The *Persians* dramatizes the growth of *hybris* into *atê*, which culminates in a harvest of spectacular lament.

Part of this message was familiar to the audience. Darius voices the wisdom of the sixth-century Athenian poet and lawgiver Solon, Athens' 'father', who stressed that wealth derived from *hybris*, even though men honour it, does not come 'in good order' (*kata kosmon*), but 'is swiftly mixed up with *atê*' (*Elegies* fr. 13.7-13 [West]).[19] Solon was remembered for the warning 'look to the end' (fr. 13.16-32; Herodotus 1.32.9, 86.4-5). Darius reveals the end of *hybris* to the audience: the bones of unburied corpses and lament. He explains the outcome of the new phenomenon of imperialism in terms of the primitive sentiments of the Greek poetic tradition. Even before Solon, the *Odyssey* had warned about the loss of *olbos* through invasion (*Odyssey* 17.419-44). What is new is the dramatic form the *Persians* gives to this message: it exhibits how *koros*, insatiability, and *hybris*, violence towards others, are realized in *atê* and insatiable, self-mutilating lament.

R.P. Winnington-Ingram argues that the *Persians* is torn between two explanations of the Persian disaster: the Persians think that *olbos* and divine envy are responsible, but Darius sees that *hybris* is responsible.[20] It is preferable to synthesize these two explanations. *Olbos* is not the cause of Xerxes' disaster; *koros* and *hybris*, which drive the acquisition and validation of wealth as *olbos*, are responsible.[21] Persian imperialism is the cause of the tragedy: its fundamental lack is justice.[22] The metaphor of flower, fruit, and harvest underscores the difference between agriculture and imperialism as sources of *olbos*. The former produces *olbos* in its just and divinely sanctioned form.[23] The latter violently diverts it from others and, as Solon warned, 'sooner or later is mixed up with *atê*'. Persia deployed its excessive surplus to dispossess others. Darius' final injunction, 'let no man, disdaining his present fortune (*daimôn*), pour out his great *olbos* by desiring others' ' (825-6) warns against imperialism as a kind of *koros/hybris* which destroys *olbos*. Again, Darius has a Homeric parallel (*Odyssey* 18.138-42).

A tale of two cities

Olbos is a function of justice, which insures productivity in both the agricultural and life-cycles. *Hybris* disrupts these cycles. The poet Hesiod urged his brother Perses to be just and not to 'increase *hybris*' (*Works and Days* 213). *Hybris*, he warned, leads to 'disasters' (*atai*), and ultimately brings calamity and barrenness to a city. 'Ultimately' is the operative term, for justice wins out over *hybris* 'in the end' (217-18). In a just city, crops, flocks, trees and people flourish (225-7, 232-4). Zeus does not ordain war (228-9). The people raise their children in peace (228). Crop disease (*atê*) and famine are absent; the community enjoys the fruits of its labours in feasts (230-1). Since the land bears crops, there is no need for ships (236-7).

By contrast, Zeus ordains 'punishment' for those who practice *hybris* even if a single man in the community is the perpetrator (238-41). To such a city, Zeus brings the 'pain' of famine and plague; the people perish (242-3). Women do not give birth; the number of households decreases (244-5). At one time or another, Zeus exacts payment, destroying a large army, city wall, or ships at sea (245-7).

Hesiod's cities of justice and *hybris* underlie the difference between Darius' and Xerxes' reigns in the *Persians*. In Xerxes' reign, Zeus wrecked the Persian fleet and destroyed the entire army (532-6). Women are 'yoked alone' (133-9) bereft of husbands (286-9, 537-45); the 'youth' (*hêbê*) and 'blossom' (*anthos*) of Asia perish (59-60, 252-5, 511-12, 669-70, 733, 918-30, 978-9); households go extinct (978-83). Hesiod's Myth of the Ages is also a subtext for this difference (*Works and Days* 109-201). The Persians interpret the time of Darius as a Golden Age (*Works and Days* 109-26) of unbroken tradition, wealth, wisdom, benevolence, and the absence of suffering.[24] Darius' *olbos* is unsurpassed; he lived like a god among the Persians (709-12). Xerxes' reign is analogous to the Silver Age, a time of *hybris* and failure to honour the gods (*Works and Days* 127-42), when men do not live long past youth (*hêbê*, 132-4).[25]

It is true that the blame of Xerxes enhances praise of Darius.[26] But the recreation of Darius' reign as a lost Golden Age, an object of longing, can also elicit the audience's yearning for the past. The stark rupture in Persia between Darius and Xerxes, depicted primarily as the difference between land and naval empire, evokes the memory of pre-Salamis Athens, a time before ships, when Athens' city wall, temples, fields, and homes were intact. Warfare became a constant reality in post-Salamis Athens. Ships, a sign of productive lack created by *hybris* in Hesiod's scheme, are the city's most prominent possession. Darius arises to condemn his son as an aberration in Persian history, the only king to 'completely empty out this city of Susa' (761); but Athens' disaster echoes in his words. Darius speaks with the paternal voice of the Greek poetic tradition. As will become clear in the second stasimon, the Athenians are Darius'

110

heirs: they acquired the empire he won and Xerxes lost in the naval battle at Salamis.

Failure to understand?

The Persians barely respond to Darius' prophecy (843-6) and ignore it in the *kommos*. Pericles Georges interprets this lack of response as the key to the drama: the Persians do not understand Darius' message 'because barbarians are uncomprehending by nature'.[27] R.P. Winnington-Ingram, whose interpretation Georges adapts, suggests that 'Aeschylus must have hoped that his audience would be more perceptive. Yet the course of fifth-century history may well make us doubt whether the lesson of Zeus *kolastês* ('punisher') was really grasped by the Athenians'.[28] Clearly, Darius' message does not get through: Xerxes never receives it; the chorus does not teach him self-control and 'to stop harming the gods' (829-31); the Queen does not return with a *kosmos* and soothe Xerxes with words (832-8, 846-51). Since the internal audience hardly interferes in the prophecy and explanation, however, Darius' final speech effectively addresses the audience of the play.

'Remember Athens and Greece'

Darius orders his audience to bear witness to the 'penalties' (823) the Persians paid for *hybris*, adjuring them to 'remember Athens and Greece' (824). This command alludes to an oral tradition of his response to the burning of Sardis. Darius was so obsessed with vengeance that he instructed a servant to remind him three times when he served his meal, 'master, remember the Athenians' (Herodotus 5.105.2; cf. 6.94.1).[29] The call to 'remember the Athenians' is an oath of vengeance which the Persian destruction of Athens fulfilled. Aeschylus' Darius reminds the audience of his response to the sack of Sardis, but ironically reverses its meaning: his command to 'remember Athens and Greece' interdicts Persian aggression against Greeks.

The signature of Aeschylus' tragic vision is the ambiguity of violence perpetrated in the name of a society's highest values.

Persian vengeance is a *drama* that provokes a more severe *pathos*, just as the Athenian/Ionian *drama* at Sardis provoked the disproportionately harsh destruction of their cities and temples. The Persian *pathos* is intertwined with Athens': it is an evacuation, a sack, the fulfilment of a double oracle, a simultaneous destruction and salvation through boat-bridges/ships, the worst disaster in the history of the city, and a realization of the call to 'remember Athens' for the destruction of temples. The *kommos* will add another echo – lament for a lost harvest. Adopting the voice of the Greek poetic tradition, Darius speaks across cultures.[30] *Hybris*, *atê*, and lament is not an exclusively Persian sequence.[31] Rather, it is the oldest Greek pattern of deviant intention, action, and divine punishment, which Persian imperialism exemplifies.

Holding the unaccountable to account

The Queen declared her son 'not accountable to the *polis*' (213-14). Darius explains that 'Zeus punishes intentions that are too arrogant, a heavy chastiser' (827-8). The word for 'chastiser', *euthynos*, suggests the mechanism for holding officials at Athens accountable, *euthynai*.[32] Some argue that the *Persians* projects such democratic oversight into the cosmos.[33] But the play transcends particular political systems.[34] Xerxes is politically unaccountable; even so, he must answer to Zeus, who maintains order in the cosmos. All mortals, whether the Great King or the Athenian demos, are accountable to Zeus. Democracy is not immune to the cycle of conquest, wealth, and *olbos* or to the sequence of *hybris*, *atê*, and lament.[35] In the aftermath of the Persian destruction of Athens, the equation of precious metal and subject cities with *olbos* became an Athenian collective ideal. The gleam of wealth and power can ensorcel the masses and their leaders as readily as it can kings and their subjects (Solon *Elegies* frr. 4, 6 [West]; Herodotus 5.49, 97; 6.132; Thucydides 6.24.3). The upshot of the Darius-episode is that successful military hegemony makes a community increasingly liable to *hybris* and *atê* over time.

5. The Synoptic Moment

Seeing the end of the drama: Xerxes' rags

Darius enjoins the chorus to teach Xerxes 'to be sensible' and 'to stop harming the gods with arrogant audacity' (829-31). Ordering the Queen to return to the house and to retrieve a 'fine garment' (*kosmos*), he instructs her to meet Xerxes with it and to soothe him with words: Xerxes' clothing is torn to shreds 'because of grief over his misfortunes' (832-8). The conclusion of the drama pivots on verbal remedies and Xerxes' investiture with a new *kosmos*. Like every other significant stage action in the play, however, they will be pre-empted. Rather than appear before the audience in new clothes, soothed and rehabilitated, Xerxes will lament his rags (1030) and order the elders to tear their robes (1060).

The stress on Xerxes' clothing derives from Greek conventions of poetic and dramatic representation.[36] Investiture and divestiture are basic forms of visual meaning, especially to achieve closure. Bacchylides' *Dithyramb* 17, a narrative of struggle for authority between Minos, king of Crete, and the Athenian hero Theseus, contains a positive version of the failed performance of the *Persians*.[37] The poem depicts Theseus proving his paternity from Poseidon: he dives into the sea and dolphins speed him to the house of Poseidon's wife, Amphitrite, who cloaks him in a purple linen mantle and puts her wedding crown on his head. Theseus emerges dry from the sea and Athenian youths aboard ship rejoice in ritual shouting and singing. The hero in his new garb appears as saviour of his people from Minos' *hybris*. The challenge arose out of Minos' touching an Athenian maiden, whom Theseus defended. In the absence of his father, a mother-substitute (his mother is Aethra) endows Theseus with symbols of his paternity, proving his right to restrain Minos' *hybris*.[38] By withholding Xerxes' new *kosmos*, the play contrasts him with the figure of the liberator, protector, and defender against *hybris*, around whom the group unites. The play's refusal to provide a new *kosmos* for Xerxes may imply a *kosmos* for the Greeks who defeated him; a *kosmos* was the aim of praise poetry of the Persian Wars (Simonides *Plataea* fr. 11.23, restored).

Investiture is a rite of integration into the group and transition to a new status. In Aeschylus' *Eumenides*, the Erinyes first

appear in clothing (*kosmos*) inappropriate to wear 'at the statues of the gods or the houses of men' (55-6). After Athena
persuades the Erinyes to become powers of fertility, harmony,
and justice in Athens, the Athenians welcome them into their
community and honour them with new 'red-dyed robes', re-
deeming the bloodshed and violence of the trilogy, and
symbolizing the transformation of the Erinyes from curses into
blessings (1025-31).[39] The comic stage employs this device. The
chorus of the *Knights* invests the Sausage-Seller with a frog-
green garment at the end of the play as he enters the Council
chamber for a feast (Aristophanes *Knights* 1404-6; cf. 861-6;
Wasps 1122-73). This is the theatrical moment Darius orders
the Queen to enact; against the gradient of his and the Queen's
wishes, the drama refuses to fulfil it.

Darius the hedonist?

Readers of the *Persians* question Darius' authority, arguing
that the audience would have received him as a self-serving
despot or that, as the king who became a god through conquest,
he embodies the *hybris* at the heart of Persian culture.[40] There
is no way to rule out this reception of Darius' first two speeches.
Yet it fails to take into account Darius' third, prophetic speech,
which has the authority of the Greek tradition of poetry and of
Solon in particular. Why does Darius speak so sensibly?

Darius' parting words, 'rejoice, elders, even in woes, giving
daily pleasure to your soul, since wealth is no benefit to the
dead' (840-1) have cast further doubt on his authority.[41] These
words express the outlook of drinking songs and of comedy.
Such advice, however, is typical of what the dead or the dying
tell the living.[42] Darius' recommendation of pleasure and contentment addresses Persia's insatiability; they are part of the
remedy the chorus expects Darius to provide (631-2). The Golden
Age – a time of feasting – associated with Darius is defined by
sufficiency and contentment rather than by excess and insatiability. From the perspective of Greek sympotic poetry, pleasure
is the focus of human life. Simonides asked, 'What human life or
what tyranny is desirable without pleasure? Without it, not even
the life of the gods is enviable' (*PMG* fr. 584).

Solon wove the themes of wealth, pleasure, and contentment into his elegies, equating those who possess great wealth with those who have enough for comfort, take a wife in season and have a child. 'This' he declares, 'is wealth for mortals. No one goes into Hades possessing countless goods, and you could not escape death by making payment ...' (*Elegies* fr. 24 = Theognis *Elegies* 719-28 [West]). Darius' last words echo the view of mortality expressed in sympotic poetry, the songs of the drinking and feasting group which are a model for the *polis*.[43] The sympotic tenor of Darius' parting words elaborates his earlier warning, in which *olbos* was a cup of wine 'wasted by desiring others' ' (824-6).[44] Greek sympotic poets expressed a similar view of the Persian invasion. 'Let us drink', Theognis urges, 'sharing pleasant conversion with one another, having no fear of war with the Persians' (763-4; cf. 773-82 [West]).

Critics similarly read the Queen's response to Xerxes' return in rags as an indictment of the barbarian mentality.[45] After Darius returns to Hades, the elders express their grief for the barbarians' multitude of present and future woes (843-4). The Queen seconds their grief (845-6) and describes what distresses her the most: the dishonour to her son's person (846-7). She is not so much obsessed with 'sartorial display' as with what Xerxes' rags symbolize, dishonour to her son and the royal *oikos*.[46] Hence she resolves to follow Darius' orders, getting a robe (*kosmos*) and meeting her son as he returns (849-50).

The following stasimon implies that Athens is heir to the empire Darius conquered and ruled, but Xerxes lost. It reinforces the status of Darius *in loco patris* and underscores the idea that empire is patrimony.

Torn empire: the second stasimon

Darius returns to the underworld.[47] The Queen exits to fetch Xerxes' *kosmos*. The chorus is alone in the orchestra and sings the second stasimon. The chorus enumerates the city-states that Darius conquered and ruled and Xerxes lost after his defeat at Salamis. The ode explores in geographical terms the image of Xerxes' torn robe, which symbolizes the rupture between Xerxes and Darius and the loss of the Persian empire.[48]

Although there is a causal connection between Xerxes' defeat at Salamis and the loss of Persian holdings listed in the ode, the majority of them remained under Persian control between Salamis and Xerxes' return to Asia. The chorus envisions events outside of dramatic time, between 479 and 473, as if they happened directly after Salamis. In keeping with its visionary character, the metre of the song is lyric dactylic.[49]

Picking up the conclusion of the first stasimon, which envisioned the disintegration of Persia's Asian empire (584-94), the ode laments the reversal of Persian power in Thrace, the Hellespont, Ionia, and the Aegean islands, including Rhodes and Cyprus. With the exception of the cities of Cyprus (892-7), the cities enumerated in this stasimon were likely members of the Athenian empire in 472.[50] Some of them, such as Lesbos, Samos, Chios, Naxos, and perhaps Tenos and Lemnos, provided ships (880-6, 891). Others, such as Paros, Myconos, Andros, Icaros and mainland Ionia were likely tribute-payers (885-902).

The first strophe reinforces the image of Darius' reign as a Golden Age, focusing on empire as 'the great and good life of ruling cities' (852-3). The chorus reiterates and expands the range of Darius' epithets, broadening the schism between the old and new Persian orders. The 'old king' was 'completely sufficient' (854-6), 'causing no harm' (855; cf. 555, 663-4 = 671-2), 'invincible' (856) and 'godlike' (857; cf. 157, 633-4, 643, 651, 654-5, 711). The antistrophe stresses the success of Persian armies during Darius' reign: they were 'honoured' (858) and kept fortified cities under control. Successful in their wars, they returned to flourishing homes 'without suffering' (861-4).[51] The elders return to a theme of the parodos and first stasimon: the Persians' divinely sanctioned success as a land power, penetrating walled fortifications and driving settled populations from their homes (87-107, 555-7). Persia's era of imperial domination enforced by siege power has ended. It is now Athens', whose ability to collect tribute was based upon siege power of a different kind: blockades which induced starvation.

The following three strophic-antistrophic pairs detail Darius' conquests and additions to the Persian empire in the Greek world and its periphery. This topic is often an occasion for *praeteritio*, calling attention to something by declining to speak about it.[52] The chorus offers a detailed list of the cities Darius conquered and ruled, and in some cases, reconquered during and after the Ionian revolt.

Crossing water boundaries symbolizes the *hybris* of imperialist desire in the *Persians*. The chorus proclaims that Darius took the cities in this ode, 'neither crossing the passage of the Halys River nor stirring from his hearth' (865-8). For Herodotus, the Halys demarcates the empire of Lydians from that of the Medes and articulates Asia into two geographical and political units (1.72). Darius personally remained within his natural, religious, and cultural limits; he was a just king and as a consequence, his people flourished. This is a theme associated with Hesiod's city of justice (*Works and Days* 225-37). Some consider this praise of Darius actually a 'sneer' against him as a 'stay-at-home'.[53] In the *Persians*, however, Darius 'acquired great wealth for his children with the point of the spear' (754-5) and claims to have 'invaded many times with many an army' (780). Darius' presence in Persia while increasing his empire is a sign of power, like Zeus in Aeschylus' *Suppliants,* who accomplishes his aims without effort or motion (91-103; cf. Xenophanes frr. 20-2 D-K). Such conquest contradicts the premise that the Persian empire's divinely sanctioned sphere is Asia.

The earliest inscriptions enumerating the cities that paid tribute to Athens date from 454. Lists of first-fruit offerings to Athena from the tribute, a sixtieth of the payment, they lack a geographical format. The sequence of cities in the lists differs from year to year; this probably reflects the order in which they paid.[54] In 442 the tribute-paying cities were grouped into five districts: Ionia, Hellespont, Thrace, Caria, Islands.[55] This order becomes fixed, although the sequence of cities paying within each district varies. The second stasimon of the *Persians* roughly includes these five districts, though in a different order: Thrace, Hellespont, Islands, Caria, Ionia. In the anapaestic prelude to the parodos the chorus listed high tribute-payers – Lydia, Mysia, Babylon, Egypt – as fearsome allies (33-55). The principle of payment governs the order of districts in this ode. Thrace is consistently the highest paying district in the Athenian empire in the period 453-434, followed by the Hellespont, the Islands, Caria, and Ionia.[56] This ranking probably obtained in 472.

Thracian and Hellespontine districts

The chorus first lists 'river cities of the Strymonian Gulf (*pelagos*), neighbours of Thracian huts' (869-71) as cities Darius captured and which obeyed him. Translating *pelagos* as 'lake', some think that the lines refer to a branch of the Paeonians who dwelled in Lake Prasias in huts built on stilts (Herodotus 5.16).[57] This is unlikely. Megabazus was unable to conquer these Paeonians (5.12-16). It is more likely that the chorus refers to settlements on the Gulf of Strymon near the Strymon River, such as Eion.[58] The chorus begins with the Gulf of Strymon because it was a cardinal point of Athens' empire, a chief source of tribute and raw materials and the westernmost bulwark against Persian reprisal.

The antistrophe claims that fortified settlements 'outside the *limnê*' on the continent obeyed Darius (872-5). For those who identify the 'Strymonian *pelagos*' with Lake Prasias, this refers to land 'outside the lake'. Again, this is improbable. Although the word *limnê* normally refers to standing water, in poetry it can designate the sea (e.g. Aeschylus *Suppliants* 524-30) and Sophocles uses it to mean 'gulf' (*Women of Trachis* 636). The word here refers to the Gulf of Strymon. There were numerous fortified settlements between the Gulf of Strymon and the Hellespont. Herodotus lists them from east to west as he narrates Xerxes' route across Thrace to Greece (7.106-9; cf. 6.46-8; 8.120).[59]

The antistrophe concludes by noting that settlements on the Hellespont, Propontis and the mouth of the Black Sea were subject to Darius. These were also cardinal points of Athenian imperialism: they provided access to commodities from the Black Sea, enabling Athens to exploit its naval power by controlling the flow of these commodities to the Aegean. The Persians gained them after the invasion of Scythia and then regained them after the Ionian revolt.

Islands, Caria, and Ionia

The third strophe and antistrophe detail the islands Darius ruled. The first group adjoins the coast of Western Anatolia; the chorus describes them from the perspective of the mainland

(880-2). Lesbos, Samos, and Chios have pride of place (883-5). These islands were early allies of Athens; each manned its own fleet during Aeschylus' lifetime. The author of the Aristotelian *Constitution of the Athenians* calls them the 'sentinels of empire' (24.2). Chian insurgents pushed for Ionian liberation after the battle of Salamis (Herodotus 8.132). Samians swore oaths to enter the Greek alliance under Spartan leadership before the battle of Mycale (9.91-2) and led the revolt at battle of Mycale (9.103.2). Lesbos and Chios joined the Greek alliance under Spartan leadership after Mycale, along with 'the other islanders who happened to be campaigning with the Hellenes' (9.106.4).

Herodotus does not identify these 'other islanders', but of the islands the chorus mentions next, Naxos and Tenos were probably among them. The admiral of the four triremes the Naxians sent to Xerxes' fleet, Democritus, joined the Greeks at Salamis (Herodotus 8.46.3). A trireme from Tenos also left the Persians to fight with the Greeks at Salamis (8.82.1). The Naxians had their name inscribed on the 'Serpent Column'; the Tenians were added later.[60] It did not take long for either island to become a tribute-paying subject of Athens. Naxos was the first island to revolt, perhaps around 465 (Thucydides 1.98.4). There are no records for Naxos' tribute payments until 447, when it paid $6\frac{2}{3}$ talents, a sizable sum. Tenos paid three talents in 449, the earliest date for which we have records.

The appearance of Myconos, Paros, and Andros (885-6) in the third strophe is surprising. They are part of the Cyclades; but they had little claim to importance. Myconos probably paid tribute from the start. When its records are first extant in 451, it pays $1\frac{1}{2}$ talents. Neither Paros nor Andros enjoyed good relations with Athens. Herodotus reports that the Parians joined neither side in the battle of Salamis, but awaited the outcome on the island of Cythnos, one of only six Aegean islands to risk fighting on the Greek side but unnamed in this ode (8.67.1). Themistocles extorted a large sum of money from Paros after the battle of Salamis (8.112.2). As is the case with all the islands, tribute figures are sketchy, but the Athenians exacted a heavy toll from Paros. In 449 the island paid $16\frac{1}{5}$, a huge and punitive sum. Andros was also subject to Athenian reprisal for medism (8.111, 121.1). Themistocles' unsuccessful siege of the island frightened Paros into offering payment. Herodotus surmises that other islands also paid (8.112.2). Myconos was probably one of them.

The third antistrophe treats a mixed geographical range of islands and peninsular Cnidus, spanning the Ionian, Island, and Carian districts. The chorus' description of islands farther from the Asian coast (890-3) applies to the first three: Lemnos, Icaros, and Rhodes. The Athenians established a foothold on Lemnos in the early fifth century (Herodotus 6.136-40). Lemnos sent ships to Xerxes' fleet. Antidorus' ship escaped to the Greek side at the battle of Artemisium (8.11.3) and fought with the Greeks at Salamis (8.82.2).

Icaros was probably in the Persian ambit in 490 when the Persians sailed beside it on the way to Eretria and Marathon (Herodotus 6.95.2). We have no record that the island paid tribute as a whole. Two of its towns paid separately in the Ionian district, indicating the presence of Athenian settlers on the island. Rhodes, a Dorian island, likewise endured Athenian settlers, paying as separate towns in the Carian district. Its major towns paid large sums.

The most interesting cities in this catalogue are those of Cyprus: Paphus, Soli, and Salamis, 'whose mother city is the cause of these laments' (892-7). According to Herodotus, the Cypriots 'gave themselves' to the Persians and invaded Egypt with Cambyses' navy in 525 (3.19.3). The cities Salamis and Soli were the spiritual centre of the island's revolt from Darius in 499/98 (5.110). Onesilus of Salamis was a force behind the resistance, putting him at odds with his brother Gorgus, the pro-Persian king of Salamis (5.104). When Onesilus was killed in the fighting, his brother Gorgus returned to Salamis, saving the city from Persian reprisal (5.110-15). Soli was not so fortunate. It withstood a Persian siege for four months before succumbing (5.115.2). Herodotus does not mention Paphus in connection with the Ionian revolt, but archaeological evidence suggests that it revolted and was taken after the Persians built a siege mound (a Persian specialty).[61] Cyprus as a whole sent 150 ships to Xerxes' fleet (7.90). Paphus sent a contingent (7.195), as did Salamis, whose king Gorgus accompanied the expedition (7.98). In 478, the Greeks under Pausanias 'campaigned against Cyprus and subdued much of it' (Thucydides 1.94.2; Diodorus 11.44.2). The liberation did not last long. The cities of Cyprus never became part of the Athenian empire.[62] The chorus may express Athens' desire for Cyprus' inclusion in the empire. It may recall Salamis' role in the Ionian revolt, linking it with Athenian Salamis' role in defeating the Persians. It could also recall a history of Cypriot medism.

Finally, the chorus details the loss of mainland Ionia in an epode. Cyrus 'conquered all Ionia by force' (771); the chorus refers to Ionia as the 'Ionian inheritance' (898-9, *klêros*). According to Herodotus, Cyrus' son Cambyses considered Ionians and Aeolians 'inherited slaves' (2.1.2). The cities of Ionia had been, as the chorus says 'wealthy and populous' (898-9). Miletus in particular was 'the jewel of Ionia' at the turn of the fifth century (Herodotus 5.28). It had gone over to Cyrus without a fight in 535 (1.143.1). The chorus recalls Ionian collaboration: the territory was the source of an 'inexhaustible strength of armoured men' and of 'allies of all sorts' (901-3), a description of Ionian conscripts (cf. 54). The Ionians provided 100 ships to Xerxes' fleet (Herodotus 7.94).

The ode straddles a line between recalling the Thracian, Hellespontine, island and Ionian failure to defend their freedom against Darius and proclaiming their liberty after the battle of Salamis – where many fought on the Persian side. It represents the reversal of Persian imperialism in the Aegean. The chorus asserts that this reversal is an act of the gods in naval fighting (903-7). The catalogue projects Athenian naval power, recalls Ionian suffering under the Persians, and is an exemplum of the evanescence of naval empire. It is significant that the chorus prefaces the reversal with 'now ... in turn' (903-5): such alternation is characteristic of naval power. Athens' empire is an inheritance from Darius which Xerxes squandered; the Athenians are Darius' heir. Their challenge is to avoid the example of Xerxes.

6

A Harvest of Tears

The *kommos*

Xerxes enters alone, unannounced, and in torn robes (1030), wearing a virtually empty quiver (1019-24).[1] He may have entered on a covered wagon (1000-1), but he is on foot throughout the episode.[2] This is the moment we have awaited; this is the event the play defers until the end: Xerxes' homecoming (*nostos*). How will he be reincorporated into his realm? Will he compound his woes, as the Queen feared when she first considered his return? (529-31). Will the chorus teach him 'self-control' and 'to stop harming the gods' (829-31) as Darius demanded? Will the Queen return with a new *kosmos* for her son? (849-51).

The *Persians* ends with a *kommos*: a sung lament between actor and chorus.[3] Readers are divided over how to interpret it. S.M. Adams calls it a 'satyr-play' and 'appendage' to the drama, which is 'lighter in mood' than the preceding scenes.[4] Michael Gagarin reads the *kommos* as offering 'rehabilitation' as well as 'support and comfort' to Xerxes.[5] David Schenker suggests it recreates the 'proper relationship between a king and his people'.[6] The *kommos* is the play's dramatic climax.[7] It exhibits the *telos* of the tragedy and of the Persian empire, staging the 'harvest of tears' Darius described as the fulfilment of *hybris* and *atê* (821-2), and realizing the play's verbal images as symbolic action on stage. Paradoxically, the effect of this re-enactment is the renewal of Xerxes' *hybris*: he takes control of the elders and commands them to mutilate their bodies in mourning before they escort him to the palace (1038-77). Xerxes regains his grip on Persia; but the *kommos* turns Persian *hybris* upon itself, demonstrating how enslaving imperialism is fulfilled in the self-directed aggression of lament.

The *kommos* is based on eastern ritual laments for two kinds of unseasonable loss: a lost harvest and the death of a king's only son in an attempt to save crops from devastation. Herodotus' account of the original eastern imperialist, Croesus of Lydia, includes a narrative of this type. Croesus' heir Atys is killed by an errant javelin while he tries to subdue a wild boar destroying Mysian fields (1.36-45).[8] This loss forms part of Croesus' saga: he claimed to be the 'most blessed' (*olbiôtatos*) man, but loses his heir, *olbos*, and empire (1.6, 1.26-92).[9] Although the *Persians* is not a tragedy of this type, it is an ironic variation of this pattern. Xerxes loses his *olbos* and empire, but unlike Croesus' son Atys, Darius' son Xerxes is the sole survivor. The young king survives, but loses 'the entire youth' of his empire (670). The *kommos* mourns the loss of these noble youths, 'the *hêbê* of the land' (922-4).

Laments for Adonis, a model for the women's laments reported in the first stasimon, are also of similar type to those of the *kommos*. A royal son killed in a boar hunt, Adonis is lamented at the height of summer; his death coincides with the loss of the harvest.[10] At Athens, women mourned Adonis in private ceremonies held on roof-top gardens.[11] They planted lettuce, fennel, barley or wheat in pots, watching them sprout and wither in the summer heart. They then used these as biers for the lamented effigy of Adonis, dumping both into springs or the sea.[12]

As Marcel Detienne notes, 'the greenness of Adonis guaranteed no harvest at all'.[13] Pointing to the proverb, 'more fruitless than the gardens of Adonis', Gregory Nagy interprets Adonis as a figure for '*hybris* in the botanical sense'.[14] Adonis is a figure of luxuriant but unsustainable growth which ends in lament. Indeed, Adonis embodies the 'flowering of *hybris*', 'harvest of tears', and loss of *hêbê* and *anthos* that characterize the Persian tragedy. That his garden and effigy end up in springs or the sea parallels the fate of Persia's 'youth' and 'flower', whose corpses litter the sea and springs. Xerxes' yoking of the Hellespont, a fruitless 'marriage' which leaves Persian wives 'yoked alone', bringing barrenness to Asia, evokes Adonis as a 'negative image of marriage and fertile union'.[15]

It is uncanny that while Athenian men were voting to invade

Sicily in 415, tradition had it that Athenian women were celebrating the Adonia, lamenting the effigy of the lost youth,
proleptically lamenting the lost 'flower' of Athens about to
invade Sicily.[16] Walter Burkert interprets the ritual of Adonis as
'play-acting the failure of planting in order to ensure by contrast
the success in reality'.[17] The *kommos* of the *Persians* serves an
analogous ritual function: lament for the loss of a fleet and an
empire is an apotropaic ritual against the same fate for Athens.[18]

The image of lost youth as a lost flower/harvest, standard in
ritual lament, is crucial to the *kommos* both in its figural and
literal meanings.[19] The Persians mourn the loss of their noble
youth as a metaphorical lost harvest; the Athenians mourn the
literal destruction of their land.[20] The Persians caused the loss
of two Athenian harvests (Herodotus 8.142.3), hampering agricultural production for the next generation.[21] Thucydides
claims that the Athenians had only just recovered in 431 when
the Spartans began to ravage Attica (2.16.1). The Persian and
Athenian *pathos*, depicted as parallel but opposed throughout
the play, intersect in the *kommos*.

Xerxes' naval imperialism destroys natural value.[22] The de-
ceptive radiance of precious metal supplants it, seducing
individuals and communities into the pursuit of monetary
wealth that has no limit.[23] Money is problematic as a principle
of growth and renewal. Aristotle views it as an unrestricted
potential for increase deriving from a desire unrestrained by
political and moral values.[24] Money is a principle of insatiability
without limit; empire has a similar structure (cf. Thucydides
6.18.3). The *Persians* dramatizes the *telos* of empire as its
termination; the play exhibits its insatiability as fulfiled by insatiable lament.[25] Thucydides develops this dimension of empire in
his *History*: imperialism 'cashes in' the lives of its citizens for
eternal glory, a process whose fulfilment is mounds of unburied
corpses, killed both by plague and by failed invasion (2.34-54;
7.59-87; cf. 818-22).

We lack the music, dance, gestures, masks, costumes, and
other material components of the *kommos* that would enable us to
appreciate its full impact. The words and metre are merely its
skeleton. Even so, they convey a sense of the emotional power of
the play's ending and of Aeschylus' dramatic technique.

Male lament

Ritual lament is a female performance in fifth-century Athenian culture.[26] Solon's laws allegedly proscribed female self-mutilation in lament.[27] Male lament inverts proper gender roles. Such an inversion is both a generic feature of tragedy – the most virile heroes, Heracles and Ajax, decry that they have become women – and a function of the Greek construction of barbarian culture as feminized.[28] Herodotus' Persians tear their clothing in 'boundless lament' (3.66.1; 8.99-100; cf. 9.24).

Yet is possible to overstate the barbarian emotionalism of the *Persians*. Old men perform ritual laments in the Greek tradition. In Euripides' *Andromache*, Peleus exhorts himself to tear his hair and to beat his head in lament for his grandson Neoptolemus (1209-11). The archetype of the old man in lament is Priam, who smears his head and neck with dung while mourning Hector's death (Homer *Iliad* 24.159-65). Plato's critique of tragedy in the *Republic* focuses on male lament. The most self-controlled men in the audience experience lament with vicarious pleasure, even though in their everyday lives they pride themselves on enduring grief and resisting lament – this is something women do. Tragedy liberates their repressed desires to lament (*Republic* 605a8-606c1; cf. 387d1-388e3). The *kommos* of the *Persians* is an example of tragedy's capacity to evoke the yearning for lament in a society demanding its suppression.

The *kommos*, then, need not be interpreted primarily as a spectacle of Persian effeminacy which reinforces the audience's sense of cultural and military superiority. Barbarian emotionalism is its enabling condition rather than its meaning. The *kommos* is a public lament for communal suffering (944-7).[29] It may be difficult for us to imagine the original audience lamenting the same thing as the Persians – the loss of empire, the annihilation of an unburied nobility, the crushing naval defeat, the blow to Xerxes and Persia, the disgrace of Xerxes' torn robes and empty quiver. The *kommos* fosters identification with such lament by locating the audience between past and future grief for its own suffering. It activates the construction of the Persian *pathos* as a displacement of Athens' *pathos* and evokes contemporary Athenian imperialist practices as sources of identification. It is likely that the Athenians lost more citizens in battle in the period from 480 to 472 than in their entire previous history.[30] Herodotus claims that during the reigns of Darius, Xerxes, and his son Artaxerxes, 'there were more woes for Greece than in the 20 generations before Darius' (6.98.2).[31] Pain and suffering (*ponos*) are the stuff of imperialism which binds Persians and Athenians.

Anapaestic prelude: Xerxes' fall and the lost harvest

Spoken of in the third person throughout the drama, Xerxes enters lamenting his own fate (909-10).[32] Unlike the audience, he does not understand that the invasion was a predictable and predicted disaster.[33] Xerxes remains similarly uninformed about the future (913). He interprets his fate as the work of a 'savage-minded' and arbitrary 'divinity' which 'trampled the race of Persians' (*daimôn*, 911-12, cf. 515-16, 921, 942-3, 1005-7). We see the principle of *drama* and *pathos* enacted upon Xerxes' entrance: the trampler enters as the trampled.

The Queen's dream offers a model for Xerxes' confrontation with paternal authority after his fall: he tears his robes in disgrace. In the staged drama, his body goes slack when he sees Darius' contemporaries (913-14) and he yearns for the invisibility of death (915-17). Xerxes' slack body personifies the dissolution of 'royal might' (589-90) and the loosening of the 'yoke of force' that holds his empire together, allowing free speech to emerge (591-4). The chorus speaks freely. Xerxes' entrance realizes the chorus' prophecy in the first stasimon. Xerxes calls the elders 'citizens' (914; cf. 555-7); they speak as citizens. The elders' reception of Xerxes reverses their awe-struck reception of his parents (150-8, 694-702).

Taking up Xerxes' lament for the savage divinity, the chorus mourns 'the good army and the great honour of Persian rule and the ranks (*kosmos*) of men the divinity cut down' (918-21).[34] Xerxes' new *kosmos* can symbolically replace the *kosmos* of men 'cut down' and restore the grandeur of his empire, but the play does not stage such a renewal. Rather, it stresses the identity

126

of Xerxes' torn robes and the noblemen he expended in the invasion that destroyed his empire.

The chorus develops the agricultural metaphor of the verb 'cut down': 'the earth laments the native youth (*hêbê*) killed by Xerxes, stuffer of Hades with Persians' (922-4). The native *hêbê* is a harvest, the 'flower (*anthos*) of the land', which Xerxes reaps and crams into Hades (926). The Persian king celebrated himself as the guardian of agricultural bounty.[35] Early Greek poetry linked the bounty of land and water with the justice of the king (Homer *Odyssey* 19.107-14).[36] In Aeschylus' *Eumenides*, the Erinyes will both punish injustice at Athens and promote the fertility of the land, people, flocks, and waters (900-1020; cf. Aeschylus *Suppliants* 625-709). In the *Persians*, the outcome of the king's *hybris* is a harvest of death. Persia's material excess defies the space of the living and of the dead. The narrows of Salamis could not contain the fleet; Greek soil could not feed the army. Hades barely contains the Persian dead.

The play's stress on *hêbê* is also a function of this *hybris*. Youthful power and exuberance, *hêbê* is the season in the human life-cycle when *hybris* and *atê* blossom.[37] The 'flower' (*anthos*) of Persian men likewise resonates with this theme: 'flower of *hêbê*' is a trope for physical maturity and beauty, while 'flower of *atê*' describes the burgeoning of disaster.[38] Darius made this connection explicit (821-2); the *kommos* develops the idea in verbal and visual images.

In the Queen's dream, Xerxes falls, his father pities him, and he tears his robes. In the staged drama, Xerxes sees the chorus, his body goes slack, and he probably falls. While the chorus describes Asia on its knee (929-31), Xerxes may be on his.[39] The image derives from wrestling.[40] The chorus fell to its knees as the Queen entered. The Queen feared that great wealth, raising a cloud of dust, might 'overturn with its foot the *olbos* Darius won' (163-4). The staging of Xerxes on his knee enacts this cluster of verbal images as a visual image on stage. Seeking divinity and worshipped as a god, Xerxes appears as a fallen mortal trampled by the gods. Xerxes' entrance re-establishes the proper order between mortals and immortals.

Xerxes' confession and the
Mariandynian mourner

Xerxes begins to sing in lyric anapaests, making himself the focus of lament. He confesses that he has 'become an evil (*kakon*) to my race and to the land of my fathers' (932-4). A term of blame, the word *kakon* contrasts Xerxes with Darius, who 'causes no evil/harm/woe' (*akakos*, 663-4 = 671-2, 855). The messenger, the chorus, and Darius blamed Xerxes. The *kommos* begins when Xerxes assumes personal responsibility for the disaster.

The chorus picks up Xerxes' confession, promising to welcome him in his homecoming with a 'Mariandynian mourner's evil-omened cry' (937).[41] Many accounts of Mariandynian mourning ritual circulated in antiquity.[42] At the height of summer, the Mariandynians lamented the loss of a royal youth, variously named Mariandynus, Bormus, or Borimus. The latter two were the object of farmers' laments (Pollux *Onomasticon* 4.54-5; Athenaeus *Banquet of the Sophists* 14.619F). The chorus wails the lament of a Mariandynian mourner because this dirge is proverbial for mourning accompanied by a double-reed pipe, particularly in the Ionian mode.[43] Perhaps it is also a slave's lament: the Mariandynians indentured themselves to the Megarian colonists of Heraclea (Athenaeus *Banquet of the Sophists* 6.263C-E). Lamenting the tragic intersection of the life- and agricultural-cycles and encompassing both farmers' laments and mourning for the premature loss of a royal heir, the figure of the 'Mariandynian mourner' fuses the Persian and Athenian *pathos* of a 'lost harvest'.

Xerxes yearns to make himself the object of lament. He approves of the chorus' intention to sing a dirge (941-2), but defines its object as his change of fortune (942-3). Tears of lament are a refrain in the opening sequences (940, 949). For whom does the chorus weep? The elders declare that they will sing a lament 'honouring the sufferings of the people and the sea-beaten grief of the *polis*, of the race' (944-7; cf. 546-7). The chorus sings a public lament for Persia's naval defeat, bewailing the abandonment of the Persian nobility in Greece, unburied and unlamented.

6. A Harvest of Tears

Ionian Ares and longing

In the second strophe, the metre changes to Ionic *a minore*. Xerxes names the malicious divinity who defeated him 'Ionian Ares': he 'despoiled' the Persians of their lives, 'cutting down the night-black plain of the sea and the unfortunate shore' (950-4). The Greek word 'cutting down' refers to the destruction of crops that functions as a prelude to infantry battle. Xerxes depicts the death of his men as a destroyed harvest.[44] Ionic *a minore* finally appears as the metre of Persian lament for defeat at the hands of the Ionians, which voices shared Ionian/Persian suffering.

The chorus demands to know where 'those who stand beside you in battle' are (956-7). The elders treat Xerxes as a hoplite-initiate, an ephebe, who swore an oath not to 'abandon the man beside me in battle'.[45] Ephebes swore before divine witnesses and by wheat, barley, grape-vines, olives, and figs. Their duty was to protect the crops and the harvest. The lament depicts Xerxes' disgrace from the double perspective of lost nobility and lost harvest. It recalls the Persian defeat in terms that suggest failure to perform the function of the farmer, citizen, and nobleman: to protect the food supply.

At the end of the third antistrophe, the elders focus on the Persian elite which attended Xerxes' chariot (1000-1). The theme is longing; the subtexts are the anapaestic list of leaders in the parodos (21-59) and the messenger's iambic trimeter catalogue of leaders who died at Salamis (302-30). The *kommos* reprises the spoken catalogues of names in the lyric register, making the absence of Xerxes' men palpable in song and dance.

The elders ask about two leaders they named in the parodos, Pharandaces (958, 31) and Susiscanes (960, 35), whose fates remain unknown. They also mention previously unnamed leaders (959-60). Xerxes explains that the men died when their Phoenician ship sank at Salamis and admits that he abandoned their corpses (962-6; cf. 303). The antistrophe names four men listed in the parodos. With the exception of Misistras (971, 30), the messenger reported their deaths: Ariomardus (968, 321, 38), Tharybis (971, 323, 51), and Artembares (972, 302, 29). The elders also ask about two others, Pharnuchus (967, 313) and

Lilaeus (970, 308), whom the messenger already reported dead. Adding generic epithets to their names, the chorus gives the impression of longing for real people.[46]

Xerxes confesses that these men 'looking at primeval, hated Athens, all in the single plash of a wave, wretchedly breathe their last breath on land' (974-7), dying like fish out of water. The indignity of their death is that their last sight was the land of Athens. Xerxes relives the final instant of their lives, a recreation made more chilling by fact that the actor who plays Xerxes (Aeschylus?) looks out at 'primeval Athens' while he utters these lines.

The chorus is mortified that Xerxes abandoned 'the prime (*aôton*) of the Persians, your eye trusted in everything' (978-9).[47] The word translated as 'prime' refers to the best part of anything, but applies particularly to fine wool or linen fabric. Like the words *kosmos* (920-1) and *anthos* (926) it draws attention to Xerxes' rags as a symbol of the obliterated Persian nobility and empire, and reminds us of the Queen's concurrent attempt to replace them.[48] 'Eye' has a meaning similar to *aôtos* – the best and vital part of something. It completes the theme of Xerxes' 'evil eye', the malignant gaze that brings death and barrenness. Xerxes abandoned his 'eye' – the best part of his society; yet he returns as the 'eye of his house', the rightful heir who continues his lineage (168-9).[49] Batanochus' only beloved son (his name has dropped out of the manuscripts) is a pointed contrast (980-1): he is the sole heir of a line which includes four named generations (981-3). His line goes extinct with his death.[50]

The lament peaks in the third antistrophe. Xerxes experiences the longing that afflicts the land of Asia, Persian wives, the *polis*, and the chorus (991-2; 60-3, 133-9, 511-12, 541-5). Rather than use the keyword 'longing' (*pothos*) Xerxes uses a metonymy: the wryneck (*iunx*), a bird that functioned in Greek erotic magic (988-9).[51] Tied to a wheel and spun around while incantations were chanted to lure back a lost lover, the *iunx* indicates Xerxes' desire for a magical retrieval of the dead, as the Persians recalled Darius from Hades. Xerxes assimilates his 'noble companions' (*hetaroi*, an Ionic form) to lovers, suggesting laments for Adonis.[52] The word *hetaroi* implies bonds of private friendship that are prized more highly than the public good and are potentially subversive of it. Xerxes' longing assumes a marked aristocratic form. The play exhibits the resolution of imperialist desire in painful longing. Xerxes' desire – to yoke two beautiful women to his chariot (181-99), to capture Athens (233), to appropriate others' *olbos* out of discontent with his own *daimôn* (824-6) – is realized in tortured longing for what is absent, dead, and irretrievable.

Concluding the third strophe, the chorus expresses astonishment that the men it named do not accompany Xerxes' curtained chariot (1000-1). According to Herodotus, after he left Sardis for Greece, Xerxes moved from his war chariot to his curtained chariot (*harmamaxa*) 'whenever the whim seized him' (7.41.1). While travelling in this vehicle – an emblem of luxuriant excess – Xerxes was attended by his best soldiers, 22,000 living symbols of his power and grandeur. If the *harmamaxa* is on stage, it symbolizes the absence of Xerxes' elite corps, the 'noble ranks', 'blossom', 'eye', and 'prime' 'cut down' in the invasion. The final transformation of the Persian war chariot and chariot yoke – images of Persian imperialism – the unattended *harmamaxa* stands for the nullification of Persia's excess and luxuriance in military defeat. It is all that remains of a massive surplus expended in the invasion.

Atê, the blow of defeat, and lost *olbos*

The fourth strophe and antistrophe contain a sharp change of metrical and speech forms. With a few exceptions, the metre is lyric iambic and the dialogue consists in one-line utterances. Xerxes and the chorus perform the lament which continues to the exodos. The subject gradually changes from what is absent – the king's 'eye' – to what is present, Xerxes' virtually empty quiver and torn robes, visual proof of his *atê*. The fourth strophic/antistrophic pair articulates the chiastic structure of the *kommos*. At first opposed as accuser to accused and diverging metrically (908-1001), the chorus and Xerxes unite in a single voice of pain (1002-15), before gradually disengaging, first as spectators to spectacle (1016-37), then as slaves to master (1038-77).

The fourth strophe begins as the play does, marking the beginning of the end: the statement that leaders of the army 'have gone' (1002; cf. 1-2). Now attention focuses on the orchestra where over two myriads of men should be escorting Xerxes' curtained chariot. The leaders 'are gone without a name' (*nônymoi*, 1003). Despite three catalogues of names, the Persians vanish 'without a name', that is, without glory. Lists of names cannot compensate for ignominious death – as invaders seeking to enslave Greece, as slaves of the king, as archers willing to kill but unwilling to risk their own lives, as unburied corpses.[53]

The 'namelessness' of the named Persian dead completes the theme of lost *olbos*. *Olbos* implies forms of immortality (see Herodotus 1.30-3; cf. Homeric *Hymn to Demeter* 480-2). The transmission of a lineage and reproduction of an *oikos* is a kind of immortality – denied to Batanochus' line (980-3). The transmission of one's name and acts to posterity, *kleos*-immortality, is a higher form. In the *Odyssey*, Agamemnon pronounces Achilles 'blessed (*olbie*) son of Peleus, Achilles like the gods, you who died far from Argos in Troy' (24.36-7). *Olbos* includes glorious death in battle, honour from gods and men, and physical memorialization (24.37-92). But its essence is the retention of a glorious name after death: 'So not even dying did you lose your name, but always you will have good *kleos* upon all men, Achilles' (24.93-4). The Persians' names are sounds without glory.

The 'blow' dealt to Persia is also related to the themes of *atê* and lost *olbos*. The messenger announced the disaster as 'in a single blow great *olbos* has been ruined' (251). The naval battle at Salamis is a concrete manifestation of this blow (408-32, 906-7) and a form of *atê*: 'disasters (*atai*) of deadly war' (652-3; cf. 1037). In the fourth antistrophe, Xerxes and the chorus embody this 'blow' as a sympathetic unity, making it visible as a physical and emotional state. Xerxes exclaims that the blow of defeat has struck down a lifetime of good fortune (1008).[54] The chorus completes his statement: 'we have been struck – for it is clear to see' (1009), probably signalling gestures that imitate the reception of a blow. Xerxes completes their utterance: 'by new, new, woe, woe' (1010). Xerxes and the chorus use the first-person plural verb, 'we have been struck' (1008-9) to mark their union in grief.[55] 'New woe' binds the young king and the elderly chorus as 'strange and new woes' bound the chorus and Darius in the necromantic hymn (665-6).

The lament re-enacts the naval defeat. In the parodos, the chorus depicted Xerxes as a monstrous invading force, all hands and sailors (83). Now Xerxes' body is his fleet and army. He proclaims 'I ... have taken a blow to my army of such a number' as if his army were part of his body (1014-15). The chorus sets up Xerxes' mime by bewailing the unlucky encounter with 'Ionian sailors', exclaiming that 'the Persian race is unfortunate in war' (1011-13; cf. 950-4).

The chorus asks Xerxes what has survived (1016). Xerxes answers with a question, 'Do you see this remnant of my outfit (*stolê*)'? (1019).[56] The word *stolê* means equipment, armament, and clothing; its use points to the equivalence of symbol and reality. Xerxes' royal outfit is his invading force, his nobility, and his empire.[57] All that remains of them is his nearly empty quiver (1020). Described as a spent treasure chest (1022), the quiver makes visible the syndrome by which the Persians confuse countable objects – money, men, and materiel – with power and promiscuously expend men and resources in a self-defeating performance. Like the *harmamaxa*, the quiver is the remnant of an excessive surplus; it embodies Xerxes' *atê* and lost *olbos*. Because of his prodigious expenditure, Xerxes stands alone and defeated.

But self-defeat is not the full story. The chorus replies, 'the Ionian people does not flee in battle' (1025). The 'Ionians' are the naval people who defeated Xerxes (950-4, 1111-13), and Xerxes declares them 'very martial' (1026). The *kommos* stages a kind of recognition scene. While lamenting their *atê* and lost *olbos*, the defeated Persians come to realize the character of the victorious Ionians. This type of recognition differs from those of the previous episodes, which involved understanding how events realized previous representations of them.

'Pain for us but joy for our enemies'?

Xerxes reports that he witnessed (from a distance) an 'unexpected catastrophe' (1026-7). The chorus pre-empts him, asking, 'Do you mean the routed naval host?' (1028). Xerxes had the best perspective on the battle (466-7). He returns to Persia both as cause of the disaster and as authoritative witness, bearing visual testimony of defeat. He confesses: 'I tore my robes at the occurrence of disaster' (1029-30). Xerxes embodies a defeat and grief unsatisfiable in lament. The elders exclaim '*papai papai*' in agony, articulating their emotional distress as physical pain (1031). Xerxes is unsatisfied by this expression. He corrects the chorus: '*papai*, alas, but even more than *papai*' (1032). Throughout the play we have heard of Xerxes' transgressions of limits – of nature, culture, and humanity. Salamis was the single greatest slaughter in human history (431-2); the dead at Marathon were not enough for him (473-7); he was not content with his *daimôn* (824-6). This exchange stages insatiability – *koros* – as a moment of supremely unsatisfiable lament. Trying to satisfy Xerxes, the chorus begins to utter 'yes, double and triple [the pains]', but Xerxes completes their thought: 'the pain [for us]; but joy for the enemy' (1033-4). The Homeric phrasing of this sentiment may enhance the audience's sense of heroic achievement (Homer *Iliad* 3.51, 6.82, 10.193). But is the audience actually meant to feel joy at this lament?

Some might take Xerxes' words literally as a cue for their own response, but the situation is more intricate. Xerxes has yearned for death (915-17), confessed to being an evil to his race and fatherland (932-4), relived his men's dying moments (974-7), experienced longing shouting from his heart (988-91), re-enacted the blow inflicted on his navy (1008-37), and displayed his spent quiver (1019-24). He and the chorus have named the Ionians the victor (950-4, 1111-3, 1025-30). He is a paragon of humility in defeat. What is the appropriate emotional response to this spectacle?

Aristotle thought that a man's deserved downfall and the *pathos* of enemies could evoke 'humane feeling' (*Poetics* 1453a27-1454a15), but not pity and fear, which require undeserved suffering and moral parity between the sufferer and spectator.[58] Greek cultural norms reserve pity for unmerited suffering. Pity is also incompatible with 'one's own pain'.[59] Several factors combine to undermine these norms in the *kommos*. Xerxes' defeat and Athens' destruction are two sides of the same 'lost harvest'; premature death, lament, and reversal of fortune are pitiable, particularly when they affect a noble *oikos*' ability to reproduce itself; the audience, owners of the most powerful navy in the Aegean, takers of tribute, enslavers of populations, heirs of Darius' empire, are vulnerable to the same sort of tragedy. It is appropriate to respond to this moment the way Odysseus responds to his enemy Ajax's plight in Sophocles' *Ajax*: we need not look past ourselves to see that we are no more than spectres or insubstantial shadows.[60] As the spectators witness Xerxes' lament, they realize that they are a single sea-borne invasion removed from a harvest of tears.

The paradigm of the *Iliad*, which ends with ritual lament for Hector's death and the hero's burial, determined the horizons of response to a defeated enemy.[61] The *Persians* stages the outcome of *hybris* in a 'harvest of tears', a fact in harmony with the nature of the cosmos.[62] The Persian *pathos* could happen to any imperialist invasion. At this moment, the *kommos* unites two contradictory elements of the play, the depiction of Xerxes' particular defeat and the use of his defeat to instantiate generally applicable laws. Readings that insist the *kommos* elicits only Schadenfreude or a sense of invulnerability based upon freedom, democracy, and Greek ethnic identity in effect argue that the play's depiction of the catastrophic outcome of Persian *hybris* encourages Athenian *hybris*. Aristotle recognized that 'those who are in great good fortune' are immune to fear (Aristotle *Rhetoric* 1382b34-1383a3) and incapable of considering their future suffering (1385b29-32). Likewise, those who 'consider themselves super fortunate' do not pity, but 'are hybristic' (1385b19-21).[63] There is reason for seeing this kind of response as inappropriate to the *Persians*: the Persian and Athenian *pathos* are parallel and intersecting (Athens does not enjoy 'great good fortune'); the play depicts naval imperialism as particularly vulnerable and stages laments for naval defeat.

Catharsis and the renewal of *hybris*

And yet Xerxes' *hybris* is unexpectedly renewable. Xerxes' moment of insatiable grief is transformative; it effects a kind of catharsis. Xerxes realizes his identity as pathetic witness and cause of the disaster. Then he seizes control of the chorus; with a single exception, his every utterance is an imperative. Harry Avery argues that Xerxes receives his *kosmos* at line 1038; this motivates him to take control of the chorus.[64] Such silent stage action rarely occurs in Athenian drama; words confirm significant stage events. Indeed, there can be no *kosmos* in any sense of the word for Xerxes. This is the point of the drama. There is no 'world-order' for him to control, no 'battle-order' that can conquer the Greeks for him, no 'noble ranks' to function as an alter-ego and living sign of his power, no 'glory', 'empire' or 'ornamental robe'. The final staging of the Persian inability to act *kata kosmon* is the Queen's failure to enter with a new *kosmos* for her son.

The *kommos* brings the narrative full circle, staging Xerxes' return. It shows the cyclical nature of the sequence *hybris*, *atê*, and lament: a renewal of *hybris* follows the cathartic recognition of *atê* in a harvest of tears. The chorus does not reincorporate Xerxes into his kingdom as an honoured and praiseworthy king. He reintegrates himself by force. But now he rules an empire of tears. George Devereux observes that 'In mourning for something lost, one regularly *further increases* one's losses: mourning is inseparable from self-aggression'.[65] The *kommos* displays the transformation of *hybris* into mourning, stressing the ultimately self-defeating character of *hybris* by exhibiting its fulfilment in self-directed aggression. The question that hangs over the drama is whether Xerxes will redirect his *hybris* outward, or whether he will learn moderation and stop harming the gods. While the *Persians* establishes closure as drama, its insertion into the historical process remains open-ended.

Exodos

The text becomes a series of stage directions and statements of performance. Xerxes orders the elders to weep for the disaster, to start the procession off stage towards the palace, and to shout in responsion to himself (1038-40). The dirge is an asymmetrical exchange between the king and his subjects. The elders call Xerxes 'master' (*despotês*); they are his slaves (1049; cf. 169). Recalling Xerxes' confession that he is *kakon*, the elders describe their cries as a 'wretched (*kakan*) gift of wretched (*kakôn*) cries for wretched cries (*kakois*)' (1041).

Xerxes orders the chorus to make rowing gestures, beating their heads in lament as a 'favour' (*charin*) to himself (1046), a kind of tribute. The ritual gesture of rowing ferries the dead across the Acheron to Hades by sympathetic magic (Aeschylus *Seven against Thebes* 854-60; cf. *Libation Bearers* 423-8; Euripides *Trojan Women* 1235-6).[66] The chorus' blows to the head make a sound like the plash of an oar striking water (*Seven against Thebes* 855-6). Since none of the Persian dead received burial, the chorus' rowing does not have the ritual function of transporting them to their final resting place. Rather, it re-enacts the sailors' rowing to the 'Hades' that 'hated Athens' was for them.

Xerxes orders the elders to beat their chests and to shout a Mysian lament (1054) before commanding them to 'ravage (literally: 'sack') their white beards' (1056). We see the double reversal of Persian aggression: the Persian sackers are sacked and then 'sack' their own bodies, re-enacting their defeat in lament (65, 177-8, 714, 807-12). Even if the elders' masks are not bloodied, the verbal image of Matallus of Chrysa's bushy beard stained royal purple with blood (316-17) enables the audience to imagine bloodied beards. In the antistrophe, Xerxes orders the elders to pluck the hair from their heads and to lament the army (1062). Again, we witness a double reversal prepared by verbal imagery. The omen of the hawk and eagle figured Xerxes' flight and the reversal of his aggression: the Persians now 'pluck' their own heads as the hawk 'plucked' the cowering eagle's head (207-10), though the verb for plucking in the *kommos* may also suggest the fate of Persia's bowmen, since it applies more particularly to drawing a bowstring or plucking a stringed instrument.

Between the hair and beard pulling, Xerxes communicates his condition to the elders, ordering them to tear their 'flowing robes' (1060-1). We witness as theatrical spectacle the image which began its dramatic life as the chorus' sensation of fear for the reality they now lament (114-19). The image circulates from chorus to actors and grows increasingly objective. The Queen declared that 'worry tears my heart too' (160) and saw Xerxes tear his robes as a response to his father's pity in her dream (197-9). The messenger witnessed Xerxes rending his robes as he gazed upon a 'depth of woes' after Psyttalia (465-8). The agent himself, Xerxes, confessed that he tore his robes when he witnessed the catastrophe (1030). Finally, verbal image becomes theatrical fact: the elders tear their robes, replicating their fearful sensation in the parodos as a ritualized gesture of lament. Xerxes' shame and humiliation before his father; the loss of his 'eye', empire, *olbos*, and subsequent longing; the disgrace of total defeat, the pain of wives lamenting their husbands and the grief of childless parents (60-4, 114-25, 133-9, 286-9, 537-45, 579-83) – these the elders tear into their robes as an act of obedience and mourning. The transformation of verbal into visual images is an integral part of theatrical meaning: spectators witness the *pathos* in symbolic form, feeling and understanding more than they see because of its verbal preparation.

Xerxes orders the elders to keep lamenting as they exit (1068). Despite luxurious slippers, the chorus finds Persian soil 'hard to tread upon' (1072-3). The chorus and Xerxes lament men destroyed 'by triple-banked boats' (1074-5). Neither Persians nor Athenians can forget that Xerxes' invasion was a 'lost harvest'. Substituting for Xerxes' young escorts, killed in the prime of their lives, the elders escort Xerxes to his palace, bearing the marks of the tyrant's *hybris* on their persons (1076-7). François Hartog observes, 'the *despotês* ['master'] exercises his power over people's bodies .... The king cuts, mutilates, and marks the bodies of his subjects'.[67] The *pathos* of the drama, first 'unfolded' as if written on papyrus and 'read' on the stage (253-5, 294-5) is re-enacted and reinscribed on the bodies of the chorus in the *kommos*.

Interpreting and Reinterpreting the *Persians*

The *Persians* as tragedy

Scholars generally agree that the *Persians* is not Aeschylus' finest tragedy. Critics fault the drama for having 'no action and no plot' and for lacking subtlety and depth.[1] Others claim that the play could not engage the sympathetic emotions of the audience: pain for the Persians is joy for the audience. The *Persians* is contested as tragedy. This chapter discusses critical appraisals and interpretations of the play. Then it examines responses to the *Persians* in Greek poetry before sketching treatments of the narrative from the Renaissance to the present.

Ulrich von Wilamowitz-Moellendorff's claim that the *Persians* consists of three self-contained acts, each a drama in itself transpiring in its own location, has influenced subsequent appraisals of the play. 'It is very much worth realizing', Wilamowitz advises, 'that Aeschylus in 472 still could construct a tragedy without any unity of plot and action.'[2] Most scholars have reacted against this view. S.M. Adams incorporates Wilamowitz's idea of three dramas into a positive interpretation of the play's structure. He argues that the *Persians* is a condensed tetralogy, a tragic 'symphony' composed of three movements and a *kommos*, which substitutes for a satyr-play.[3] In the first movement, the chorus and Queen are torn between anxiety and confidence; in the second, the *daimôn* causes disaster; in the third, Darius explains that the tragedy is the result of *hybris* rather than the work of a *daimôn*. Adams' model of a symphony is fruitful; however, its movements are better considered *hybris*, *atê*, and lament: this sequence recurs in different keys from the parodos to the exodos of the play. The comparison of the *kommos* to satyr-play is inapt.

R.P. Winnington-Ingram offers a nuanced version of Adams' hypothesis.[4] The *Persians* has three 'panels': the first (parodos and first episode) and the third (*kommos*), express the idea that malicious divinities cause woe to mortals who attain excessive prosperity; the middle panel (Darius-scene) shows that prosperity does not attract divine malice: Zeus punishes *hybris* to preserve the cosmic order. Winnington-Ingram considers the *kommos*' failure to incorporate Darius' message and its return to the outlook of the first panel meaningful. Darius' observations, he contends, 'change everything'; but Xerxes and the chorus continue to blame the *daimôn* for the catastrophe.[5] Winnington-Ingram perhaps demands a philosophical discussion instead of the theatrical response to Darius' message which the *Persians* offers: the *kommos* stages the realization of *hybris* in lament, re-enacting the *pathos* of the drama as symbolic action on stage.[6] Lamenting their *atê* and lost *olbos* the Persians come to realize a more powerful 'reaper', Ionian Ares. The raw emotion of the *kommos* exhibits the law of *drama* and *pathos* as dramatic spectacle. Winnington-Ingram makes too rigid a distinction between the play's *daimôn*-centered view of the tragedy and the moral/religious view; they are complementary. No one holds *olbos* responsible for attracting an envious *daimôn*; the play implicates the Persian mode of producing *olbos* through conquest in the tragedy.

H.D.F. Kitto identifies the 'lack of a clear focal point in the action' as the play's weakness.[7] The *Persians* features no fatal decision; its characters and chorus are weak. The introduction of a second actor disrupts the balance of the tragedy, making its core difficult to find.[8] Is the play the tragedy of Persia? Kitto thinks not: 'the play ... is ... the tragedy of Xerxes' sin'.[9] The notion of sin has no place in a discussion of Greek tragedy, however loosely the term may be used. And it seems obvious that the *Persians* is the tragedy of Xerxes, his family (Darius and the Queen), his kingship, and his empire, which has catastrophic results for his nobility, subjects, allies, and the 'entire barbarian race'.

Readers interpret the *Persians* as a tragedy about Xerxes'

and the Persians' reversal of fortune, particularly their loss of *olbos*, dramatized as a movement from foreboding to realization.[10] They stress the interplay of verbal and visual imagery – the yoke, the torn robe, the bow and arrow, the chariot – and the play's development of theme through repetition and enactment as spectacle. William Thalmann in particular has shown how Xerxes' rags symbolize 'the wreck of Persian *olbos*' and 'how the yoke of Persian power has been shattered'.[11]

While it is easy to describe the *Persians* as a formal tragedy, it has proved rather more difficult to show that the *Persians* fulfils the rhetorical function of a tragedy – that it arouses pity, fear, and related emotions.

Is the *Persians* tragedy?

Aristotle differentiated poetry from history on the grounds that the former depicts 'the sorts of things that can happen and what is possible according to likelihood or necessity' while history represents 'what happened' (*Poetics* 1451a36-1451b5). In his view, poetry is 'more philosophical and more serious than history' because what it represents is 'more universal' (1451b5-10). Aristotle allows that historical poetry can represent 'the kinds of things that were likely to happen' (1451b29-32). The problem for the interpretation of the *Persians* is whether the play dramatizes the 'kinds of things that can happen' or merely 'what happened'.

Aristotle's definition of tragedy is relevant: 'tragedy is the imitation of a serious and complete action that has magnitude ... of people acting and not through narrative, accomplishing through pity and fear the catharsis of such emotions' (*Poetics* 1449b24-8). Both pity and fear require the spectators' sympathetic awareness and consciousness of their own vulnerability. The *Persians* induces fear from its memory of Xerxes' invasion, the prospect of another invasion, and by prompting reflection on the fictionalized fall of Persia's empire. The play's depiction of the Persian *pathos* as symmetrical and antithetical to the Athenian *pathos* is a strategy to arouse pity. The form of the Persian *pathos* is similar to Athens', but different enough to provide the distance for pity until the *kommos*, when the two briefly intersect, releasing the tensions of pity, fear, and longing.

141

The *Persians* is often read as a tragedy in form and performative occasion but as an epinician, a praise poem for the victory over the Persians, in function.[12] J.D. Craig puts the case succinctly:

> ... is it likely that the Athenians were going to ... extend to the Persians that measure of sympathy which would lead to the tragic *katharsis* of pity and terror in view of their sufferings? It would be safer not to apply that principle at all. The *Persae* is unlike any other dramas .... They were to witness the punishment of *hybris*, and the chastisement was to be at their own hands.[13]

Craig finds support for his position in Aristophanes' portrayal of Aeschylus in the *Frogs*: the tragedian declares that his *Persians* taught the Athenians 'always to desire to defeat their enemies, because it glorified the best achievement' (1026-7).

Craig does not offer a more general interpretation of the play, but it is possible to extend his reading: the myth of the *Persians* is that the Athenians defeat *hybris*. This was an essential part of Athenian democratic self-understanding throughout the fifth century.[14] This myth justifies Athens' empire as a form of moral leadership. In this perspective, the *Persians* would not be tragedy in any meaningful sense but a projection of group identity; the fictionalized fall of the Persian empire would be an act of praise for the Athenians who vanquished it.[15] But one should take this interpretation a step further: the *Persians* projects Athenian moral leadership because it recognizes the limits of human power in the cosmos. In particular, it depicts the limits of naval imperialism. Xerxes' *atê* and 'disease of the mind' consist in his attempt to enslave the Hellespont and 'to dominate all the gods, especially Poseidon' (744-51). While the play recalls the liberation of Greece, it also dramatizes the vulnerabilities of naval imperialism, both reassuring the 'allies' and warning the Athenians about the limits of empire. Because it recognizes the humanity of Xerxes' delusion, the tragedy and the laws it instantiates apply to mortals rather than merely to barbarians.

This is the crux of the matter. Recent versions of the patriotic hypothesis read the play as a construction of Greek civic and ethnic identity which dehumanizes the Persians. Tragedy articulated the institutions, myths, rituals, and ideologies which enabled Athenian society and politics.[16] Such self-definition required the identification and containment of the 'other'. Edith Hall reads the *Persians* as the first extant manifestation of what Edward Said terms 'orientalism' in western culture, the set of discourses by which the West 'knows' the East, and lays the groundwork for domination.[17] Hall interprets the play as exhibiting Persians and barbarians not merely as 'slaves' under a divine king who monopolizes power and glory, but as deficient in humanity, intelligence, courage, and virility.[18] She allows for dissonance between the play's 'orientalism' and its reception, pairing the play's depiction of the barbarian 'other' with opportunities for the spectators' 'covert exorcism of their own psychological pain'.[19] But Hall reads the *Persians* as crowning Athens' greatness with the sort of invulnerability that characterizes Persian *hybris* in the play (e.g. 87-107).[20] This presents a paradox: the *Persians* dramatizes the fall of the Persian empire as a result of *hybris* to instil a sense of eternal superiority in the audience. Craig's reading poses a similar problem. Awareness of and respect for the divinely imposed limits of human power as clarified by the Persian disaster temper the celebratory element of the *Persians*.

Recent historical readings of the play restrict audience responses to Schadenfreude and exclude audience identification with both the Persians and their *pathos*. Pericles Georges reads the *Persians* as a drama of the 'purest barbarian ethos'. Xerxes is 'beneath tragedy'. The elders are incompetent, war-mongering, effeminate, untrustworthy, disobedient slaves. The Queen is masculine. The Persians are incapable of comprehending the moral and religious meaning of their defeat and show 'autistic belligerence'. The play urges the audience to continue the war.[21]

If the *Persians* is about the 'pure barbarian ethos' why does it not stress the continuity of this ethos? Why is Medus' son a model of self-control (767) and Cyrus 'blessed' (768) and 'well-intentioned' toward the gods (772)? Why is Darius glorified? The historical Darius would have illuminated the 'pure barbarian ethos' more clearly than Aeschylus' Darius, who depicts

Xerxes as an aberration. It is difficult to see how the *Persians* urges war. Darius legitimates Persian rule in Asia (762-4) and interdicts further invasion of Greece (790-2). The play's fiction of total defeat – all men of military age die, all ships are lost, and the empire will fall – is difficult to square with a call to war. What remains to fight? Finally, what limits such an interpretation? Should we say that the *Persians* erotizes Persian women in lament as a call to Greeks to invade and seize them? (cf. Homer *Iliad* 2.354-6, 3.298-301). Georges is right to stress that the *Persians* is open-ended – Xerxes does not receive a *kosmos* or Darius' message; his proposed rehabilitation does not take place within dramatic time. There is a possibility that Xerxes may continue to 'harm the gods'. But the *kommos* depicts Xerxes' *hybris* as confined to a pathetic remnant of elders. The audience of the play receives the message intended for Xerxes.

Thomas Harrison reads the play as an assertion of Hellenic cultural superiority and a supremely optimistic projection of Athenian naval imperialism which 'immunises' the audience against the barbarian *pathos*.[22] If this reading is right, the *Persians* would form part of the cultural matrix enabling such disastrous Athenian ventures as that in Egypt (460/59-454 BC) and against Sicily (415-413 BC). It would promote the delusion that only 'barbarians' suffer total defeat in sea-borne invasions of conquest and appropriation.

On the other side are those who consider the *Persians*' 'patriotic' element tangential to its meaning and read the play as canonical tragedy.[23] Some stress that the *Persians* attributes the punishment of *hybris* to the gods, not to the Greeks.[24] Others point to the dignity of the Persians, their heroic quality, or the mildness with which Aeschylus depicts them (given that they destroyed Athens) as signs that the play eschews triumphalism.[25] Against such interpretations it may be said that the Persians lament their defeat at Ionian hands (563, 950-1, 1011-12, 1025-37). Divine and human responsibility are compatible and mutually reinforcing; dignity accorded the Persians can also serve patriotic purposes.[26] Xerxes cues the audience's response to his pain as 'joy for my enemies' (1034). It is difficult to deny that the play differentiates Greeks and Persians as victor and vanquished and as slaves and free. Nor is it difficult to see that some, perhaps most, in the audience might have experienced the play as a triumph staged as a tragedy. But there is more to this tragedy than patriotic celebration.

It is possible to synthesize the play's epinician and tragic perspectives. As Gregory Nagy notes, the function of epinician is two-fold: to praise victory and to warn against the seductions of *hybris* and tyranny.[27] The *Persians* implies praise for victory but also conveys insight into the dangers of *hybris* and empire.[28] Three features of the tragedy are important in this regard: Zeus holds mortals accountable for overweening ambition (827-8); malicious divinities abet human delusions (93-101, 360-1, 724-6, 742); the cosmos vindicates its order independently of mortals (495-507, 744-51). The *Persians* does not imply that only barbarians commit *hybris*; it uses Xerxes' invasion of Greece as a paradigmatic expression of it. The Persian tragedy exemplifies a tendency of human nature.

The *Persians* includes multiple and inconsistent perspectives which spectators would have to balance. Michael Gagarin reads the play as a synthesis of two perspectives: a tragic, Persian perspective, which might evoke sympathy, and a triumphant, Greek/Athenian perspective, which celebrates victory and experiences Schadenfreude. Although his interpretation is weighted in favour of the victorious perspective, Gagarin finds warning implicit in the drama.[29] The dual-perspective model is helpful, but probably too simple. The Persians speak sometimes as Persians, sometimes as Greeks; characters within the play do not speak from a single perspective. The Queen differs radically from Darius in her interpretation of Xerxes' motives. Darius depicts Xerxes as an anomaly; the Queen locates him in an imperialist society which requires the validation of royal wealth as *olbos* by conquest (159-72, 753-8). Darius speaks as a character whose motive is to deny responsibility for the disaster and as a voice of objective reality.

A majority of interpreters find a balance of contradictory perspectives and meanings in the *Persians*. Simon Goldhill detects an epinician impulse in the play's construction of Salamis as a conflict of political systems which vindicates the cosmic order; yet he takes the play's staging of a *kommos* for the Persians as an attempt 'to develop a complex understanding of recent events of Athenian history, and to raise questions about a response to the victory'.[30] Christopher Pelling sketches the parameters of audience response to the *Persians*, from Schadenfreude to shock, as the play explores and affirms the Greek-barbarian antithesis. He argues that the play enables the Athenians to realize their collective self-identity by experiencing pity rather than disregard when confronted with their enemy's suffering.[31] Rush Rehm stresses the play's focus on death as bridging the gulf between Persian and Greek.[32] A sympathetic Athenian response implies 'that grief and loss can draw together even mortal enemies, opening a space that preempts, rather than defines, a category like 'the "Other" '.[33] Thus 'Aeschylus validates barbarian suffering and makes their grief available to an audience who might otherwise wish to denigrate or minimize it'.[34]

The riddle of Darius

The Darius-scene is the central variable for interpreting the *Persians*. Many readers consider Darius a mouthpiece for Aeschylus.[35] Darius' wisdom, however, is traditional; no one can take credit for it. Bengt Alexanderson argues that Darius is merely another character in the drama: ignorant of the present, knowledgeable of the future because of oracles, but not because he possesses a higher wisdom.[36] Still others consider him a self-serving despot who tries to distance himself from the disaster he fathered.[37] Interpretations of Darius run the gamut to an extent unparalleled for any other character in the drama.

Darius is the play's central fiction. He is a unity composed of contraries: he is both a god and a man; a Persian who bridged the Bosporus to invade the Scythians, he excoriates his son for bridging the Hellespont to invade Greece; he ordered Ionians treated as non-persons for revolting and their temples destroyed for burning the temple of Cybebe, yet he condemns Persian looting of statues and destruction of Greek temples and altars; he limits the sphere of Persian imperialism to Asia and is depicted as holding an empire within its proper limits, yet the play praises him as conqueror and ruler of an Aegean empire outside of those limits (865-97); he represents the history of

146

Persian imperialism as moderate, just, and divinely sanctioned while condemning *hybris*; the chorus depicts the Persian empire as maintained by force (586-94) and constituted by practices, such as city-sacking and enslavement by tribute-exaction, that qualify as *hybris*. My solution has been to view Darius as a transcendent paternal figure, both Xerxes' and Athens' father, who speaks with the voice of the Greek poetic tradition, embodies wisdom born of suffering, shares guilt with those he condemns, and still finds a place for pity. He loudly criticizes his son for ignoring his commands, seeking to dominate the sea, and destroying Greek sacred property; but he silently reminds the Athenians of their *drama*, the burning of Cybebe's temple as an explanation of their *pathos*, and warns them of the outcome of *hybris*.

*

The situation of tragic performance is complex; any interpretation of a tragedy should allow for this complexity. A tragedian has multiple allegiances: to his art, to the inherited traditions of poetry, to his class and status group, to his city, to Greece, to victory in the tragic competition. The *Persians* does not have a single interpretation. It offers variable messages to different segments of the audience, depending upon *polis*-affiliation, status, class, knowledge of history, and familiarity with the poetic tradition. Many agree that the *Persians* is an implied encomium. But this does not do justice to the Persian perspective. The play formulates the Persian *pathos* as symmetrical and opposed to the Athenian – evacuation, sack, fulfilment of prophecies of disaster and salvation, attribution of salvation to what enabled the disaster (bridges/fleet), punishment for the violation of temples, lament for a lost harvest. Envisioning the *telos* of naval imperialism in lament for ships and men, while depicting victory at Salamis and implying the formation of an Athenian empire, the *Persians* is a memory of victory/defeat and a prophecy of how empire falls. A similar contradiction is apparent in the play's construction of the Persians. They lack freedom, equality, and equal access to power, occupying the negative space of the Athenian socio-political identity. But their story is a human paradigm: a tale of *drama* and *pathos*; a story of how the cycle of conquest, wealth and *olbos* is a formula for the loss of *olbos*; a narrative and enactment of *hybris, atê*, and lament; a prophecy of the tragedy of empire as patrimony and succession; a myth of Zeus' intervention to hold mortals accountable for extra-legal crimes.

The following sections explore the terms Aeschylus' *Persians* established as constitutive of the Persian tragedy in Timotheus' *Persians* and in the counter-tradition of Attic comedy, where Persians figure ridiculed Athenians or appear in Golden Age fantasies. Then the discussion turns to versions of the narrative in Renaissance Italy, enlightenment Europe and America, and finally in post-World War II revivals and adaptations. Appropriated by Christians in the Middle Ages, Xerxes figures the menace of Turkish imperialism in the Renaissance before making a transition to romantic villainy and heroism in early modernity, and finding a place in the discourse of fascism, imperialism, and war in the West after World War II.

Timotheus' *Persians*: the king's great escape

Timotheus' (*c*. 460-350) *Persians* was discovered on a papyrus roll in Egypt in 1902; its 240 or so fragmentary verses may comprise up to half of the poem.[38] Prior to this, the poem was known from Plutarch's quotations and notices in late authorities. Plutarch cites it as a patriotic poem, quoting a dactylic hexameter line from the proem: 'making a great, celebrated *kosmos* of freedom for Greece'.[39] The subject of 'making' in this line is debated, but I suspect it is Timotheus, who locates his song in the tradition of poetic commemorations of the Persian Wars as a *kosmos*, perhaps following Simonides (*Plataea* fr. 11.23, restored).[40] According to Plutarch, the singer Pylades' performance of Timotheus' *Persians* at the Nemean games in 205 BC renewed the glory of the Persian Wars, inducing its auditors to feel as if they were living its glory in the present (*Life of Philopoemen* 11.3-4).

The *Persians* is a kitharodic nome, metrically complex astrophic lyrics accompanied by the kithara. According to Julius Pollux, the kitharodic nome has seven sections (*Onomasticon* 4.66). The papyrus includes three of them: central narrative (*omphalos* or 'navel'), poetic 'seal' (*sphragis*), where the poet imprints his signature on his work, and epilogue.[41] The date and place of the *Persians'* first performance are unknown. Most scholars place its first performance between 412 and 395, considering the period from 410 to 408 most likely.[42] Euripides' *Orestes*, performed in 408, is crucial to the dating. In it, a Phrygian slave reports Orestes' 'sacrifice' of Helen and chaos in the palace (1369-1502).[43] Because he sings astrophically, scholars argue that Euripides imitated Timotheus' Phrygian (140-61) and that the *Persians* must have been first performed before 408.[44]

Such lines of influence are difficult to determine. The song's first performance fits better between 396 and 394 when the Spartan king Agesilaus led an invasion of the Persian empire.[45] The pretext for the invasion was the belief that the Persian king, Artaxerxes II, was preparing to launch a fleet into the Aegean to invade mainland Greece.[46] The Spartans entrusted Agesilaus with both land and sea command against Persia in 395 (Xenophon *History of Greece* 3.4.27-9; Plutarch *Life of Agesilaus* 10.5-6). The theme of the *Persians* plays into the pretext for the Spartan invasion (cf. Timotheus fr. 790 *PMG*).

First performance is more likely toward the end of the invasion in 394, and Ephesus is the best location.[47] Agesilaus operated out of Ephesus; Timotheus' suppliant Phrygian claims 'my Artemis, great god, will protect me at Ephesus' (160-1). This is the only Greek city besides Miletus named in the extant poem; the line has an ironic bite if uttered at Ephesus. Agesilaus turned Ephesus into an immense 'workshop of war'.[48] He put the economy on a wartime footing and held contests for his warriors, who crowded the gymnasia and marketplace. He orchestrated a spectacle of barbarian effeminacy to instil contempt for the enemy in his troops (Xenophon *History of Greece* 3.4.16-18; *Agesilaus* 1.25-8). His heralds announced the sale of captured barbarians naked. Xenophon writes: 'And so when the soldiers saw they were white from never taking off their clothes, soft and never toiling because always riding on chariots, they thought that the war would be no different from fighting women' (Xenophon *History of Greece* 3.4.19; *Agesilaus* 1.28). Timotheus' poem gives voice to this spirit, depicting naked barbarians (98-103, 132-9) and describing the 'white-armed hands' with which Lydians embrace Cybele in supplication and lament (126). The named peoples of his song are those the Spartans plundered – Phrygians, Mysians, and Lydians. Timotheus strips them of their clothes and their dignity.[49]

Many have assumed that because the poem is about the battle of Salamis – not named in the extant poem – the song was first performed at Athens.[50] But this is unlikely. Timotheus, a Milesian, would not have announced that his city and those of the twelve Ionian cities hailed 'from the Achaeans' while performing at Athens (234-6).[51] That Ionians are Athenian colonists is a cardinal point of Athenian ideology (Herodotus 1.147; Euripides *Ion* 1575-88; Thucydides 1.2.6). The 'noblest' and 'purest Ionians', those of the twelve cities of which Timotheus calls Miletus pre-eminent (235-6), departed from the Prytaneum of Athens (Herodotus 1.146.2; 7.95.1).[52] Achaean heritage expresses Ionian self-definition as a people from the Peloponnese and places Ionians under 'the great leader of Sparta', as Timotheus styles Sparta in his epilogue (207; cf. Xenophon *History of Greece* 3.1.3).[53] Spartans used this title of themselves (Herodotus 7.228.3; Thucydides 1.128.7; cf. Simonides *Plataea* fr. 11.32-4). The 'leader of Sparta' leads Greece. No poet would name Sparta in this way at Athens. Timotheus' *Persians* contests Aeschylus' *Persians*, which created a fused Athenian/Ionian identity under Athenian hegemony.

Timotheus' topography of battle and flight is so vague, the absence of divine, heroic, and human figures associated with Salamis so conspicuous, and the fighting described so unlike traditional narratives of Salamis, that the poem as we have it hardly corresponds to the Athenian idea of Salamis.[54] Battles fought against the Persians are condensed into a single naval battle, which itself is partly assimilated to the naval battles that created Sparta's current land and sea hegemony. The prominence of javelins in the naval fighting is crucial in this regard (21-8; cf. 162-5). Neither Aeschylus nor Herodotus mentions this weapon's use among those fighting on the Greek side at Salamis (cf. Herodotus 8.90.2-3). The javelin was antithetical to the Athenian concept of naval warfare as the skill of manoeuvring and ramming. Aeschylus' account of the battle stresses this skill (417-18). His sailors do not even have weapons: they kill the enemy with fragments of their wrecks (424-6). The javelin was characteristic of the Dorian practice of 'fighting land battles at sea' which enabled them to defeat Athens in the harbour of Syracuse in 413.[55] It figures Peloponnesian prowess. Some argue that Timotheus narrates a typical naval battle and is not interested in history, but it is likely that he narrates a symbolic naval battle and presents a synoptic view of history.[56]

The yoking of the Hellespont associates Timotheus' *Persians* with traditional narratives. A drowning barbarian tells the sea, 'already, insolent sea, you had your furious neck yoked down in a linen-bound shackle' (72-4; cf. 114-18), combining descriptions of the bridge in the parodos of Aeschylus' *Persians* as a 'yoke on the neck of the sea' and a 'linen-bound boat-bridge' (68-9, 72) with Darius' image of the bridge as 'shackles' (747). The barbarian treats the sea as a unity, addressing the straits of Salamis as if they were the Hellespont.

Aeschylus' depiction of Salamis is present throughout Timotheus' *Persians*.[57] Timotheus' narrative conception – defeat, flight, lament – is Aeschylus'. The papyrus starts with a ramming episode: sailors pop off the deck and the Greeks upend barbarian ships by ramming them (1-20; cf. Aeschylus *Persians* 303-30, 417-19). Like Aeschylus, Timotheus envisions shores and promontories clogged with corpses (94-7).[58] The essence of Salamis, the shattering of the Persian fleet in the narrows (Aeschylus *Persians* 413-16) also features in Timotheus. In Aeschylus, the Greek fleet menacingly sounds out the 'depths of the sea', as it strikes the waves in rhythm (Aeschylus *Persians* 396-7). Timotheus' drowning barbarian vomits out the 'depths of the sea' in a menacing torrent of words (72-85).

Timotheus condenses Persian *hybris* and the Dionysiac violence that destroys it in his portrait of this drowning barbarian (60-85).[59] Playing on the equivalence of drunkenness, rough seas, and drowning, he uses sympotic imagery to characterize the barbarian.[60] Water 'is poured' into his alimentary tract; 'surging up from his mouth', it 'seethes over' like wine (61-5).[61] The verb meaning 'seethe over' is cognate with the word for a woman driven mad by Dionysus, a *thyias*.[62] Timotheus' language suggests wine and Dionysiac madness, but the sea-water itself is 'without Dionysus' (62), paradoxically producing the *hybris* of intoxication.

'Making himself like the sea, the mutilator of his body' (70-1), the drowning man vents shrill arrogance (66-81). His *hybris* and madness mirror his portrait of the sea; the sea-water he vomits reifies his torrent of words (83-5). Timotheus was a master of mimetic effects. His depiction of a barbarian imitating the sea while his watery vomit mirrors his words marks his own imitative musical effects.[63]

The narrative of the naval defeat culminates in the performance of lament, but Timotheus shifts the lamenters' perspective to the future. Barbarian combatants mourn their impending deaths at the scene of battle (98-139). Thucydides approximates this pathos in his narrative of the Athenian naval defeat in the Syracusan harbour. Athenian hoplites lament and consider 'how they will be saved' (7.71). Timotheus' Lydians look for a 'sweet escape from death' (119-20) and desire to supplicate Cybele. Aeschylus visually connected *proskynêsis* with Asia and Xerxes on their knees in defeat. Timotheus links defeat and supplication, placing oneself at the mercy of another under the protection of the gods by falling and clasping his or her knees.[64] A Lydian imagines himself falling at the knees of Cybele, his 'mistress'. Embracing her darkly clad body with 'white-armed hands' (121-6), he laments his death and the fate of his corpse, 'a pitiable feast for flocks of birds who eat raw food' (128-39). Timotheus does not narrate his fate. He intensifies the pathos, but deprives the barbarians of humanity.

This scene segues into Greeks capturing barbarians. Timotheus describes one capture. A 'Greek armed with iron' seizes a Phrygian 'by the hair' (140-4). The Phrygian 'entwines' himself around the Greek's knees and begs for his life in pidgin Greek (145-61). He will go back and live at Sardis, Susa, or Ecbatana. Artemis will protect him at Ephesus – a city teeming with Greek soldiers and mercenaries. Timotheus is similarly silent about his fate.

The Greek rout overtakes the scene. Barbarians throw away their javelins (161-5) and tear their faces in grief (166). The *pathos* finally reaches the Persians, who lament in their style, tearing the 'beautifully woven garments (*stolê*) on their bodies'

152

(167-70). The 'shrill lament of Asia' reaches the king's entourage, which resounds with lament, 'looking upon their future *pathos* with fear' (169-72). Timotheus' narrative of the past merges with the current Spartan invasion.

Finally, the king appears (173-4). He is unnamed. He sees the disorderly flight of his army, and 'falling on his knee he mutilates his body' (176). Timotheus transfers Aeschylus' image of Xerxes' falling and tearing his robes in the Queen's dream to the king's response to defeat. Like Aeschylus' Xerxes, Timotheus' king focalizes the *pathos*: he 'seethes like waves at his fate' (177), a technique applied to the drowning barbarian. The sea embodies *hybris* and lament, two sides of the same reality. Timotheus retains Aeschylus' depiction of *hybris* as fulfilled in lament.

The king's lament in Timotheus recapitulates Aeschylus' *kommos*. He bewails 'the fall of houses' (178), a theme Aeschylus linked to Xerxes, 'the eye of the house' who survives at the cost of his 'trusted eye' (Aeschylus *Persians* 979).[65] He laments the Greek navy's destruction of the 'populous youth (*hêbê*) of my ships' (180-1; cf. Aeschylus *Persians* 512, 669-70, 733). Timotheus also depicts the loss of men as a lost harvest, a central image of the *kommos*. The king compares the Greek ships which destroyed Persia's 'youth' to Sirius, the Dog Star, whose rising signals the heat that withers crops, sickens men, and marks the time for laments for such figures as Adonis.[66] Then he segues into an image of his ships on fire (182-5). Referring to Aeschylus' *kommos* and to the current invasion of Sparta, Timotheus' king predicts future laments 'on Persian land' (185-6) and apostrophizes his fate (187-8).

After his lament, the king orders four horses yoked to his chariot and his carts loaded 'with *olbos* beyond count' (190-2). The command subverts Aeschylus' *Persians*: the tragedy imagined Xerxes' 'yoke' shattered at Salamis (188-9) and Persia's *olbos* 'overturned' (164), 'destroyed' (252), and 'poured out' (825). Timotheus' king orders his tents burned, contradicting Herodotus, who reports that Xerxes left his tent and furniture with Mardonius for the Greeks to capture at Plataea (9.82). Timotheus' king stints the Greeks of his wealth (194-5).

Does this ending imply that the king retained his *olbos* from his earlier defeat and that the Spartans can march to Susa and strip him? Or does it question the idea of narrating the Persian defeat as a great victory? We hear the insane and pathetic voices of barbarians from the fringes of the Persian empire – but we do not witness the king lamenting his lost *olbos*. Timotheus' ending hints at the underlying reality of fourth-century Greece: the king's '*olbos* beyond count' financed the Spartan navy that captured the Athenian fleet at Aegospotami in 405 and was funding a resurgent navy aimed at driving the Spartans from the sea.[67] This happened at the battle of Cnidus in 394.[68]

The royal *olbos* described at the end of the *Persians* both made and destroyed the 'great leader of Sparta'. Bribing leaders of Thebes, Corinth, and Argos with 50 talents of gold while Agesilaus was in Ephesus, Artaxerxes II solidified a land and sea alliance against Sparta, forcing Agesilaus to return to Greece to defend his home-base (Xenophon *History of Greece* 3.5.1-4.2.8). What began self-consciously as a new Trojan War – Agesilaus attempted to replicate the sacrifice Agamemnon made at Aulis (Xenophon *History* 3.4.3-4; Plutarch *Life of Agesilaus* 6.4-6) – was shaping up as yet another internecine war.

The golden race: *Persians* in comedy

If tragedy depicts the other as the self, comedy depicts the self as the other. In comedy, Athenians are depicted as Persians, who signify Athens' aristocratic, luxurious, effeminate, money-oriented, imperialist culture. In Eupolis' *Maricas* of 421, the Athenian politician Hyperbolus appears as Maricas, a word Darius used to address the reader of his inscriptions.[69] Likening Maricas to Xerxes crossing the Hellespont, the play's chorus parodies Aeschylus *Persians* 65: 'the city-sacking Maricas has already crossed' (Eupolis *Maricas* fr. 207 K-A). The *Maricas* styles Hyperbolus, a litigious merchant-politician-imperialist and *bête noire* of comedy, as Xerxes.[70] A contemporary of Eupolis, the comedian Plato, has a character quote Xerxes' refrain in the exodos of the *Persians*, 'shout now in response to me' (fr. 226 K-A = 1040, 1048, 1066). We do not know what comedy the quote comes from, but Plato's *Hyperbolus*, a play ridiculing Hyperbolus as a slave, foreigner and villain who wins the lottery to become a member of the Council ahead of his master, who is an alternate, is a good possibility.

Comedy drew out golden-age themes associated in Aeschylus' *Persians* with Darius' reign and generally with the wealthy cultures of the East. Aeschylus' Xerxes is a 'godlike man of a golden-born race' (79-80); Persia (3, 9, 159), Lydia (45), and Babylon (53) are associated with 'much gold'. In Aeschylus, gold finances an invasion aimed at appropriating the freedom and silver of the Greeks; its radiance implants delusions of power and divinity. Gold symbolizes a culture which mistakes signs for realities, confuses pageantry and luxury with power, and produces a false sense of *olbos*; this culture seduces Xerxes into seeking to transcend human nature.[71] In comic golden-age scenarios, sign and reality, culture and nature, man and divinity, gold and *olbos* are fused. The central idea of the Golden Age is the presence of 'all good things' which come 'on their own': no labour is required.[72] Such a Golden Age is 'automatic'. Hesiod's 'golden race of mortal men' is the progenitor of the concept (*Works and Days* 109-26). H.C. Baldry considers the comic *topos* a way of ridiculing old fantasies.[73] Ian Ruffel, by contrast, interprets it as an 'expression of radical popular idealism'.[74] This may be; but the comic Golden Age is never far removed from dystopia.

Old comedy's staging of Persians illuminates the sympotic and festive ideals which Aeschylus, Choerilus, and Timotheus invert to fashion images of Persian *hybris* and defeat.[75] The utopian component of old comedy is an ideal of community realized in the feast and symposium to the exclusion of war, politics, and litigation. Labour and sometimes slavery are absent. Aeschylus' Darius espouses this ideal. Herodotus constitutes his Persians in a version of this scenario (1.125-6). If the Persians follow Cyrus they will become 'free', enjoying feasts, avoiding slavery and servile labour – in short, they will have 'all good things' (1.126.4-6).[76] Throughout Herodotus' *Histories*, Persians are associated with enormous feasts and excessive wine (1.133, 212.2; 3.34; 7.118-19). The rulers of an empire are a feasting/drinking group that enjoys 'all good things'.

Pherecrates, a contemporary of Aristophanes, was credited with a comedy entitled the *Persians*, dated between 427 and 416.[77] The comedy had definite golden-age elements, though we have no precise idea of how Persians functioned in the play. They could have figured the luxury of wealthy Athenians or Asian plenty and primitivism which satisfied utopian yearnings. Wealth is certainly a theme of the play. At one point the chorus of Persians denies it has any need for farming, craftsmen who support it (including a yoke-maker), seeds or vine-poles. They will enjoy 'all good things' without labour: 'rivers of black broth' containing rich cakes and the best bread 'will gush on their own from the founts of Wealth' (fr. 137.1-5 [K-A]). The ever-flowing river of goods gushing through the Golden Age can be read against Aeschylus' tragic images in the *Persians* such as 'wave of woes' (599-600), 'fount of woes' (743), 'flood of the Persian army' (87-92, 412), the freezing and thawing Strymon (495-507), and Xerxes' attempt to 'stop the sacred, flowing Hellespont' (745-6).[78] A natural limit of mortal power, the river flows with unnatural goods in the comic Golden Age. Zeus' rain nourishes a bounteous river; nature and culture, land and sea, plants and animals are undifferentiated (fr. 137.6-10 [K-A]). Man will not labour. The comedy involves abundant feasting and tableware of precious metals (fr. 134 [K-A]).

In comedy Xerxes and Persians are vehicles for fantasies about imperialist greed, lack of manliness, the pleasures of luxurious feasting, drinking, and culture as natural bounty. Aeschylus located a Golden Age in Persia: Xerxes' defeat marks its end.

The Turkish menace:
Apollonio's *Xerxes' Invasion of Greece*

In 1461, the Florentine merchant Giovanni Rucellai commissioned Apollonio di Giovanni to paint decorations for his daughter's bridal chest (*cassone*).[79] Apollonio's decorative painting, *Xerxes' Invasion of Greece*, projects Florence as the new Athens. The painting moves spatially and temporally from right to left, Asia to Europe. At the far right, prideful Xerxes (labelled SERSES) crosses a bridge over the Hellespont, which is crowded with vessels.[80] Apollonio then depicts a cavalry battle: Xerxes exhorts his troops to fight while Cimon (labelled CYMON) captures surrendering Persians, and Pericles (labelled PERICLES) marshals knights into battle. A companion panel, *The Triumph of the Victorious Greeks*, destroyed in a German raid on Bath, moves in space and time from left to right, from Salamis to Athens.[81] Beginning with a naval battle, it merges with a triumphal procession leading to Athens, whose architecture recalls ancient Rome.[82] Victorious Greeks and their leaders, one labelled TEMISTOCLES, line the procession. Not only does Athens look like Rome; the narrative unites the Salamis tradition with Vergil's description of Actium: naval victory followed by triumphal procession.[83]

Apollonio's vision of eastern defeat and western triumph draws on Boccaccio's account of Xerxes' prideful fall in the *Fates of Illustrious Men* (1360) and Petrarch's (1304-74) crusade-mongering *Rime* 28.[84] Paintings of Boccaccio's *Theseid of the Wedding of Emilia* (1339), a heroic romance exemplifying the prudence of Theseus, Duke of Athens, which also included his triumph over Scythian amazons, framed the two historical panels.[85] Apollonio's paintings comprised a complete account of Athens' triumph over the 'other' from Theseus to Pericles.

Xerxes' army figures the menace of contemporary Ottoman imperialism. Some of his soldiers wear the hats and carry the pikes of Ottoman janissaries.[86] Constantinople is visible in the distance as Xerxes crosses the Hellespont.[87] The Turks captured Constantinople in 1453, eight years before Apollonio received his commission.[88] Recalling Persia's defeat and Athens' triumph, the paintings prophesy Christian victory over the Turks.

A public reading of Aeschylus' *Persians* is an addendum to Apollonio's work. After a Christian navy's defeat of a Turkish fleet in the battle of Lepanto in 1571, citizens of the island of Zacynthus, which contributed a contingent to the Christian fleet, recited the play. The Turks replaced the Persians as the eastern vanquished foe in the imagination of the Italian Renaissance; the people of Zacynthus, an island under Venetian control, probably read an Italian translation.[89]

Xerxes as a figure of romance

The first large-scale restaging of a Greek tragedy, Sophocles' *Oedipus the King*, took place in Vicenza, Italy, in 1585.[90] The earliest adaptations of Xerxes' story appeared in opera, where

Xerxes featured as a romantic antihero. Francesco Cavalli presented a *Xerxes* in Venice in 1654 and reperformed it in Paris shortly after Louis XIV's wedding in 1660.[91] Giovanni Bononcini scored a *Xerxes* in 1694. George Frederic Handel's version, based on both Cavalli's and Bononcini's, debuted in London in 1738. Xerxes is a trouser or travesty role – a part written for a castrato. The unnatural lover and king who cannot obtain the object of his desire, Xerxes finally marries the woman who wants his throne and poses as a man – a wounded veteran – to get it. Handel's *Xerxes* closed after five performances but today is one of his most popular operas.[92]

In 1699 the English actor and playwright Colley Cibber (1671-1757) mounted a *Xerxes* at Little Lincoln's Inn Fields which was an even greater flop: it closed after one performance.[93] The tragedy depicts the transformation of Xerxes, failed invader of Greece who cannot rouse the passion to avenge his honour, into a romantic villain bent on destroying the virtue of the woman who spurned him. Cibber's Xerxes returns to Persia after his defeat to celebrate a false triumph. The Persians do not tear their clothes in lament, but 'Rend the Skies with Ecchoed Wellcomes' (I.140) for their 'triumphant' king. Xerxes uses the occasion to punish the elements that betrayed his fleet and vows to drive the chariot of the sun. Cibber recalls the myth of Phaethon as a paradigm for Xerxes' failure in Aeschylus' *Persians*.[94]

Xerxes' false triumph plays on golden-age themes of eternal spring and the freeing of slaves. His sycophantic poet proclaims 'Now we shall turn the Glass of Time,/And make it run the Golden Age again' (I.182-3). Xerxes concocts a scheme to devote himself to insatiable pleasure (I.393-4), plotting to test a woman of superlative virtue, Tamira, who spurned his love and throne, and then to rape her. The cruel hedonist uses every tyrannical ploy – murder, torture, treachery, rape, mutilation. Xerxes' 'Golden Age' becomes a time of debauchery, civil war, and mob violence.

Tamira tricks Xerxes into thinking that she will betray her husband Artabanus to gratify his lust; this disgusts Xerxes, and he no longer desires to rape her because she has no virtue to spoil. Xerxes trusts his divinity and capacity to avoid his fate to the very end. He meets Tamira's husband Artabanus in a duel; Xerxes and the virtuous general die from the blows they inflict on each another. Cibber stages tyrant-slaying as aristocratic self-sacrifice. Xerxes' death restores a military aristocracy to power. *Xerxes* fuses traditions of history, tragedy, and comedy to create a romantic tragedy.

The fusion of tragedy and romance is the theme of an anonymous American playwright's *Xerxes the Great, or The Battle of Thermopyle* (*sic*), produced in Philadelphia in 1815. The play sets Xerxes' ambition for the glory of conquering Leonidas and Sparta against Spartan republican ideals. The deposed Spartan King Demaratus returns with Xerxes to regain his throne. Sparta is divided between Leonidas' mandate to fight and die for freedom and the case for appeasing Xerxes and saving lives. Leonidas persuades an assembly that freedom is inalienable and that there is no choice but to fight for it.

As in Cibber, the play culminates in a duel. Xerxes calls the 'demigod' Leonidas to battle. Leonidas' blow shatters Xerxes' sword and causes him to fall, but Xerxes' henchman kills him. Leonidas' dying words convey the ambiguities of Xerxes' fame, which will soon turn to infamy (V.iv.21-3). The play ends with Xerxes' triumphant ride in a chariot through Sparta and the return of Demaratus to the throne. The romance of Xerxes' victory and the tragedy of Leonidas' heroic sacrifice are preludes to Xerxes' tragedy, the destruction of his 1,000 ships at Salamis (V.i.20-2).

Transcending history: Shelley's *Hellas*

In 1821, the Greeks revolted from the Ottoman empire. In 1822, Percy Bysshe Shelley published a lyrical tragedy on the subject, *Hellas*.[95] Employing the form and imagery of Aeschylus' *Persians*, Shelley's poem prophesies the fall of Islam and the Ottoman empire and the rise of a new Greece in the Christian West.[96]

An unfinished Prologue includes a divine assembly in which Christ, Satan, and Mohammed stake claims before God on how destiny should unfold at this turning point.[97] Christ proclaims the immortality of Greece and the victory of freedom over tyranny. Satan claims ownership of any empire that emerges from a reshuffling of power on earth before Christ interrupts him: 'Obdurate spirit! Thou seest but the Past in the To-come' (161-2). The prayer of *Hellas* is transcendence of the ceaselessly repeating pattern of history in a new age of western, Christian freedom.

The tragedy unfolds in five episodes. In the first, Mahmud, Sultan of the Ottoman empire, awakes unable to recall a recurrent dream. His underling Hassan arranges for him to see Ahasuerus, an ancient Jew. Probably the name for Xerxes in the *Book of Esther*, Ahasuerus allows his general Haman to extirpate the Jews from his empire, but changes course under the influence of his Jewish wife Esther.[98] He honours her cousin Mordecai, whose refusal to bow before Haman was the origin of Haman's plot. Ahasuerus allows Mordecai to wear his clothes, ride his horse, and proclaim the vengeance of the Jews throughout the empire in his name: they hang Haman and his ten sons, kill 500 enemies in Susa, and slaughter 75,000 adversaries throughout the Persian empire (*Esther* 9:1-16). The story is set in the year of Plataea and Mycale (479 BC) and constitutes a Jewish version of the Greek story of defeating the peoples of the Persian empire. Shelley's Ahasuerus stands at the intersection of Judeo-Christian and Eastern empires; he figures Xerxes, the Turks' predecessor, and the Jews, precursors of Christians.[99] Ahasuerus is the superseded power who advises his successor.[100]

Hassan and three messengers in succession deliver bad news before Ahasuerus speaks with Mahmud, enabling him to recall his dream: Mahomet II's capture of Constantinople. In Aeschylean terms, this is the 'act' (*drama*) which requires 'suffering' (*pathos*). As Mahmud's empire was born in blood so it will die (896-913). This scene realizes the Satanic principle: the vision of the 'To-come' in the past, as the future repeats and reciprocates past violence.

After Ahasuerus departs, Mahomet II emerges from the grave to inform Mahmud of Islam's collapse. Mahmud laments victor and vanquished alike in the procession of history (948-57). *Hellas* reads the *Persians* as a lament for the cycle of *drama* and *pathos*. As Mahmud mourns the impending fall of his empire, he hears shouts of victory and calls for vengeance. The Turks have gained the upper hand against the Greeks. Mahmud considers these expressions of triumph pathetic (986-8): 'I must rebuke/This drunkenness of triumph ere it die,/And dying, bring despair'. Eastern intoxication and *hybris* coalesce as in Choerilus and Timotheus. Turks celebrate the illusion of victory and call for the enslavement and slaughter of Greeks.

The chorus of captive Greek women envisions the light of Athens and Greece rising again in the West and attempts to imagine a new origin (1118-23). After contemplating Greek history and myth, particularly the fall of Troy, the women conclude that history itself must end. A new Golden Age is destined to come to the same end as the old, replicating the past in the present. The chorus orders an end to the vicious cycle of *drama* and *pathos* (1154-9).

The restoration of freedom is contingent on the renewal of pity. The chorus urges reconstruction of the 'broken' Athenian altar of Pity near the temple of Wisdom (775-6). Shelley reads the *Persians* as an attempt to elicit pity for the Persians. The basis for his utopian vision is the exchange of 'love for hate and tears for blood' (779). *Hellas* unites the ethics of tragic spectatorship with Christian morality to envision the end of history, conceived as a triumph of freedom without empire.

Restaging the *Persians*

Aeschylus was said to have restaged the *Persians* in Sicily; this tradition may have arisen as an explanation of why Dionysus misrepresents the play in the *Frogs*: there were two versions of it.[101] The Athenians voted to honour Aeschylus by allowing his plays to be reperformed after his death.[102] Aeschylus founded a theatrical dynasty: his sons Euphorion and Euaeon, both tragedians, probably restaged his plays. The most likely time for a restaging of the *Persians* is the early 420s.[103] In Aristophanes' *Acharnians* of 425, Dicaeopolis describes himself sitting in the theatre with his mouth agape, 'expecting Aeschylus' but getting a contemporary hack (9-12). The prologue of the *Acharnians* plays on the ending of the *Persians*. Eupolis' quotation in the *Maricas* can be dated to 421 and could derive from a revival; the date of Plato's quotation of the *Persians* is unknown. Further frustrating efforts at dating is the likelihood that the comedians knew the *Persians* from texts. A text was the basis for Herodotus' quotation of the play (8.68g; 728) and for his engagement with it throughout the *Histories*.

The *Persians*' anti-imperialist message and its sense that history belongs to the free made it a staple of liberation movements and a bulwark against totalitarianism. Takis Mouzendis' staging of the play at Epidaurus in 1971 was received as an act of subversion of the Junta that ruled Greece from 1967 to 1974.[104] Yet the *Persians* also held appeal for totalitarian regimes which saw their 'victory' presaged in it. The Nazis restaged the play in the winter of 1942; it was one of a series of tragedies produced as they struggled in the East.[105] Rightists in the Greek civil war of 1946-49 appropriated the *Persians* in their war against communism.[106] In 1951, leftist political prisoners interned on the island of Aï Stratis, allowed to perform the *Persians* as part of their 'rehabilitation', reclaimed the play as a tragedy and prophetic exhibition of Greek delusions of power, victory, and moral superiority.[107]

East Germany became a fruitful place for restaging the *Persians*; it was here that the play struck audiences as anti-war art. Mattias Braun's adaptation of the *Persians* as an anti-fascist play, produced several times in Germany during the period 1960 to 1969, was received as an anti-war drama contesting American involvement in the Korean and Vietnam Wars.[108] The first professional revivals of the *Persians* in New York in the early 1970s staged the *Persians* as an anti-Vietnam play.[109]

The first Gulf War in 1991 breathed new life into the *Persians*. In 1993, Peter Sellars directed a *Persians* at the Salzburg Festival, using Robert Auletta's adaptation of Aeschylus' *Persians* as a dramatization of Saddam Hussein's crushing defeat. Xerxes is Saddam Hussein (who is never named in the play). Taking place in Baghdad during the 'smart' bombing campaign of 1991, the play inverts the original play's story of a massive empire felled by tiny Greece to probe the symbiotic pathologies of eastern despotism and western culture.

The second Gulf War produced another adaptation of the *Persians*, Ellen McLaughlin's, written at the request of the late

American actor, Tony Randall.[110] To McLaughlin, the *Persians* 'warns us of the perils of conquest and imperialism – this rolling catastrophe of war, never-ending, soul-sapping, civilization-destroying ....'[111]

Aeschylus' *Persians* is today enshrined in the anti-war and anti-imperialist discourse of western culture. Xerxes personifies the threat to the western male identity and to the moral, political, and religious orders which sustain it. The quintessential loser of history, who ruins the Golden Age he inherited, Xerxes continues to haunt those who defeat him as they rebuild the ruins left in his wake, for the temptation to become Xerxes is the price of victory over him.

Notes

1. The *Persians*, History, and Historical Drama

1. See Detienne, *Dionysos at Large*; Lonsdale, *Dance and Ritual Play*, esp. 76-136.

2. Pickard-Cambridge, *Dramatic Festivals*, 57-125; Parke, *Festivals*, 125-35; Simon, *Festivals*, 101-8; Csapo/Slater, pp. 103-21.

3. ML^2 46 = Fornara 98; Isocrates *On the Peace* 8.82 = Csapo/Slater III.35A; Scholium to Aristophanes *Acharnians* 504 = Csapo/Slater III.35B; Connor, 'City Dionysia and Athenian Democracy'; Goldhill, 'Great Dionysia'.

4. See Gantz, 'Aischylean Tetralogy'.

5. Flintoff, 'Unity'; Moreau, 'La tétralogie'.

6. Broadhead, lv-lx; Gantz, 'Aischylean Tetralogy', 134.

7. The *Hypothesis* to the *Persians* reports Aeschylus' victory in 472 and it is confirmed by an inscription. For the judging of tragic competitions, see Pickard-Cambridge, *Dramatic Festivals*, 95-9; Csapo/Slater, pp. 157-65.

8. *Life of Aeschylus* 13 says he won thirteen victories. The Suda, a tenth-century AD encyclopaedia, claims he won 28 (*s.v.* Aeschylus).

9. Thalmann, 'Xerxes' Rags', 260-1.

10. For Aeschylus' biography, see Podlecki, *Political Background*, 1-7. *TrGF* 3 pp. 31-108 collects the evidence.

11. *Life of Aeschylus* 11 = Csapo/Slater I.23a. *FGE* 'Aeschylus' II identifies it as a forgery.

12. Lefkowitz, *Lives*, 67-74.

13. Athenaeus *Banquet of the Sophists* 1.21D-22A = Csapo/Slater IV.304.

14. Some think that Aeschylus played the Queen and Xerxes because they do not appear together when the drama leads us to expect that they will (e.g. Pickard-Cambridge, *Dramatic Festivals*, 138). This is an inadequate reason (Taplin, *Stagecraft*, 120). McCall, 'Aeschylus in the *Persae*', 47 argues that Aeschylus played these roles because they required his authority to win sympathy.

15. See Wilson, *Khoregeia*, esp. 71-103.

16. The *Fasti* record that Pericles produced the *Persians* (*TrGF* 1 pp. 22-5).

17. See Podlecki, *Pericles*, 1-10.

18. See Gillis, *Collaboration*, 45-58.

19. See Storey, *Eupolis*, 114-16.

20. For the extent of the Persian empire, see Briant, *Cyrus to Alexander* 172-83.

21. See Lewis, 'Tyranny of the Pisistratidae'; Lavelle, *Fame, Money, and Power*.

22. Herodotus 5.55-6; Thucydides 6.53.3-59; cf. [Aristotle] *Constitution of the Athenians* 18.

23. See Taylor, *Tyrant Slayers*; Ober, 'Tyrant-Killing'.

24. Herodotus 5.66-9; [Aristotle] *Constitution of the Athenians* 21; Andrewes, 'Reform Bill'; Ostwald, 'Reform'; Manville, *Origins*, 157-209; Ober, 'Athenian Revolution'.

25. *PMG* 893, 896, translated and discussed in Taylor, *Tyrant Slayers*, 22-35; Vlastos, 'Isonomia', and Ostwald, *Nomos*, 96-173 offer different formulations of the principle of *isonomia*.

26. Kuhrt, 'Earth and Water'.

27. Georges, 'Persian Ionia'; Murray, 'Ionian Revolt'; Briant, *Cyrus to Alexander*, 146-56.

28. For the Persian-installed tyrants, see Austin, 'Greek Tyrants'; Georges, 'Persian Ionia', 10-23.

29. Homer *Iliad* 5.59-64; cf. Thucydides 2.12.3.

30. Cybebe is a Lydian version of the goddess known in Greece as Cybele. See Roller, *God the Mother*, esp. 63-186.

31. Xerxes, Persepolis H = Kent 150-2 = Brosius 191; Briant, *Cyrus to Alexander*, 550-3, 965-6.

32. Herodotus 6.21.2 names the play as if its title were the *Capture of Miletus*, as do the later writers Plutarch (*Moral Essays* 814A-B5) and Aelian (*Various History* 13.17). Many doubt that this was the actual title.

33. Rosenbloom, 'Shouting "Fire" ', 170-2; Roisman, 'Phrynichus' *Sack of Miletus*' argues for a date after 479.

34. Dionysius of Halicarnassus *Roman Antiquities* 6.34.1; Thucydides 1.93.3. Not all agree that Themistocles was Archon or that he began to fortify Piraeus in 493/2. For the case against both, see Fornara, 'Themistocles' Archonship'. For the case in favour, see Lewis, 'Themistocles' Archonship'.

35. Forrest, 'Themistokles and Argos', 235; Podlecki, *Themistocles*, 6-7. Cf. Ammianus Marcellinus *Roman History* 28.1-3-4.

36. Else, *Origin and Early Form*, 74-5; Lloyd-Jones, 'Early Greek Tragedy', 232.

37. See Suter, 'Lament'.

38. Plato *Republic* 604e5-6, 606b1; cf. Gorgias *Helen* 11.9 (D-K); Timocles, *Women at the Dionysia* fr. 6 (K-A); Rosenbloom, 'Myth, History, and Hegemony', 101-3.

39. Aristotle *Rhetoric* 1386a-b; *Poetics* 1453a6; Konstan, *Pity Transformed*, 27-104. For the comforts of pity, see Pucci, *Violence of Pity*, 171-4.

40. Aristotle *Rhetoric* 1386a27-8; Stanford, *Greek Tragedy and the Emotions*, 21-48.

41. For the rarity of historical drama at Athens, see Castellani, 'Clio vs. Melpomene'.

42. See Grundy, *Great Persian War*, 162-94; Green, *Greco-Persian Wars*, 30-40; Burn, *Persia and the Greeks*, 236-57; Hammond, 'Expedition of Datis and Artaphrenes'; Lazenby, *Defence*, 45-80.

43. For Xerxes' invasion, see Grundy, *Great Persian War*; Hignett, *Xerxes' Invasion*; Green, *Greco-Persian Wars*; Burn, *Persia and the Greeks*; Hammond, 'The Expedition of Xerxes'; Young, 'A Persian Perspective'; Lazenby, *Defence*; Strauss, *Battle of Salamis*.

44. Maurice, 'The Size of the Army of Xerxes', argues that 210,000 people and 75,000 animals were the maximum supportable. Young, 'A Persian Perspective', counters that even these numbers would have been impossible; cf. Barkworth, 'Organization'. See further Lazenby, *Defence*, 90-2; Hignett, *Xerxes' Invasion*, 345-55.

45. ML² 23 = Fornara 55. For its authenticity, see Jameson, 'Waiting for the Barbarian', and 'Provisions for Mobilization'; Hammond, 'Herodotus VII and the Decree of Themistocles' dates the decree to September 481. Hignett, *Xerxes' Invasion*, 458-68 considers it a forgery.

46. See Thompson, 'Athens Faces Adversity'; Shear, 'The Demolished Temple at Eleusis'; 'The Persian Destruction of Athens'; Pedrizet, 'Le Témoignage d'Eschyle'.

47. Aeschylus *Agamemnon* 126-34, 338-47, 522-37, 810-29; *Seven against Thebes* 287-368; Ferrari, 'The Ilioupersis in Athens'.

48. E.g. Kitto, *Greek Tragedy*, 34.

49. Strauss, *The Battle of Salamis*, 109-11.

50. Hignett, *Xerxes' Invasion*, 403-8.

51. *FGE* 'Simonides' VIII, IX, XX(a); Simonides fr. 531 *PMG*.

52. *FGE* 'Simonides' XVI, XVIII, XX(a); cf. Pindar fr. 77; Raaflaub, *Discovery of Freedom*, 58-89.

53. See Rutherford, 'Towards a Commentary', 35-8; West, 'Simonides Redivivus'; Sider, 'Fragments 1-22 W²', 13-17 for translations of the papyrus fragments.

54. West, 'Simonides Redivivus', 3-4 suggests that the poem contained a prophecy of the Old Man of Sea.

55. See Sider 'Fragments 1-22 W²', 28-9 for text and translation.

56. For an overview of these questions, see Rutherford, 'Towards a Commentary', 38-41.

57. Brackets indicate restored or conjectured words.

58. West, 'Simonides Redivivus', 8-9 infers from *Plataea* fr. 14.5-8 the poem was performed after the formation of the Athenian empire and prophesied that Ares would drive the Persians from Asia; see also Flower, 'From Simonides to Isocrates', 66-9. I find this doubtful.

59. Lloyd-Jones, 'Notes on the New Simonides', 1; Shaw, 'Lords of Hellas, Old Men of the Sea', 180-1 connect Achilles and Pausanias. Aloni, 'The Proem of Simonides' Plataea Elegy', 98 and Boedeker, 'Paths to Heroization at Plataea', 157-8 argue that Achilles figures the collective dead.

60. Aloni, 'The Proem of Simonides' Plataea Elegy', 93-105; Boedeker, 'Paths to Heroization at Plataea'. See also Simonides' song for the dead at Thermopylae (fr. 531 *PMG*).

61. See Boedeker, 'Heroic Historiography', 124-7. Georges, *Barbarian Asia*, 58-66 views the theme as a Greek inversion of Persian propaganda, vengeance for the sack of Troy.

62. See Boedeker, 'Protesilaus and the End of Herodotus' *Histories*'; Moles, 'Herodotus Warns the Athenians'; Dewald, 'Wanton Kings, Pickled Heroes, and Gnomic Founding Fathers'; Desmond, 'Punishments and the Conclusion of Herodotus' *Histories*'; Flower/Marincola, *Histories IX*, 309.

63. Persian booty was a significant addition to Athens' wealth and an impetus to a new level of material culture. See Miller, *Athens and Persia*, 32-62.

64. Fornara 61, collects the sources. See Lang, 'Scapegoat Pausanias'; Evans, 'The Medism of Pausanias'.

65. See Briant, *Cyrus to Alexander*, 852-76; Mossé, *Alexander*, 66-72.

66. Aversion: Archilochus fr. 19 (West); desire/imitation: Hybrias fr. 909 (*PMG*). See McGlew, *Tyranny and Political Culture*, 14-51; Wohl, *Love among the Ruins*, 215-69.

67. Badian, 'Thucydides and the Outbreak', 130; cf. Fornara, 'Some Aspects', 266. For the assessment of tribute, see Thucydides 1.96.1; Plutarch *Life of*

Aristides 24.3; cf. Diodorus 11.47.1; *ATL* 3.234-43; Meiggs, *Athenian Empire*, 50-67. For Persian tribute, see Herodotus 3.90.1; 6.42; Briant, *Cyrus to Alexander*, 388-421.

68. Ehrenberg, *From Solon to Socrates*, 115; Robertson 'True Nature', 64-9. See Raaflaub, *Discovery of Freedom*, esp. 137-46 for a different view. Brunt, 'The Hellenic League', 158 describes the tribute as 'an administrative amendment'. I consider this view anachronistic. Plutarch *Life of Aristides* 24.1 claims that the alliance against Xerxes levied payments from its members, but it is more likely that each ally was self-supporting.

69. Van Wees, *Status Warriors*, 183-90. See Homer *Iliad* 3.281-91, 456-60; cf. 7.361-4. See further, Xenophon *Anabasis* 3.2.28; *Education of Cyrus* 7.5.72-3.

70. Raaflaub, *Discovery of Freedom*, 176-7 dates it the Peloponnesian War.

71. Fornara/Samons, *Athens from Cleisthenes to Pericles*, 109.

72. See *ATL* 3.185. Cawkwell, 'Fall of Themistocles', 41 sees such extortion as 'natural'.

73. Timocreon fr. 727 (*PMG*). *ATL* 3.185 interpret it as a communal penalty. Timocreon represents it as a private payment to repatriate him.

74. Robertson, 'True Nature', 74 makes the league exclusively punitive; this was one important dimension of it. Sealey, 'The Origin', likewise reduces the league to a single function, piratical raids.

75. The Persians considered Apollo the quintessential Greek god (ML^2 12 = Fornara 35); see Briant, *Cyrus to Alexander*, 491-3. For possible reflections of Delian Apollo in Athenian vase-painting of the period, see Shapiro, 'Athena, Apollo, and Religious Propaganda'.

76. Osborne, 'Archaeology and the Athenian Empire', 324.

77. See Pritchett, 'The Transfer of the Delian Treasury'.

78. Cf. Robertson, 'True Nature', 71-3.

79. Robertson, 'True Nature, Continued', 119-20. Most scholars accept a democratic league. Meiggs, *Athenian Empire*, 46-9 summarizes the consensus; cf. Rhodes, *Athenian Empire*, 6-7.

80. Scholium to Aeschines *On the False Embassy* 2.31 = Fornara 62. Badian, 'Towards a Chronology', 81-6 accepts the testimony. Thucydides, who knew the region well, omits this attempt at colonization (4.102).

81. *FGE* XL. Aeschines *Against Ctesiphon* 3.184-5 and Plutarch *Life of Cimon* 7.4-5 quote them in a different order.

82. Plutarch *Life of Themistocles* 5.4. The date is certain; the play is not.

83. Lloyd-Jones, 'Problems', 24 suggests that the *Persians* was based on a play performed with the *Phoenician Women*. The Suda *s.v.* Phrynichus names these plays *Just Men* or *Persians* or *Throne Partners*.

84. Herodotus 8.105.2; Xenophon *Education of Cyrus* 7.5.58-65; Briant, *Cyrus to Alexander*, 270-7; Hall, *Inventing the Barbarian*, 157-9; Hornblower, 'Panionios', esp. 50-7.

85. Cf. Hall, 'Asia Unmanned', 115-16.

86. This is supposedly based on Phrynichus *TrGF* 1 F10a. See Stössl, 'Aeschylus as a Political Thinker', 116.

87. Forrest, 'Themistocles and Argos', 235-7; Podlecki, *Political Background*, 14-15.

88. See Lenardon, 'Chronology'; Podlecki, *Themistocles* 197-8.

89. Nagy, *Pindar's Homer*, 176-7; Boedeker, 'Hero Cult'.

90. Plutarch *Life of Cimon* 8.5-6; *Life of Theseus* 36.2-3; Pausanias *Description of Greece* 1.17.6; Podlecki, 'Cimon, Skyros and "Theseus' Bones" '.

91. Pausanias *Description of Greece* 1.17.2-3; cf. Plutarch *Life of Theseus* 36.1.

92. Meiggs, *Athenian Empire*, 69.

93. Shapiro, 'Theseus in Kimonian Athens', 33-9.

94. Robertson, 'True Nature, Continued', 110.

95. For the chronology of the period 478-435, see Unz, 'Chronology'; Badian, 'Towards a Chronology'.

96. Thucydides 1.100.1; Plutarch *Life of Cimon* 12-13; cf. Diodorus 11.60.3-62; Meiggs, *Athenian Empire*, 73-84.

97. See Hall, *Inventing the Barbarian*, 62-9.

98. See Euben, 'The Battle of Salamis and the Origins of Political Theory', 363-8; Hall, 12.

99. For a different view, see van Wees, 'Politics and the Battlefield', 157-61.

100. For these criteria, see Finley, 'Empire in the Greco-Roman World', 1-8.

101. For the methods of the Athenian empire, see Meiggs, *Athenian Empire* 205-339; Raaflaub, *Discovery of Freedom*, 118-65. Finley, 'The Athenian Empire', 42-3 argues convincingly against a discrete change from hegemony to empire.

2. Fear

1. Winnington-Ingram, 'A Word in *Persae*'.

2. See Avery, 'Dramatic Devices', 176-7.

3. For *hybris* as vaunting and confident militarism, see e.g. Aeschylus *Seven against Thebes* 397-407.

4. Saïd, 'Tragédie et Renversement', 329. For the *Persians*' debt to Homer, see Smethurst, *Artistry*, 260-9.

5. Darius, Behistun 1.6 = Kent 119 = Brosius 44.6, lists 23 lands and peoples upon his accession. Later, he lists 30 (Naqš-i Rustam A.3 = Kent 138 and Susa E = Brosius 46.3). Xerxes lists 31 (Persepolis H.3 = Kent 151 = Brosius 191.3). See Briant, *Cyrus to Alexander*, 172-83. Herodotus 3.89-94 lists 20 tribute-bearing provinces and some 65 peoples.

6. Xenophanes *Elegies* fr. 3 (West); Herodotus 1.94.1; cf. 1.155.2-4; Kurke, *Coins, Bodies, Games, and Gold*, 165-71.

7. That the Mysians fought with the Trojans (Homer *Iliad* 2.858-61) may have influenced their inclusion. The final lament of the *Persians* is Mysian (1054).

8. Hecataeus could be Aeschylus' source for Persian tributes (Herodotus 5.36.2; cf. 5.49), though Hall, *Inventing the Barbarian*, 74-6 cogently argues that the *Persians*' debt to Hecataeus is small.

9. See Konstan, 'Persians, Greeks, and Empire'.

10. For the names in the play, see Sidgwick, 66-8; Broadhead, 318-21; Lattimore, 'Aeschylus on the Defeat of Xerxes', 84-8; Schmidt, *Iranier-Namen*; Balcer, *Prosopographical Study*.

11. Xerxes married Amestris, daughter of Otanes. He had at least one marriageable son with her in 479, Darius (Herodotus 9.108), and many sons with other women (8.103; 7.39.1). At the time of his accession, Xerxes had an infant daughter named Ratašah (Brosius 162).

12. See Hall, *Inventing the Barbarian*, 82-3.

13. *Hybris* turns to *atê* when its disastrous consequences become apparent. See Homer *Iliad* 1.202-14, 407-12; 9.16-28; Neuburg, '*Atê* Reconsidered', 502; see also Padel, *Whom Gods Destroy*, 167-202, 249-59.

14. For Typho, see Hesiod *Theogony* 820-80; [Aeschylus] *Prometheus Bound* 351-72; Moreau, *Eschyle: la violence et la chaos*, 148-50 compares Xerxes and Typho.

15. Hignett, *Xerxes' Invasion*, 441-4; Fontenrose, *The Delphic Oracle*, 124-8 believes that Aeschylus influenced Herodotus (128 n. 9).

16. I follow Müller in placing 93-101 after 113. These lines fit best after the statement of Xerxes' deviation; see Broadhead, 53-5. The translators Benardete, Smyth, and Lembke/Herington transpose the lines. For arguments against transposition, see Groeneboom, 30-1; Hall, 115-16, who does not transpose. Nor does Podlecki, *Persians*.

17. Scott, 'The Mesode', argues that the Greeks are the subject of this reflection; see also Scott, *Musical Design*, 156-7; Gagarin, *Aeschylean Drama*, 49, 183-4 n. 5.

18. Michelini, *Tradition*, 78-9. Garvie, 'Aeschylus' Simple Plots', 67-70 downplays 'the moral lesson' of the play, claiming that Aeschylus could have developed it in the parodos (67).

19. See Holtsmark, 'Ring Composition', 11-12; Miller '*Ingenium* and *Ars*' 78-81; Wilson, 'Territoriality', 53-7 for the contrast between natural and learned activity at 102-13.

20. See Rosenbloom, 'Myth, History, Hegemony', 93-8.

21. Ring composition is the basic structural element of the *Persians*. See Holtsmark, 'Ring Composition'.

22. See Herodotus 3.66.1; 8.99.2, where Persians rend their *chitônes* after Xerxes' defeat; cf. Sappho fr. 140a (Lobel/Page).

23. For linen corselets, see Page, *Sappho and Alcaeus*, 215-16; for the Ionian tunic, see Herodotus 5.88.1; Thucydides 1.6.3; Bacon, *Barbarians*, 26-31.

24. Morrison et al., *Athenian Trireme*, 169-71. Aeschylus *Suppliants* 134 calls a trireme 'a linen-stitched house'. Timotheus *Persians* 15 calls the hull of a trireme 'linen-bound flanks'.

25. For the image of the yoke, see Fowler, 'Aeschylus Imagery', 3-6; Michelini, *Tradition* 81-7.

26. For the *Persians* as a play about *hybris*, see Jones, *On Aristotle and Greek Tragedy*, 72; Kitto, *Greek Tragedy*, 36.

27. Cf. Thucydides 6.30-1, with reference to Athens' invasion of Sicily in 415.

28. See Hall, 118-19. Seaford, *Reciprocity and Ritual*, 109-14 discusses physical and ideological links between council houses and tombs of ancestral heroes. Harmon, 'The Scene of the *Persians*' sets the play at the city-gates of Susa, where eastern cities held councils and buried their dead. But the play never mentions city-gates; and the *Persians* does not demand this kind of accuracy: the play locates Darius' tomb in Susa, when in fact he was buried near Persepolis. For more on Darius' tomb, see Chapter 4.

29. Dale, 'Interior Scenes', 260-2 sees the *skênê* and the tomb as the same structure. Cf. Harmon, 'The Scene of the *Persians*', 9. Arnott, *Greek Scenic Conventions*, 58 argues that the council house and the tomb cannot be identical because *stegos* is too vague a term and the tomb is not mentioned until the second half of the play. As Taplin, *Stagecraft*, 106 notes, however, the play avoids prior preparation for the ghost-raising: it is a surprise.

30. Pickard-Cambridge, *Theatre of Dionysus*, 35.

31. Prickard, 53 and Murray, *Aeschylus*, 55 identify the *skênê* with the royal palace.

32. Taplin, *Stagecraft*, 453-4 thinks the scene changes from an imagined council chamber to Darius' tomb after the first stasimon. See also Belloni, 105-6.

33. Kitto, *Greek Tragedy,* 42; Taplin, *Stagecraft*, 452-9; Belloni, 105-6; Hammond, 'More on Conditions of Production', 11-12; West, *Studies*, 48. Hammond, 'Conditions of Dramatic Production', 425-7 thinks that a rudimentary *skênê*, a covered stall open at the front and sides, represented the council house. The belief that a *skênê* was not used rests upon an insufficient sampling of plays.

34. I agree with Wilamowitz, *Aischylos Interpretationen*, 43 and Broadhead, xlv.

35. Wilamowitz, *Aischylos Interpretationen*, 48-51 sets the action at the council-chamber, then at Darius' tomb, and finally on a country road. Cf. Broadhead, xlvi.

36. Kitto, *Greek Drama*, 37; Broadhead, xlv.

37. See Connor, 'Land Warfare as Symbolic Expression', 26.

38. Darius represented his power in terms of the spear: Naqš-i Rustam A.4 = Brosius 48.4; Naqš-i Rustam B.8h = Brosius 103.9.

39. Scott, *Musical Design*, 157-8 suggests that actors' entrances interrupt the epodes of the chorus' hymn (673-80) and the second stasimon (898-907).

40. Homer *Odyssey* 3.137-40; 8.487-91; 20.178-82.

41. Taplin, *Stagecraft*, 70-1 prefers 155.

42. Xenophon *Anabasis* 3.2.13. Herodotus says that equals kissed on the lips, near equals kissed on the cheek, and the 'far more ignoble' performed *proskynêsis* before their superiors (1.134.1). See Briant, *Cyrus to Alexander*, 222-3; Hall, *Inventing the Barbarian* 96-7; Harrison, *Emptiness of Asia*, 87-8; Couch, 'Proskynesis'.

43. Herodotus 7.56.2, 203.2 deny Xerxes' divinity; Gorgias fr. 5a (D-K): 'Xerxes is Zeus of the Persians'; Gow, 'Notes', 134-6.

44. For differing views of this metre in the play, see Drew-Bear, 'Trochaic Tetrameter', 385-93; Michelini, *Tradition* 41-64.

45. Georges, *Barbarian Asia*, 83 sees this as the Queen's 'dark side', but it typifies the female perspective in Greek thought. Cf. Sancisi-Weerdenburg, 'Exist Atossa', 24: 'there is really nothing Persian in her behaviour'.

46. See Broadhead, 260-3; Michelini, *Tradition*, 88-92; Hall, 122-3. My interpretation is closest to Fowler, 'Aeschylus' Imagery', 8 and Gagarin, *Aeschylean Drama*, 180-1 n. 35.

47. Sansone '*Persae* 163', 115-16 relates the image to wrestling, and like Belloni, 111, argues that the dust arises from a fall. I think that *Ploutos* churns up the dust in its aggression and *olbos* is subverted by its defeat.

48. Groeneboom, 46-7; Thalmann, 'Xerxes' Rags', 276-7.

49. Aeschylus *Suppliants* 180: 'I see dust, the voiceless messenger of an army'; *Seven against Thebes* 78-82.

50. Paired at *Iliad* 16.594-6; 24.534-42; *Odyssey* 14.204-6. For the meaning of *olbos* and *olbios* ('blessed', 'prosperous') in Homer, see *Odyssey* 4.204-11; 7.146-50; 24.36-94.

51. See Theognis *Elegies* 373-82 (West), which berates Zeus for allowing hybristic and unjust men *olbos* while good and just men are poor.

52. Hesiod *Theogony* 968-74; Homeric *Hymn to Demeter* 480-9; Homeric *Hymn to Gaea*. See further Chapter 5.

53. See Immerwahr, *Form and Thought*, 154-61; Chiasson, 'The Herodotean Solon'; Harrison, *Divinity and History*, 31-63.

54. *Anandros* means without a husband (289), without men (298), without manliness or courage (cf. *anandria*, 755). Most take *chrêmatôn anandrôn* to mean 'wealth without men', e.g. Michelini, *Tradition*, 88-90, who translates 'a mass of unmanned possessions' (89). Belloni, 112-13 takes it to mean 'wealth without a man' (i.e. Xerxes); Broadhead, 262-3, thinks the train of thought includes both. I agree with Hall, 122 that *plêthos* means 'the masses', but I take

chrêmatôn anandrôn to mean 'wealth without manliness', that is, 'not derived from conquest'. Groeneboom, 47-8 notes that the Queen relates a man's 'excellence' (*aretê*) to wealth.

55. Cf. Thalmann, 'Xerxes' Rags', esp. 276.

56. For 'eye' as the source from which grapes grow, see Alcman fr. 93 (*PMG*); Ion of Chios *Elegies* fr. 26 (West). Xenophon *Oeconomicus* 19.10 uses 'eyes' of the shoots of fruit trees. See Sophocles *Electra* 417-23 for an image involving a cognate idea.

57. For the 'eye of the house' as the male heir, see Aeschylus *Libation Bearers* 934. Hall, 122 interprets 'eye of the house' as the master's presence which ensures the proper use of wealth. Xenophon *Oeconomicus* 12.19-20 relates this concept to the Persian king. Belloni, 112 sees the Queen's double fear as embracing wealth in the absence of a master and the inability to generate power from that wealth. But the idea underlying the Queen's fear is that Xerxes is irreplaceable as *despotês*: neither the Queen and Darius nor Xerxes has a son to succeed him.

58. Herodotus depicts Xerxes' birth from Atossa, daughter of Cyrus, as decisive for his accession (7.3.4). Aeschylus calls her 'Queen', never stating her name or parentage.

59. For these metaphors, see Aeschylus *Libation Bearers* 807-11; cf. 130-1, 859-65, 961-4.

60. See Moreau, 'L'oeil maléfique'.

61. Aeschylus *Suppliants* 713-18; Morrison et al., *Athenian Trireme*, 148-9 n. 22.

62. Belloni, 115; Sancisi-Weerdenburg, '*Yaunâ*'.

63. 187, 255, 337, 391, 423, 434, 475, 844. For this loan word meaning 'mumble' or 'stammer', see Hall, *Inventing the Barbarian*, 3-19.

64. See Cartledge, *The Greeks*, 45-6.

65. See Hall, 123 for a different view.

66. Bacchylides *Dithyramb* 18.2 for 'delicately living Ionians'. See further Xenophanes *Elegies* fr. 3 (West); Antiphanes *Woman of Dodona* fr. 91 (K-A); Alty, 'Dorians and Ionians', 7-11.

67. Herodotus 8.65.4-5; cf. 7.10, 19, 37.2, 46.1, 101-3, 209.2; 9.42.

68. Gow, 'Notes', 137.

69. See Broadhead, 78; Moreau, 'Le songe', 40-1. Meier, *Political Art*, 75 thinks they figure Greece and all barbarian lands. But why are they 'sisters of the same race'? Prickard, 58 and Smyth, *Aeschylean Tragedy*, 65 take them as personifications of mainland and eastern Greeks.

70. Herodotus 7.61, 150.2-3, 220.4; cf. 6.53.4; Georges, *Barbarian Asia*, 66-71.

71. Sommerstein, *Aeschylean Tragedy*, 76-7; Moreau, 'La tétralogie', 133.

72. Psychoanalytic interpreters of the dream, Caldwell, 'The Pattern of Aeschylean Drama', 78-83 and Devereux, *Dreams in Greek Tragedy*, 1-23 read it to mean that Xerxes wants to 'possess' his mother and that this is her ambivalent desire too.

73. See Sancisi-Weerdenburg, 'Exit Atossa', 27-30.

74. Burned: Aeschylus *Agamemnon* 88-96; Aristophanes *Wealth* 661. Poured: Aeschylus *Libation Bearers* 92.

75. Gow, 'Notes', 138-40; Harrison, *Emptiness of Asia*, 146-7 n. 50.

76. See Mikalson, *Herodotus and Religion*, 114-25. Moreau, 'Le songe', 39, 46-7 suggests that Apollo appears as the god of prophecy and as the god whose temple at Delphi the Persians sought in vain to pillage (Herodotus 8.35-9).

77. Aelion, 'Songes et prophéties', 136-7.

78. See Knox, ' "So Mischievous a Beaste" '.

79. The *magi* were a Median tribe which functioned as ritual experts in Persia (Herodotus 1.101). See Briant, *Cyrus to Alexander*, 245-6.

80. Groeneboom, 63; Briant, *Cyrus to Alexander*, 297-9 relates it to the royal hunt.

81. The image was traditional in the Near East. See Briant, *Cyrus to Alexander*, 230-2, 297-300; 'Darius seal' = Brosius 43.

82. Herodotus balances Athenian and Spartan responsibility for the victory. See Harrison, *Emptiness of Asia*, 61-2.

83. Cf. Goldhill, 'Battle Narrative', 190-1.

84. See Kantzios, 'The Politics of Fear', 14-15.

85. Hall, 128 considers the messenger's haste 'a jibe ... at the speed with which the Persians fled from Greece'.

3. *Pathos*

1. See Avery, 'Dramatic Devices', 173-8; Harrison, *Emptiness of Asia*, 74-5.

2. The quoted phrase is from Harrison, *Emptiness of Asia*, 115, who finds pleasure in the slaughter an essential part of the play's Persian perspective. By contrast, Sommerstein, *Aeschylean Tragedy*, 82 thinks that Aeschylus reminds the audience of 'their own atrocities'.

3. See Groeneboom, 67; Turner, *Athenian Books*, 9-10.

4. Clairmont, *Patrios Nomos*, 1.7-15 dates the origin of the practice to the late 470s. For the possibility that these names were read aloud, see Ebbott, 'List of the War Dead', 93-4.

5. See Barrett, 'Narrative and Messenger', 550-4 for the Homeric echoes of this line.

6. See Taplin, *Stagecraft*, 85-7.

7. Cf. Smethurst, *Artistry*, 116-17.

8. Seaford, *Reciprocity and Ritual*, 339 n. 31. For the Persians' cloaks, see Flintoff, '*Persians* 277'.

9. Moreau, 'La tétralogie', 133, for instance, finds an absence of hatred in the play.

10. Cf. Euben, 'Battle of Salamis', 365.

11. A sixth, Amistris (320), may be identical to Amistres (21).

12. Herodotus claims that they fought at Plataea (8.113.2-3; 9.31.3). See Lattimore, 'Aeschylus on the Defeat of Xerxes', 87.

13. See Herodotus 9.122.3; Thomas, *Herodotus*, 103-14; Wohl, *Love among the Ruins*, 174-88.

14. I agree with Broadhead, 115; Morrison et al., *Athenian Trireme*, 56-7 on the numbers 1,000 and 300. Others add the fast triremes to the rest to arrive at 1,207 and 310 respectively, e.g. Hignett, *Xerxes' Invasion*, 345-50; Lazenby, *Defence of Greece*, 172-4.

15. See e.g. Homer *Iliad* 22.209-13. Fowler, 'Aeschylus' Imagery', 7 connects the scale with the play's yoke imagery. The beam of a balance is called a 'yoke'.

16. Winnington-Ingram, 'Zeus in *Persae*', 2-3 considers it too 'parochial'; Hall, 'Asia Unmanned', 129-30 thinks that attributing salvation to a female goddess would undermine the polarity between Greek (male) and Persian (female). The 'Themistocles Decree' entrusts the evacuated city 'to Athena who guards Athens and to all the other gods' (ML^2 23.4-6 = Fornara 55.4-6).

17. See further, Euripides *Trojan Women* 25-7.

18. For this proverb, see Alcaeus frr. 112.10, 426 (Lobel/Page). Cf. Sophocles *Oedipus Tyrannus* 56-7; Thucydides 7.77.7.

19. See Detienne/Vernant, *Cunning Intelligence*, esp. 11-26.

20. Herodotus 1.32; 3.40.2; 4.205; Xerxes: 7.10e, 46.4; 8.109.3; cf. Aeschylus *Agamemnon* 459-74, 1331-42; Mikalson, *Herodotus and Religion*, 150-2; Shapiro, 'Herodotus and Solon', 350-5.

21. In Herodotus, Xerxes orders his Phoenician generals decapitated after they complain about Ionian betrayal at Salamis (8.90.1-3).

22. Hall, 137, adopting a suggestion of Craig, 'Interpretation', 100, argues that 374-83 refer to the Greek navy. The messenger, however, is not an omniscient narrator and does not know what the Greeks are doing. The nocturnal confidence and good order of the Persians as they await the fleeing Greeks set up the reversal when the Greeks appear for battle at daybreak. Herodotus reports that the Persians squandered their energies at their oars all night (8.76), just as in the messenger's account (382-3).

23. Thucydides 4.125-6; 7.29-30, esp. 29.4.

24. See Aeschylus *Seven against Thebes* 78-180; [Aeschylus] *Prometheus Bound* 114-27.

25. Xenophon *Anabasis* 4.3.19 (women shriek), 31-4; 5.2.14.

26. E.g. Herodotus 8.64-5, 84.2; Plutarch *Life of Themistocles* 13.2-3, 15.1.

27. *FGE* 'Simonides' XVI = Fornara 60; Herodotus 8.77.2.

28. For the 'light of freedom', see Aeschylus *Libation Bearers* 807-11. Benveniste, *Indo-European Language and Society*, esp. 262-7 argues for a radical connection between 'growth' and the root of *eleutheria*, *(e)leudheros*.

29. Aeschylus *Seven against Thebes*, 69-77, 287-368; cf. Sophocles *Women of Trachis* 282-5.

30. Herodotus 6.44.3; 8.89.1-2, 129.2; Thucydides 7.30.2; Hall, 'Drowning', 49-56.

31. Hall, 'Drowning', 66-7 argues that the *Persians* uses 'elaborate periphrases and metaphors' to indicate the barbarians' inability to swim.

32. See Detienne/Vernant, *Cunning Intelligence*, 296-7.

33. Aeschylus condenses two Homeric models, *Iliad* 16.401-10 and *Odyssey* 22.383-9. The latter is especially apt: not only does the sun kill the suitors/fish, but the suitors violated Odysseus' *oikos* as the Persians violated Athens' *polis*.

34. For thorough discussions of Psyttalia, see Saïd, 'Pourquoi Psyttalie'; Harrison, *Emptiness of Asia*, 97-102.

35. Pausanias *Description of Greece* 1.36.2 numbers the Persian dead on Psyttalia at 'nearly 400'. Hignett, *Xerxes' Invasion*, 238 n. 7 rejects this number.

36. Plutarch *Life of Aristides* 9.2 says that Aristides and the hoplites who occupied the island performed this function for the Athenians.

37. Georges, *Barbarian Asia*, 84 reads 463 as 'poetic vengeance' for Aeschylus' brother Cynegirus, who died after his arm was severed by an ax while he tried to strip the ensign from a Persian ship at Marathon.

38. Plutarch *Life of Aristides* 9.1-2 claims that some 'distinguished' Persians were taken alive and that three of Xerxes' nephews were sacrificed to Dionysus 'who eats raw flesh'. See also Plutarch *Life of Themistocles* 13.2-3.

39. MacDowell, '*Hybris* in Athens', 16-17; Cairns, '*Hybris*' 7-8.

40. See also Plutarch *Life of Aristides* 9.1-2.

41. Fornara, 'Hoplite Achievement', 51-4 bases his claim that Herodotus' version is a fiction on the desire to glorify hoplites, but Aeschylus accords even more glory to hoplites/light-armed troops than Herodotus. See van Wees, 'Politics and the Battlefield', 174 n. 16.

42. Georges, *Barbarian Asia*, 84. For Pan, see Bourgeaud, *Cult of Pan*, 133-62. Pausanias *Description of Greece* 1.36.2 describes roughly carved statues of Pan on the island.

43. See Salanitro, 'Il pensiero politico di Eschilo nei Persiani'. Saïd, 'Pourquoi Psyttalie', 65-6; Harrison, *Emptiness of Asia*, 97-8 are preferable.

44. Saïd, 'Pourquoi Psyttalie', 68; Harrison, *Emptiness of Asia*, 97.

45. For tragedy's stance toward nobility, see Griffith, 'Brilliant Dynasts'; 'King and Eye'. Van Wees, 'Politics and the Battlefield', 159 takes this as a diminution of the sailors' 'military credit'.

46. See Thucydides 3.97-8: Demosthenes does not return to Athens after losing 120 hoplites in battle – all roughly the same age and 'the best men in war'.

47. See [Aristotle] *Constitution of the Athenians* 26.1; Rhodes, *Commentary*, 326-7 finds this implausible because of the navy's lower-class base. But all classes contributed to the navy, and the rich were called upon to fund and command individual ships. See further, Isocrates *On the Peace* 8.86-9; Rosenbloom, 'Empire and its Discontents', 263.

48. See Ober, *Mass and Elite*, 11-17.

49. Herodotus 8.90.4; cf. 7.212.1; 8.87-8; Diodorus 11.18.3.

50. See Badian, 'Herodotus on Alexander I'.

51. Herodotus 8.30-2; cf. 7.203.1; 9.31.5. For the Serpent Column, see ML^2 27 = Fornara 59; *ATL* 3.95-110.

52. Hall, 144 considers the theme the Persians' inability to handle physical hardship because of their 'soft' land and climate.

53. Lincoln, 'Death by Water', tries to show that this episode combines the science and ethnology of the day to depict the Persians as an inferior people to the Greeks.

54. See Horsfall, 'Aeschylus and the Strymon', 503-5.

55. Herodotus 6.44.2-3; 7.34-5, 42.2, 188-92; 8.12-14, 37-9; cf. 8.129.

56. Scholium to Aeschines *On the False Embassy* 2.31 = Fornara 62.

57. Cf. Fowler, 'Aeschylus' Imagery', 7.

58. Taplin, *Stagecraft*, 92-8 revives previous suggestions of transposing 529-31 to after 851 and recommends emending 529; Thalmann, 'Xerxes' Rags', 261-7 refutes these expedients.

59. Cf. Dworacki, 'Atossa's Absence', 104-5.

60. Homer *Iliad* 13.484; 24.347-8; *Odyssey* 10.277-9; Hesiod *Theogony* 986-91; Mimnermus *Elegies* fr. 1 (West).

61. Tyrtaeus fr. 10.15-32 (West); Solon *Elegies* fr. 24.6 (West); Euripides *Helen* 12-13.

62. Evanescence: Mimnermus *Elegies* frr. 2, 5.4-5 (West); Theognis *Elegies* 985-8, 1069-70, 1129-32 (West). Death in battle: Homer *Iliad* 16.857 = 22.363; Anacreon *Tetrameters* fr. 2 (West); *FGE* 'Simonides' XLVI, XLIX. Ares, paradoxically, is 'giver of blossoming *hêbê*' (Homeric *Hymn to Ares* 9).

63. For marriage as the mutual enjoyment of *hêbê*, see *Odyssey* 23.209-12.

64. For the negative connotations of *habros* and its derivatives after the Persian Wars, see Kurke, 'Politics of *Habrosynê*', 97-106.

65. See Bordaux, 'Lecture du Premier Stasimon', 77.

66. Cf. Bordaux, 'Lecture du Premier Stasimon', 80. See further, Thalmann, 'Xerxes' Rags', 282; Hall, *Inventing the Barbarian*, 62-76.

67. See Momigliano, 'Sea-Power in Greek Thought'.

68. For losses at Egypt in 454 (closer to 100 ships), see Robinson, 'Thucydidean Sieges'; for Drabescus, see *ATL* 3.106-10; Cyprus seems to be a fiction. Sicily is more or less accurate.

69. See Parker, *Miasma*, 226-7; Vermeule, *Aspects of Death*, esp. 179-88.

70. Bordaux, 'Lecture du Premier Stasimon, 78.

4. A Tragedy of Succession

1. See Taplin, *Stagecraft*, 99-100.

2. For the Queen's second entrance as a 'mirror scene', see Taplin, *Stagecraft*, 98-107.

3. For these offerings, see Alexiou, *Ritual Lament*, 7-8; Hall, *Inventing the Barbarian*, 89; Ogden, *Greek and Roman Necromancy*, 169-70.

4. Such kennings often refer to food. See Timocles *Heroes* fr. 13 (K-A); Wilkins, *The Boastful Chef*, 241-3.

5. Groeneboom, 133. A 'pure' cow has never been yoked and is fit to dedicate to the gods (Homer *Odyssey* 3.380-4).

6. Cf. Aeschylus *Libation Bearers* 127-8.

7. See Scholium B to *Persians* 614; Roller, *God the Mother*, 66-9.

8. Hall, 151 considers these ingredients typical of Asian femininity and fecundity; see also Hall, 'Asia Unmanned', 123-6.

9. Gaea: Homeric *Hymn to Gaea*; Demeter and Kore: Homeric *Hymn to Demeter* 480-9; cf. Hesiod *Theogony* 969-74.

10. Pedrizet, 'Le Témoignage d' Eschyle', 74-9, though it is unlikely that 811-12 refer to ancestral graves.

11. Georges, *Barbarian Asia*, 102-9 considers the Queen masculine and the chorus effeminate.

12. Cf. Wiles, *Tragedy in Athens*, 96.

13. Cf. Ogden, *Greek and Roman Necromancy*, 166-7.

14. Hammond, 'Conditions of Dramatic Production', esp. 405-30; 'More on Conditions of Production', 5-9, 16-22.

15. Pickard-Cambridge, *Theatre of Dionysus*, 35; Taplin, *Stagecraft*, 117.

16. Arnott, *Greek Scenic Conventions*, 58-9.

17. Taplin, *Stagecraft*, 117.

18. Wiles, *Tragedy in Athens*, 79.

19. Taplin, *Stagecraft*, 115 sees Darius' quasi-divine authority as part of the dramatic fiction of the *Persians*. Harrison, *Emptiness of Asia*, 89 considers the raising 'barbarous blasphemy'. Pelling, 'Aeschylus' *Persae*', 14-16 negotiates between these views.

20. Scott, *Musical Design*, 155-6 notes that the rhythmic pulse of the hymn is difficult to find.

21. For the Greekness of the hymn, see Hall, *Inventing the Barbarian*, 89-90; cf. Ogden, *Greek and Roman Necromancy*, 129-32.

22. See Haldane, 'Barbaric Cries', 43-4.

23. See Moritz, 'Refrain in Aeschylus', 189-95, esp. 194.

24. See Groeneboom, 141-2; Broadhead, 170; Hall, *Inventing the Barbarian*, 120-1.

25. See Groeneboom, 142-3; Belloni, 193. The word 'mound' in 659 has prompted the theory that Darius arose from behind a mound, but as Taplin, *Stagecraft*, 117 notes, the word also means 'tomb'.

26. Smethurst, *Artistry*, 132-3.

27. See de Romilly, *Magic and Rhetoric*, esp. 3-7.

28. Taplin, *Stagecraft*, 116-19, 447-8.

29. Smethurst, *Artistry*, 132.

30. Hammond, 'More on Conditions of Production', 16-22; see further, Broadhead, 309.

31. Hammond, 'Conditions of Dramatic Production' 430-2; 'More on Conditions of Production', 16-22 with plate 1; Wiles, *Tragedy in Athens*, 79 n. 78; Green, *Theatre in Ancient Society*, 17-18.

32. Webster, *Greek Theatre Production*, 17, 165-6 envisions such a staging. For Darius' entrance as a *deus ex machina*, see Rehm, *Play of Space*, 239. In general, see Mastronarde, 'Actors on High'.

33. Smethurst, *Artistry*, 133 notes the 'doubling' of the first and second halves of the *Persians*; see also Michelini, *Tradition*, 74.

34. Line 683 is controversial. Hall, 157 suggests that the chorus sings its hymn on the ground, beating and scratching the earth. Darius, however, describes the chorus as 'standing near my tomb' while lamenting (686-7). Groeneboom, 146-7 identifies the subject of the first two verbs in 683 as *polis*.

35. Cf. Couch, 'Three Puns', 272-3.

36. Moreau, 'Le songe', 39 notes that the *Persai* are 'in reality destroyers of themselves'.

37. See Munson, 'Artemisia in Herodotus', for the irony of a woman's uttering these lines.

38. Hignett, *Xerxes' Invasion*, 208-10 considers it disastrous; Strauss, *Battle of Salamis*, 101-2 thinks it 'good but incomplete'.

39. Harrison, *Emptiness of Asia*, 90 finds Darius' late wisdom characteristic of his false authority and sees an implicit contrast between Darius and Themistocles as interpreters of oracles.

40. Conacher, '*Persae*', 23.

41. See Broadhead, lv-lvi.

42. See Michelini, *Tradition*, 144.

43. Cf. Pelling, 'Aeschylus' *Persae* and History', 18-19.

44. Gagarin, *Aeschylean Drama*, 47 argues that bridging the Hellespont is not necessarily an impiety in the play: only Darius interprets it this way.

45. Lloyd-Jones, *Justice of Zeus*, 88 is an exception.

46. Broadhead, 188 suggests that 'hammer-beaten shackles' are the anchors used to secure the ships parallel to the current.

47. Timotheus *Persians* 73-4 refers to Xerxes' bridge as 'linen-bound shackles'.

48. For the relationship between 'toil' (*ponos*) and value, see Rosenbloom, 'From *Ponêros* to *Pharmakos*', 338-9 with n. 193.

49. Rosenbloom, 'Empire and its Discontents', 250-3. See Thucydides 2.39-46, 60-4; Euripides *Suppliants*; Isocrates *On the Peace*.

50. Wallinga, 'The Ancient Persian Navy', 71-2; Briant, *Cyrus to Alexander*, 107-61.

51. For the imperative to increase inherited *olbos*, see Euripides *Autolycus TrGF* 5.1 F282.4-6.

52. Smethurst, *Artistry*, 136; Georges, *Barbarian Asia*, 87; Harrison, *Emptiness of Asia*, 80-1.

53. See Rosenmeyer, *Art of Aeschylus*, 295-9.

54. Saïd, 'Herodotus and Tragedy', 141-5 sees Xerxes strictly as an anomaly in the Persian tradition.

55. For empire as the *ponos* of the fathers, see Thucydides 2.36.2, 62.3; cf. Aristophanes *Wasps*, 1098-101, 1114-21.

56. See Hunter, *Past and Process*, esp. 228-30.

57. For the *hybris* of Persian imperialism, see Cairns, '*Hybris*', 13-15.

58. Cf. Caldwell, 'The Pattern of Aeschylean Drama', esp. 83. Xerxes' status as a tragic figure is denied. See Lattimore, *Poetry of Greek Tragedy*, 38: 'As for Xerxes: who cares about Xerxes? Is there anything dramatic about a man getting so precisely what he deserves? (I merely ask)'; Georges, *Barbarian Asia*, 87: 'No tragic significance inheres in the fate of the totally blameworthy' and 'Aeschylus' Xerxes is beneath tragedy' (88). Fisher, *Hybris*, 262 contends that to the extent the *Persians* is about the 'gradual revelation of the punishment of *hybris*' it is not tragedy.

59. Golden, *In Praise of Prometheus*, 35-6 for lack of conflict; Kitto, *Greek Tragedy*, 42 for lack of choice.

60. See Strauss, *Fathers and Sons in Athens*, 130-78.

61. Rosenbloom, 'Empire and its Discontents', 253; cf. Rood, 'Thucydides' Persian Wars', 149.

62. See Raaflaub, 'Stick and Glue'; Tuplin, 'Imperial Tyranny'. For Athenians as Persians, see Tuplin, *Achaemenid Studies*, 172-7.

63. E.g. Gagarin, *Aeschylean Drama*, 53; Thalmann, 'Xerxes' Rags', 282 n. 68.

64. ML^2, p. 42 = Fornara 41 D1.

65. See Brenne, 'Ostraka and the Process of Ostracism', 21-2; 'T1: Ostraka', 87-90.

66. ML^2 26 I = *FGE* 'Simonides' XX(*a*).

67. Craig, 'Interpretation', 100 sees only how Darius' condemnation 'brings home ... the full extent of their victory'.

68. Briant, *Cyrus to Alexander*, 19 points out that the Persian king is the chief of 'the people in arms' and 'one of the Achaemenid king's ideological justifications was his aptitude for war and for leading armies'.

69. [Aristotle] *Constitution of the Athenians* 26.1 is confused, but plausibly claims that during the Kimonian period (*c*. 476-461) generals were elected 'because of their fathers' reputations'. For known Athenian generals, see Fornara, *Athenian Board of Generals*.

70. Cyrus, Murghab A-C = Kent 116; cf. Brosius 4. For Darius, see, e.g. Behistun 1.2-3 = Kent 119 = Brosius 44.I.2-3.

71. See e.g. *FGE* 'Simonides' XXIV; Thucydides 1.132.2.

72. E.g. ML^2 24, 26; *FGE* 'Simonides', XV.

73. Tuplin, 'Persians as Medes'.

74. For Herodotus' depiction of the Median kings, see Brown, 'Mêdikos Logos'.

75. Herodotus 1.126-30; 210.2-3; 3.82.5; 7.2.

76. Sidgwick, 63 thinks that Medus 'telescopes' the first three Median kings and the son of Medus is Astyages. Broadhead, 192, 278-9 believes that Medus is Cyaxares and his son is Astyages; cf. Balcer, *Herodotus and Bisitun*, 38-9; M.L. West, 'Sham Shahs', 183.

77. Herodotus 3.25-38; 5.25; see Lloyd, 'Herodotus on Cambyses'.

78. For this model, see Plato *Laws* 694c-696a = Brosius 106.

79. Darius, Behistun 1.11 = Kent 120 = Brosius 35.

80. Darius, Behistun 1.14 = Kent 120 = Brosius 35.

81. Prickard, Sidgwick, Broadhead, Page, and Belloni exclude it. West restores it. Hall follows West. See M.L. West, 'Sham Shahs', 184-8.

82. Hall, 162.

83. Schütz, *Commentarius*, cited by M.L. West, 'Sham Shahs', 185 suggested this explanation. See Rose, 146; Prickard, 112; Belloni, 213.

84. Hall; Georges, *Barbarian Asia*; Harrison, *Emptiness of Asia*.

85. Kitto, *Greek Tragedy*, 38-41; Winnington-Ingram, 'Zeus in *Persae*', 10-11; Conacher, '*Persae*', 24-5.

86. Herodotus 4.1, 83-98, 118-44; Briant, *Cyrus to Alexander*, 141-6.

87. Broadhead, xiv-xviii, xxviii-xxix; Winnington-Ingram, 'Zeus in *Persae*', 14; Saïd, 'Herodotus and Tragedy', 140.

5. The Synoptic Moment

1. Georges, *Barbarian Asia*, 92 thinks the chorus displays an 'unreasoning will to empire'.

2. Winnington-Ingram, 'Zeus in *Persae*', 12. Gagarin, *Aeschylean Drama*, 47-8 interprets *hybris* exclusively as collective Persian guilt in the play.

3. Cf. Georges, *Barbarian Asia*, 83.

4. Winnington-Ingram, 'Zeus in *Persae*', 14; Michelini, *Tradition*, 74.

5. For *drama* as action that entails reciprocal treatment, whether good or bad, see Snell, *Aischylos und das Handeln*, esp. 14.

6. See *Agamemnon* 532-3, 1562-4; *Libation Bearers* 313-14; cf. *TrGF* 3 F456.

7. This text is difficult. I follow Groeneboom, 168-9 and Belloni, 218-20. For other views, see Broadhead, 202-4; Hall, 164; Podlecki, 'Three Passages', 3.

8. Contrast *Agamemnon* 338-47, 459-74, 750-82.

9. Georges, *Barbarian Asia*, 87-8.

10. For perversion of ritual in tragedy, see Seaford, *Reciprocity and Ritual*, esp. 368-405.

11. The Greeks considered Plataea a Spartan victory: Simonides *Plataea* frr. 11.25-45; 13.8-13; Pindar *Pythian Ode* 1.75-8; Thucydides 1.69.1.

12. Lattimore, 'Aeschylus on the Defeat of Xerxes', 91 calls it an 'insignificant mopping-up operation'.

13. Pucci, 'Euripides: The Monument and the Sacrifice', 165-6; cf. Connor, 'Land Warfare as Symbolic Expression', 22-4.

14. MacDowell, '*Hybris* in Athens', 21 defines *hybris* as 'having energy or power and misusing it self-indulgently'; cf. Cairns, '*Hybris*', 22-5. Fisher, *Hybris*, 1 stresses that *hybris* is 'the serious assault on the honour of another, which is likely to cause shame, and lead to anger and attempts at revenge'.

15. Michelini, '*Hybris* and Plants', 35-9; *Tradition*, 96-8; Fisher, *Hybris*, 119-21.

16. MacDowell, '*Hybris* in Athens',16; Fisher, *Hybris*, 375-85.

17. Michelini, '*Hybris* and Plants', 39-44; Nagy, 'Theognis and Megara', 60-3; Helm, 'Aeschylus' Genealogy of Morals', 23-34.

18. Fisher, *Hybris*, 260 identifies 'intentional acts of enslaving imperialism and sacrilege' as the critical feature of Xerxes' *hybris*; cf. Broadhead, 204-5.

19. See further Hesiod *Works and Days* 320-6, 352; Bacchylides *Dithyramb* 15.47-63; Theognis *Elegies* 153-4; 198-202 (West); Katz Anhalt, *Solon the Singer*, 82-97.

20. Winnington-Ingram, 'Zeus in *Persae*', esp. 1-2.

21. See Aeschylus *Agamemnon* 776-82; Nagy, 'Theognis and Megara', 54-63; *Pindar's Homer*, 243-9; Katz Anhalt, *Solon the Singer*, 11-114; Cairns, '*Hybris*', 7-8, with reference to Aristotle.

22. For the injustice of imperialism, see Herodotus 1.5-6; 3.21.2; 7.16a; Thucydides 2.63.2; Balot, *Greed and Injustice*, esp. 99-135.

23. See Xenophon *Oeconomicus* 5.12; [Aristotle] *Economics* 1343a25-b2.

24. 102-7, 555-7, 642-77, 780-6, 852-67. For Persia and the Golden Age, see Chapter 7.

25. Alexanderson, 'Darius', 9; cf. Nagy, 'Theognis and Megara', 62-3.

26. Saïd, 'Darius et Xerxès', 31-6.

27. Georges, *Barbarian Asia*, 88.

28. Winnington-Ingram, 'Zeus in *Persae*', 14-15.

29. I agree with Craig, 'Interpretation', 100; Harrison, *Emptiness of Asia*, 59 that Aeschylus inverts an oral tradition; Saïd, 'Darius et Xerxès', 31-5; 'Herodotus and Tragedy', 138 thinks that Herodotus inverts Aeschylus.

30. Cf. Smethurst, *Artistry*, 250-1.

31. Hall, *Inventing the Barbarian*, 70-3, 100 treats the moral-religious explanation of Xerxes' defeat as an 'ethnological' explanation. See further, Georges, *Barbarian Asia*, 86; Harrison, *Emptiness of Asia*, 102.

32. In 472, this function was probably under the jurisdiction of the Areopagus, a Council of ex-Archons. See Ostwald, *Popular Sovereignty*, 40-2, 55-62.

33. Meier, *Political Art*, 74.

34. Theognis *Elegies* 39-40 (West) envisions a tyrant arising to straighten out a corrupt city as 'corrector' (*euthyntêr*). In the *Persians*, the king of Asia wields the 'governing (*euthyntêrion*) sceptre' (764). Democracy is not essential to the idea.

35. Harrison, *Emptiness of Asia*, 109 claims that 'democracy and piety ... immunise the Athenians from the dangers of Persian imperialism'. Georges, *Barbarian Asia*, 111 asserts that freedom and competition in the *polis* 'will contain – or ignore – such violent and impetuous natures as Xerxes' '. That the opposite was the case was the subject of Greek discourse from Hesiod to Plato. See Balot, *Greed and Injustice*; Ober, *Political Dissent*, 104-21; cf. Rood, 'Thucydides' Persian Wars', 158.

36. Keaveney, 'Xerxes' New Suit', 240-1 suggests that the *Persians* plays on Persian royal rites of investiture: the king-initiate removes his own clothing and dons a garment Cyrus wore, assuming the power of the kingship. See Plutarch *Life of Artaxerxes* 3.1-2; Briant, *Cyrus to Alexander*, 523-4, 959.

37. See Barron, 'Bakchylides, Theseus, and a Woolly Cloak'. Bacchylides *Dithyramb* 17.18-23 and *Persians* 160, 767 are similar; Bacchylides' poem is probably earlier.

38. For this moment as a *topos* in the vase painting of the period, see Shapiro, 'Theseus in Kimonian Athens', 39-40. A version of this story was painted in the Temple of Theseus (Pausanias *Description of Greece* 1.17.3).

39. Goheen, 'Aspects of Dramatic Symbolism', 122-6; Macleod, 'Clothing in the *Oresteia*'.

40. For the first view, see Gagarin, *Aeschylean Drama*, 52; Kantzios, 'The Politics of Fear', 13-14; for the second, Georges, *Barbarian Asia*, 111; Harrison, *Emptiness of Asia*, esp. 86-91.

41. For Hall, 165, it suggests ' "oriental" preoccupation with sensual self-gratification'.

42. Euripides *Alcestis* 323; *Heracles* 502-13; Anonymous Tragic Fragment *TrGF* 2 F95.

43. See Murray, 'The Greek Symposion in History'; Levine, 'Symposium and *Polis*'.

44. Timotheus and Choerilus elaborate sympotic images of the Persian defeat. See Chapter 7.

45. E.g. Hall, 165: 'Nothing more powerfully conveys the audience's view of the obsessiveness of Persian sartorial display'; cf. Sidgwick, 49; Harrison, *Emptiness of Asia*, 81.

46. Thalmann, 'Xerxes' Rags', 264, 269-70, 278; Rehm, *Play of Space*, 248.

47. Anderson, 'The Imagery of the *Persians*', 174 suggests that Darius remains on stage during the final lament, pitying his son.

48. See Thalmann, 'Xerxes' Rags', 269-78.

49. Scott, *Musical Design*, 156 links the dactyls with 'the political context at the end of the first stasimon'. Dale, *Metrical Analyses*, 4 connects the metre with Homeric catalogue poetry.

50. Lloyd-Jones, *Justice of Zeus*, 89 calls the ode a 'veiled encomium of the Athenian empire'.

51. See West, *Studies*, 90-1; Broadhead, 280-1 for the textual problems here.

52. Darius listed only Cyrus' conquests in Western Anatolia (770-1); see Herodotus 7.8.a1; Thucydides 2.36.4.

53. Sidgwick, 51; Hall, 167 compares Darius with Aegisthus.

54. Meiggs, *Athenian Empire*, 237.

55. Meiggs, *Athenian Empire*, 244.

56. For the figures, see Meiggs, *Athenian Empire*, 524-30.

57. Sidgwick, 51; Gow, 'Notes', 155. *ATL* 3.207 suggests a reference to islands off Thrace, but the epithet 'river' or 'fresh water' rules this out; see Broadhead, 217-18.

58. For the Thracian district as it might have been at the origins of the Athenian empire, see *ATL* 3.214-23. The chorus omits Pallene, possibly because it came under Persian influence during Xerxes' reign (Herodotus 8.126-9).

59. See Tuplin, 'Xerxes' March from Doriscus to Therme'.

60. ML^2 27 = Fornara 59.

61. Meiggs, *Athenian Empire*, 481.

62. Meiggs, *Athenian Empire*, 482-4.

6. A Harvest of Tears

1. That Xerxes enters in rags has often been denied. See Taplin, *Stagecraft*, 122 and n. 1.

2. Taplin, *Stagecraft*, 123 excludes the wagon from the scene; see also Rehm, *Play of Space*, 249 with n. 61, 388. If the wagon is present, it symbolizes the absent 'flower of the Persians' (252) which Xerxes lost in the invasion.

3. *Kommos* derives from the verb *koptô*, which means 'beat' or 'strike'. Aristotle defines a *kommos* as 'a shared lament between actors and chorus' (*Poetics* 1452b24-5).

4. Adams, 'Salamis Symphony', 53; cf. Prickard, 120-1. Georges, *Barbarian Asia*, 87 considers the *kommos* 'satyr-play Grand Guignol'.

5. Gagarin, *Aeschylean Drama*, 41-2.

6. Schenker, 'The Queen and the Chorus', 292-3.

7. Broadhead, xxxiv; Rehm, *Play of Space*, 249; cf. Prickard, 121: 'Xerxes' absurdities seem to form the climax of the play'.

8. For Atys as a doublet for Phrygian Attis, consort of Cybele, see Vermaseren, *Cybele and Attis*, 88-92; cf. Reed, 'Sexuality of Adonis', 335.

9. See Chiasson, 'Herodotus' Use of Tragedy in the Lydian *Logos*'.

10. Alexiou, *Ritual Lament*, 55-7.

11. The earliest evidence for the Adonia at Athens dates from the 430s or 420s, but as Simms, 'Mourning and Community', 124 points out, it may have been adopted much earlier. Ritual lament for Adonis, in which girls tore their *chitônes*, was already part of Sappho's repertoire (fr. 140a Lobel/Page).

12. Burkert, *Structure and History*, 107. Simms, 'Mourning and Community', 129-33 interprets the gardens as funeral biers for the effigy of Adonis. Reed, 'Sexuality of Adonis', 320 thinks they were dumped into springs only.

13. Detienne, *Gardens of Adonis*, 106.

14. Nagy, *Pindar's Homer*, 285 n. 48; 'Theognis and Megara', 60-3. Detienne, *Gardens of Adonis*, 119.

15. See Detienne, *Gardens of Adonis*, esp. 116-19.

16. Aristophanes *Lysistrata* 387-98; Plutarch *Life of Alcibiades* 18.5; *Life of Nicias* 13.11; cf. Simms, 'Mourning and Community', 136-7.

17. Burkert, *Structure and History*, 107; Detienne, *Gardens of Adonis*, 109.

18. Pavlovskis, 'Aeschylus Mythistoricus', 21.

19. See Alexiou, *Ritual Lament*, 195-7.

20. Athenian communal claims to nobility are bound up with the view of themselves as an autochthonous people, sprung from the land they inhabit. See Loraux, *The Invention of Athens*, 149-55. This dovetails with the socio-economic requirement of land ownership for nobility.

21. See Robertson, 'Wooden Wall', 15 n. 28.

22. Cf. Rehm, *Play of Space*, 245-6.

23. The desire for wealth is unlimited: Solon *Elegies* 13.71-76 = Theognis *Elegies* 227-32 (West); Theognis *Elegies* 596, 1158-9 (West); Aristophanes *Wealth* 186-97; Xenophon *Ways and Means* 4.7; Seaford, *Money and the Greek Mind*, 165-9. In Aeschylus *Agamemnon* 750-81, *hybris* is infinitely self-replicating.

24. Aristotle *Politics* 1256b40-1258b9.

25. Hall, *Inventing the Barbarian*, 83-4 stresses '*excessive* mourning' as 'barbaric'. Cf. Prickard, 120. Such excess is also a function of the magnitude of the *pathos* (Rehm, *Play of Space*, 385 n. 29) and the insatiability of imperialism.

26. Alexiou, *Ritual Lament*, 14; Holst-Warhaft, *Dangerous Voices*, 118-19.

27. Alexiou, *Ritual Lament*, 14-23; Foley, 'The Politics of Tragic Lamentation', 103-8; Seaford, *Reciprocity and Ritual*, 74-86. Hall, 169 and Georges, *Barbarian Asia*, 102 point out that the lament the men perform in the *kommos* exceeds what was legally allowed women in Athens.

28. For feminization as essential to drama, see Zeitlin, 'Playing the Other'. For barbarian culture as feminized, see Hall, 168-9.

29. For public lament, see Seaford, *Reciprocity and Ritual*, 139-43.

30. For early Athenian warfare, see Frost, 'The Athenian Military before Cleisthenes'.

31. Cf. [Aristotle] *Constitution of the Athenians* 26.1, which claims that Athenians died by the 2,000 or 3,000 in this period.

32. Cf. Smethurst, *Artistry*, 142.

33. Winnington-Ingram, 'Zeus in *Persae*', 13-14.

34. Groeneboom, 184 relates the image to cutting down flowers. The verb *epikeirô* also means 'check growth by cutting' and fits the idea of curtailing excess.

35. See Briant, *Cyrus to Alexander*, 233-9.

36. See West, *Hesiod: Works and Days*, p. 213. Herodotus depicts the Persian royal curse in these terms (3.65.6-7).

37. Hesiod *Works and Days* 127-39; Theognis *Elegies* 629-32 (West).

38. *Anthos* of *hêbê*, e.g. Homer *Iliad* 13.484; Hesiod *Theogony* 988; Solon *Elegies* fr. 25 (West); Theognis *Elegies* 1003-12 (West). *Anthos* of *atê*: Solon *Elegies* fr. 4.35 (West); cf. Aeschylus *Agamemnon* 658-60.

39. Taplin, *Stagecraft*, 123 uses this as evidence that Xerxes did not arrive by covered wagon, but it can also be evidence that he dismounted.

40. Groeneboom, 184-5.

41. See Moritz, 'Refrain in Aeschylus', 194.

42. See Alexiou, *Ritual Lament*, 58-60.

43. This was the subject of popular song (*PMG* 878). For the Ionian mode as 'slack', and 'soft' see Csapo, 'The Politics of the New Music', 232-5, 243-4.

44. Broadhead, 230 likens the scene to a meadow whose flowers are culled.

45. Tod, *Greek Historical Inscriptions*, 2.204 = Harding 109A; Siewert, 'The Ephebic Oath', 107 sees a reference to the oath in this passage.

46. Smethurst, *Artistry*, 143 observes that the bare epithets give the impression 'that the men are truly dead'.

47. *Aôton* is Page's emendation.

48. For *anthos* meaning the 'nap' of fine cloth, see Borthwick, 'The "Flower" of the Argives and a Neglected Meaning of *Anthos*'.

49. 'Eye' may suggest what the Greeks believed were the Persian king's spies, his 'eyes and ears'. See Aristophanes *Acharnians* 91-2; Herodotus 1.114.2; Xenophon *Education of Cyrus* 8.2.10-12; Briant, *Cyrus to Alexander*, 343-4.

50. Batanochus' son is called 'sweetest' (*alpistos*). Hesychius *Lexicon* glosses this word as 'beloved' (*agapêtos*), a term used of an only male child.

51. See Gow, 'Iunx, Rhombos, Turbo', 3-5; Johnston, 'The Song of the *Iunx*', 180-9. Faraone, *Ancient Greek Love Magic*, esp. 55-69 sees *iunx* here as 'a generalized magic spell' (25 n. 107).

52. For Adonis and the *iunx*, see Detienne, *Gardens of Adonis*, 83-9; Reed, 'Sexuality of Adonis', 344.

53. Rehm, *Play of Space*, 243 sees the Persian names as 'a form of epic unforgetting that makes their dying immortal'.

54. Reading with West, *Studies*, 94-5.

55. See Avery, 'Dramatic Devices', 181-2; Garvie, 'Aeschylus' Simple Plots', 71.

56. In Plutarch *Life of Artaxerxes* 3.1-2, the Persian royal garment is a *stolê*; see also Timotheus *Persians* 167-72.

57. See Saïd, 'Tragédie et renversement', 341.

58. See Segal, 'Catharsis, Audience, and Closure', 164-5; cf. Konstan, *Pity Transformed* 46-7.

59. See Konstan, *Pity Transformed*, esp. 34-43.

60. Pelling, 'Aeschylus' *Persae* and History', 18-19 compares Odysseus' pity for his enemy Ajax at Sophocles *Ajax* 121-6, for which, see Hesk, *Ajax*, 44-7.

61. See Frye, *Anatomy of Criticism*, 391; Rutherford, 'Tragic Form and Feeling in the *Iliad*'; Macleod, 'Homer on Poetry'; Goldhill, 'Battle Narrative and Politics', 193 n. 35, compares the end of the *Iliad*; Heath, *Poetics of Greek Tragedy*, 80-9, esp. 82.

62. Cf. Mitsis, 'Xerxes Entrance', 115-18.

63. See Cairns, '*Hybris*', 7.

64. Avery, 'Dramatic Devices', 182-4.

65. Devereux, *Dreams in Greek Tragedy*, 14.

66. See Lawler, *The Dance of the Ancient Greek Theatre*, 45-6.

67. Hartog, *The Mirror of Herodotus*, 332.

7. Interpreting and Reinterpreting the *Persians*

1. For the first, see Broadhead, xxxiii-xxxv; Michelini, *Tradition*, 72; for the second, Winnington-Ingram, 'Zeus in *Persae*', 15, who thinks the *Persians* may be Aeschylus' 'least great' play. Golden, *In Praise of Prometheus*, 31-6 adds lack of character development and of conflict.

2. Wilamowitz, *Aischylos Interpretationen*, 48.

3. Adams, 'Salamis Symphony'.

4. Winnington-Ingram, 'Zeus in *Persae*'.

5. Winnington-Ingram, 'Zeus in *Persae*', 14-15.

6. Rosenmeyer, *Art of Aeschylus*, 287-92, by contrast, considers this explanation of Xerxes' tragedy a failure. For a balanced view, see Conacher, '*Persae*', 5-7.

7. Kitto, *Greek Tragedy*, 42.

8. Kitto, *Greek Tragedy*, 42-3. For the second actor, see Michelini, *Tradition*, 27-40.

9. Kitto, *Greek Tragedy*, 43.

10. See Gagarin, *Aeschylean Tragedy*, 55-6; Thalmann, 'Xerxes' Rags'; Saïd, 'Tragédie et renversement'.

11. Thalmann, 'Xerxes' Rags', 277.

12. For earlier views, see Broadhead, xv; Hall, *Inventing the Barbarian*, 70-2. Harrison, *Emptiness of Asia*, appraises interpretations of the play.

13. Craig, 'Interpretation', 99. Lattimore, 'Aeschylus on the Defeat of Xerxes', is the culmination of the 'patriotic drama' tradition. Podlecki, *Political Background*, 8-26 reads the play as an encomium of Themistocles. Murray, *Aeschylus*, 115 reads the play as 'national celebration' which also induces sympathy and affection for the Persians (129).

14. See Herodotus 5.77.4; 8.3.2; Thucydides 1.94-97, 128-30; Castriota, *Ethos and Actuality*, 17-28.

15. Golden, *In Praise of Prometheus*, 36-41 argues that the *Persians* is epideictic tragedy, because its rhetorical purpose is praise and blame. The play is concerned primarily 'to *condemn* the qualities of the spirit or mind that led to the pitiful and fearful events depicted' (40-1).

16. Seaford, *Reciprocity and Ritual*, 328-405 sees tragedy as dramatizing the self-destruction of a ruling house (through perversion of ritual) to the benefit of the *polis* (through the establishment of *polis*-cult). As a 'barbarian tragedy', the *Persians* is an exception to this rule: the ruling house survives, but the entire society is ruined.

17. Hall, 11-13, 16-19; *Inventing the Barbarian*, 56-100; Said, *Orientalism*, 55-7.

18. Hall, *Inventing the Barbarian*, 69-100.

19. Hall, 19.

20. Hall, *Inventing the Barbarian*, 100.

21. Georges, *Barbarian Asia*, 85-113.

22. Harrison, *Emptiness of Asia*, esp. 109. Georges, *Barbarian Asia*, 111, credits free competition in the *polis* with this function.

23. The strongest statement of this view is Kitto, *Greek Tragedy*, 38.

24. Kitto, *Greek Tragedy*, 35-46; Broadhead, xv-xviii.

25. Murray, *Aeschylus*, 111-30; Pavlovskis, 'Aeschylus Mythistoricus'; Rehm, *The Play of Space*, 239-51; cf. Thalmann, 'Xerxes' Rags', 282.

26. Georges, *Barbarian Asia*, 83-5.

27. Nagy, *Pindar's Homer*, 181, 186-7.

28. Spatz, *Aeschylus*, 33-5; Winnington-Ingram, 'Zeus in *Persae*', 14-15; Smethurst, *Artistry*, 139-41; Meier, *Political Art*, 78; Rosenbloom, 'Crying "Fire"', 190-2; 'Myth, History, and Hegemony', 93-8; Rehm, *Play of Space*, 249.

29. Gagarin, *Aeschylean Tragedy*, 52-3 for warning. Prickard, xxvii-xxviii, contrasts the 'ideal/dramatic' and the 'real/patriotic' 'interest' of the drama. See also Groeneboom, 16-18.

30. Goldhill, 'Battle Narrative and Politics', 193

31. Pelling, 'Aeschylus' *Persae* and History', 17; for pity as an Athenian emotion, see Konstan, *Pity Transformed*, 80-1.

32. Rehm, *Play of Space*, 242-3.

33. Rehm, *Play of Space*, 250.

34. Rehm, *Play of Space*, 244.

35. See p. 102 with n. 87, p. 179.

36. Alexanderson, 'Darius in the *Persians*', 11.

37. See p. 114 with n. 40, p. 180.

38. Hordern, *Fragments of Timotheus*, 62-73.

39. *PMG* 788. Other fragments Plutarch quotes are similarly patriotic (*PMG* 789-90). Croiset, 'Observations', 328-9 observes that the papyrus does not sustain this sentiment. For the fragments, see Bassett, 'First Performance', 154-8; Hall, 'Drowning by Nomes', 58-60.

40. Bassett, 'First Performance', 155 and others take it as a reference to Themistocles. Croiset, 'Observations', 328-9 considers Zeus or Apollo the subject. Hordern, *Fragments of Timotheus*, 128-9 thinks the Athenian people is the subject.

41. See West, *Greek Music*, 356-72 for Timotheus and the music of the period. For the cultural and social background of this music, see Csapo, 'Politics of the New Music'.

42. See Hansen, 'First Performance of Timotheus' *Persae*', 135-8 for a table of conjectures.

43. Zeitlin, 'Closet of Masks', 56-67; Porter, *Studies in Euripides' Orestes*, 173-213.

44. Bassett, 'First Performance', 160-1; Porter, *Studies in Euripides' Orestes*, 200-1; Janssen, *Timotheus Persae*, 13-22; cf. Hansen, 'First Performance', 137-8.

45. The Spartans were at war with Persia from 400 BC when the Ionians requested Spartan aid. See Xenophon *History of Greece* 3.1.3; Cartledge, *Agesilaos*, 191-4, 203-18.

46. Xenophon *History of Greece* 3.4.1-3; *Agesilaus* 1.6-8; cf. Plutarch *Life of Agesilaus* 6.1.

47. Cf. Ebeling, 'The *Persians* of Timotheus', 318-19.

48. Xenophon *History of Greece*, esp. 3.4.16-19; *Agesilaus* 1.14. Cf. Plutarch *Life of Agesilaus* 9.4-5.

49. Cf. Hall, 'Drowning by Nomes', 60-5.

50. Bassett, 'First Performance', 154; Hansen, 'First Performance of Timotheus' *Persae*', 137; Wilson, 'Athenian Strings', 304-6.

51. Bassett, 'First Performance', 162 suggests that the point is to put the Spartans in their place since the Achaeans were an older people than the Dorians.

52. See further Herodotus 1.145-6; 7.94-5.

53. Cf. Croiset, 'Observations', 326. Hose, 'Response to Hall', 85-6 suggests a *polis* in the Spartan alliance as the place of performance.

54. Many claim that Salamis was named elsewhere in the poem (e.g. Janssen, *Timotheus Persae*, 13-15). It may have been; but one cannot find one-third to one-half of Aeschylus' *Persians* which lacks indications of Athens and Salamis.

55. Thucydides 7.40.5, 62, 67.2, 70. Janssen, *Timotheus Persae*, 24 suggests that the mutilated lines 4-5 describe the beams the Corinthians fitted across their bows to enable prow-to-prow ramming, another sign that the poem projects Peloponnesian naval power (though this is not Janssen's point). See Thucydides 7.34-6, 62.

56. Hordern, *Fragments of Timotheus*, 134.

57. See Croiset, 'Observations', 330-5.

58. Cf. Hall, 'Drowning by Nomes', 66-7.

59. Hall, 'Drowning by Nomes', 66-72 reads the scene as a celebration of the Greek ability to swim as a mark of cultural supremacy.

60. See Slater, 'Symposium at Sea', 168-9.

61. See Alexis *Agonis* fr. 5 (K-A).

62. Hesychius *Lexicon*, s.v. *thyias*; Timotheus fr. 778 (*b*) (*PMG*).

63. Cf. Herington, *Poetry into Drama*, 156.

64. For supplication, see Gould, 'Hiketeia'.

65. 'The fall of houses' is a quotation of Aeschylus *Libation Bearers* 50, where it refers to the house of Atreus. Many take it as a reference to Xerxes' house. I take 'houses' as a true plural referring to Persian households.

66. Homer *Iliad* 22.25-32; Hesiod *Works and Days* 582-96; Archilochus fr. 107 (West); Alcaeus fr. 347 (*PMG*); Hippocrates *Airs, Waters, Places* 11. See Detienne, *Gardens of Adonis*, 114, 120-1. It was also the season for cutting wood for ships.

67. Thucydides 2.65.12; Xenophon *History of Greece* 2.1.14-15; Diodorus 13.104.3-4; Plutarch *Life of Lysander* 4.3-5, 9.1-2.

68. Xenophon *History of Greece* 4.3.10-14, 4.8.7-11; Diodorus 14.83-4, 15.35.2; Plutarch *Life of Agesilaus* 23; Cartledge, *Agesilaos*, 218.

69. Darius, Naqš-i Rustam B.9a-9b = Kent 140. *Maricas* means 'menial', or 'boy'. See Cassio, 'Old Persian MARIKA-'.

70. For Hyperbolus in fifth-century comedy, see Rosenbloom, '*Ponêros* to *Pharmakos*', 308-12, esp. 308 n. 102. For the *Maricas*, see Storey, *Eupolis* 197-214.

71. For gold in Greek poetry, see Nagy, *Pindar's Homer*, 276-8; Kurke, *Coins, Bodies, Games, and Gold*, esp. 49-54, 61-4, 185-6.

72. See Hesiod *Works and Days* 116-18; Baldry, 'Idler's Paradise', 49-52.

73. Baldry, 'Idler's Paradise', 59-60. Cf. Carriere, *Le Carnaval et la Politique*, 85-118.

74. Ruffel, 'The World Upside Down', 473, 480, 487.

75. For Choerilus, see *Persian Wars* fr. 9 (Barnabé); Slater, 'Symposium at Sea', 161-3; cf. Bacchylides *Encomia* fr. 20B.

76. See Ceccarelli, 'L'Athènes de Périclès': Athens' empire is sometimes a Golden Age in comedy.

77. The dating is conjectural. See Baldry, 'Idler's Paradise', 55.

78. See also Pherecrates *Miners* fr. 113 (K-A); Metagenes *Persians of Thurii* fr. 6 (K-A).

79. See Gombrich, 'Apollonio', 22-3; Watson, 'Apollonio'.

80. Watson, 'Apollonio', 8 detects Sicinnus in a boat; Gombrich, 'Apollonio', 23 suggests the old man in the boat is Xerxes in disguise.

81. See Watson, 'Apollonio', 5, figure 2; Gombrich, 'Apollonio', figure 17, for photographs.

82. Watson, 'Apollonio', 13.

83. Vergil *Aeneid* 8.671-728. Apollonio depicted Vergil's *Aeneid* on *cassoni*. See Gombrich, 'Apollonio', 12-17.

84. Cf. Dante *Purgatory* 28.70-5. For Apollonio's sources, see Watson, 'Apollonio', 14-16; Gombrich, 'Apollonio', 22-3.

85. Watson, 'Apollonio', 16-21.

86. Watson, 'Apollonio', 12-13.

87. Watson, 'Apollonio', 15.

88. See Gombrich, 'Apollonio', 142-3 n. 42.

89. Hall, 2.

90. Garland, *Surviving Greek Tragedy*, 117-18; for earlier, mainly amateur productions, see 115-17.

91. See Glover, *Cavalli*, 24-8.

92. Dean, 'Handel's *Serse*', 165.

93. Viator, 'The Stage History of Cibber's *Xerxes*', 155.

94. See Eitrem, 'Necromancy', 14-16 for Aeschylus' use of the myth.

95. The *Hellas* is cited from Hutchinson, *Complete Poetical Works of Shelley*.

96. In the Preface to *Hellas*, Shelley wrote, 'The *Persae* of Aeschylus afforded me the first model of my conception, although the decision of the glorious contest now waging in Greece being yet suspended forbids a catastrophe parallel to the return of Xerxes and the desolation of the Persians'. See Erkelenz, 'Shelley's *Hellas* and Aeschylus' *Persians*'.

97. See Larissy, '*Hellas* as Allegory', 88-91.

98. The *Septuagint* translates Ahasuerus as Artaxerxes.

99. See Larissy, '*Hellas* as Allegory', 91-9; Erkelenz, 'Shelley's *Hellas* and Aeschylus' *Persians*', 321-5 sees him also as a figure for the Greeks, progenitors of western freedom and bearers of the contemporary passion for vengeance.

100. Larissy, '*Hellas* as Allegory', 98-9 views Ahasuerus as both master and slave: having experienced both, he transcends them.

101. Scholia to Aristophanes *Frogs* 1028a-b; *Life of Aeschylus* 18. Most scholars accept a Sicilian performance. See Sommerstein, *Aeschylean Tragedy*, 21-2; Podlecki, *Persians* 117-20. Around 470, Aeschylus presented *Women of Aetna* in Sicily to celebrate the refoundation of Catana as Aetna (*Life of Aeschylus* 9).

102. Scholium to Aristophanes *Acharnians* 10 = Csapo/Slater I.17B; cf. I.17C.

103. Hall, 2 suggests 425.

104. Garland, *Surviving Greek Tragedy*, 172-4.

105. Hall, 2; Garland, *Surviving Greek Tragedy*, 211; Favorini, 'History, Collective Memory, and the *Persians*', 109.

106. Van Steen, 'Forgotten Theater', 368-9.

107. See Van Steen, 'Forgotten Theater', 370-2.

108. Hall, 2; 'Aeschylus, Race, Class, and War', 175.

109. Hartigan, *Greek Tragedy on the American Stage*, 102-4; Hall, 2.

110. *San Francisco Chronicle*, 8 September 2004, E1.

111. *The Villager*, 73.7, 18-24 June 2003.

Bibliography

Abbreviations

Texts and editions of Aeschylus and the Persians

Belloni = L. Belloni (ed. & trans.) *Eschilo, I Persiani* (Milano: Università Cattolica del Sacro Cuore, 1988).

Broadhead = H.D. Broadhead (ed.) *The Persae of Aeschylus* (Cambridge: Cambridge University Press, 1960).

Groeneboom = P. Groeneboom (ed.) *Aischylos' Perser*, trans. H. Sönnichsen (Göttingen: Vandenhoeck & Ruprecht, 1960).

Hall = E. Hall (ed. & trans.) *Aeschylus Persians* (Warminster: Aris and Phillips, 1996).

Page = D. Page (ed.) *Aeschyli Septem quae Supersunt Tragoedias* (Oxford: Clarendon Press, 1972).

Prickard = A. Prickard (ed.) *The Persae of Aeschylus* (London: Macmillan, 1929, reprint of 1879 edition).

de Romilly = J. de Romilly et al. (eds) *Eschyle, Les Perses* (Paris: Presses Universitaires de France, 1974).

Rose = H.J. Rose, *A Commentary to the Surviving Plays of Aeschylus*, vol. 1 (Amsterdam: Noord-Holland, 1957).

Sidgwick = A. Sidgwick (ed.) *Aeschyli Persae* (Oxford: Clarendon Press, 1903).

West = M.L. West (ed.) *Aeschyli Tragoediae cum incerti poetae Prometheo* (Stuttgart: B.G. Teubner, 1998^2).

Translations of the Persians

Benardete = S. Benardete, *Persians*, in D. Grene and R. Lattimore (eds) *The Complete Greek Tragedies. Aeschylus II* (Chicago: University of Chicago Press, 1991^2), 44-86.

Hall = see above.

Lembke/Herington = J. Lembke and C.J. Herington, *Aeschylus Persians* (New York: Oxford University Press, 1981).

Podlecki = A. Podlecki, *The Persians by Aeschylus* (Englewood Cliffs, New Jersey: Prentice Hall, 1970).

Smyth = H.W. Smyth, *Aeschylus*, vol. 1 (London: William Heinemann Ltd., 1946).

Texts of other Greek authors

Bernabé = A. Bernabé (ed.) *Poetarum Epicorum: Testimonia et Fragmenta Pars I* (Leipzig: Teubner, 1996^2).

189

Diodorus = Diodorus of Sicily, *Library*, trans. C.H. Oldfather, 12 vols (Cambridge, Mass: Harvard University Press, 1946-67).
D-K = H. Diels and W. Kranz (eds) *Die Fragmente der Vorsokratiker*, 3 vols (Berlin: Weidemann, 1956-59[8]).
FGE = D. Page (ed.) *Further Greek Epigrams* (Cambridge: Cambridge University Press, 1981).
FGrH = F. Jacoby (ed.) *Die Fragmente der griechischen Historiker* (Leiden: E.J. Brill, 1968-).
Herodotus = Herodotus, *The Histories*, trans. A. de Selincourt (London: Penguin, 1996, revised with introductory matter and notes by John Marincola).
K-A = R. Kassel and C. Austin (eds) *Poetae Comici Graecae*, 8 vols (Berlin: Walter de Gruyter, 1983-).
Lobel/Page = E. Lobel and D. Page (eds) *Poetarum Lesbiorum Fragmenta* (Oxford: Clarendon Press, 1955).
PMG = D. Page (ed.) *Poetae Melici Graecae* (Oxford: Clarendon Press, 1962).
TrGF 1 = B. Snell and R. Kannicht (eds) *Tragicorum Graecorum Fragmenta*, vol. 1 (Göttingen: Vandenhoeck & Ruprecht, 1986[2]).
TrGF 2 = R. Kannicht and B. Snell (eds) *Tragicorum Graecorum Fragmenta*, vol. 2: *Fragmenta Adespota* (Göttingen: Vandenhoeck & Ruprecht, 1981).
TrGF 3 = S. Radt (ed.) *Tragicorum Graecorum Fragmenta*, vol. 3: *Aeschylus* (Göttingen: Vandenhoeck & Ruprecht, 1985).
TrGF 5.1 = R. Kannicht (ed.) *Tragicorum Graecorum Fragmenta*, vol. 5.1: *Euripides* (Göttingen: Vandenhoek & Ruprecht, 2004).
Thucydides = Thucydides, *History of the Peloponnesian War*, trans. R. Warner (London: Penguin, 1972, introduction and notes by M.I. Finley).
West = M.L. West (ed.) *Iambi et Elegi Graeci* (Sandpiper Books, reprint 1998).

Scholarly works and compilations of sources

ATL = B. Meritt, H.T. Wade-Gery, M.F. McGregor (eds) *The Athenian Tribute Lists*, 4 vols: vol. 1 (Cambridge, Mass.: Harvard University Press, 1939); vols 2-4 (Princeton: American School of Classical Studies at Athens, 1939-53).
Brosius = M. Brosius, *The Persian Empire from Cyrus II to Artaxerxes I*. LACTOR 16 (London: LACTOR, 2000). Cited by document number.
Csapo/Slater = E. Csapo and W.J. Slater, *The Context of Ancient Drama* (Ann Arbor: University of Michigan Press, 1994). Cited by document number unless otherwise stated.
Fornara = C. Fornara, *Archaic Times to the End of the Peloponnesian War*. *Translated Documents of Greece and Rome*, vol. 1 (Cambridge: Cambridge University Press, 1983[2]). Cited by document number.
Harding = P. Harding, *From the End of the Peloponnesian War to the Battle of Ipsus. Translated Documents of Greece and Rome*, vol. 2 (Cambridge: Cambridge University Press, 1985). Cited by document number.
Kent = R. Kent, *Old Persian: Grammar, Texts, Lexicon* (New Haven: American Oriental Society, 1953[2]).
ML[2] = R. Meiggs and D.M. Lewis (eds) *A Selection of Greek Historical Inscriptions* (Oxford: Clarendon Press, 1988[2]). Cited by document number unless otherwise stated.

Bibliography

Books, chapters, and articles

Adams, S. 'Salamis Symphony: The *Persae* of Aeschylus', in M. White (ed.) *Studies in Honour of Gilbert Norwood*. The Phoenix supplementary vol. 1 (Toronto: University of Toronto Press, 1952), 46-54. Reprinted in E. Segal (ed.) *Oxford Readings in Greek Tragedy* (Oxford: Oxford University Press, 1983), 34-41. I cite the original essay.

Aelion, R. 'Songes et prophéties d'Eschyle: une forme de mise en abyme', in *Lalies: Actes des sessions de linguistique et de littérature* 3 (1981), 133-46.

Alexanderson, B. 'Darius in the *Persians*', *Eranos* 65 (1966), 1-11.

Alexiou, M. *The Ritual Lament in Greek Tradition* (Lanham, MD: Rowman and Littlefield, 2002², revised by D. Yatromanolakis and P. Roilos).

Aloni, A. 'The Proem of Simonides' Plataea Elegy and the Circumstances of its Performance', in D. Boedeker and D. Sider (eds) *The New Simonides: Contexts of Praise and Desire* (Oxford: Oxford University Press, 2001), 86-105.

Alty, J. 'Dorians and Ionians', *Journal of Hellenic Studies* 102 (1982), 1-14.

Anderson, M. 'The Imagery of the *Persians*', *Greece & Rome* 19 (1972), 166-74.

Andrewes, A. 'Kleisthenes' Reform Bill', *Classical Quarterly* 27 (1977), 241-7.

Arnott, P. *Greek Scenic Conventions in the Fifth Century B.C.* (Oxford: Clarendon Press, 1962).

Auletta, R. *Persians* (Los Angeles: Sun & Moon Press, 1993).

Austin, M.M. 'Greek Tyrants and the Persians, 546-479 B.C.', *Classical Quarterly* 40 (1990), 289-306.

Avery, H. 'Dramatic Devices in Aeschylus' *Persians*', *American Journal of Philology* 85 (1964), 173-84.

Bacon, H. *Barbarians in Greek Tragedy* (New Haven: Yale University Press, 1961).

Badian, E. 'Toward a Chronology of the Pentecontaetia down to the Renewal of the Peace of Callias', in E. Badian, *From Plataea to Potidaea: Studies in the History and Historiography of the Pentecontaetia* (Baltimore: Johns Hopkins University Press, 1993), 73-107.

Badian, E. 'Thucydides and the Outbreak of the Peloponnesian War: A Historian's Brief', in E. Badian, *From Plataea to Potidaea: Studies in the History and Historiography of the Pentekontaetia* (Baltimore: Johns Hopkins University Press, 1993), 125-62.

Badian, E. 'Herodotus on Alexander I of Macedon: A Study in Some Subtle Silences', in S. Hornblower (ed.) *Greek Historiography* (Oxford: Clarendon Press, 1994), 107-30.

Balcer, J.M. *Herodotus and Bisitun: Problems in Ancient Persian Historiography*. Historia Einzelschriften Heft 49 (Franz Steiner: Stuttgart, 1987).

Balcer, J.M. *A Proposopographical Study of the Ancient Persians Royal and Noble c. 550-450 B.C.* (Lewiston: Edwin Mellen Press, 1993).

Baldry, H.C. 'The Idler's Paradise in Attic Comedy', *Greece & Rome* 65 (1953), 49-60.

Balot, R. *Greed and Injustice in Classical Athens* (Princeton: Princeton University Press, 2001).

Barkworth, P. 'The Organization of Xerxes' Army', *Iranica Antiqua* 27 (1993), 149-67.

Barrett, J. 'Narrative and Messenger in Aeschylus' *Persians*', *American Journal of Philology* 116 (1995), 539-57.

191

Barron, J.P. 'Bakchylides, Theseus, and a Woolly Cloak', *Bulletin of the Institute of Classical Studies* 27 (1980), 1-8.

Bassett, S. 'The Place and Date of the First Performance of the *Persians* of Timotheus', *Classical Philology* 26 (1931), 153-65.

Benveniste, E. *Indo-European Language and Society*, trans. E. Palmer (Faber and Faber: London, 1973)

Boedeker, D. 'Protesilaus and the End of Herodotus' *Histories*', *Classical Antiquity* 7 (1988), 30-48.

Boedeker, D. 'Hero Cult and Politics in Herodotus: The Bones of Orestes', in C. Dougherty and L. Kurke (eds) *Cultural Poetics in Archaic Greece* (Cambridge: Cambridge University Press, 1993), 164-77.

Boedeker, D. 'Heroic Historiography: Simonides and Herodotus on Plataea', in D. Boedeker and D. Sider (eds) *The New Simonides: Contexts of Praise and Desire* (Oxford: Oxford University Press, 2001), 120-34.

Boedeker, D. 'Paths to Heroization at Plataea', in D. Boedeker and D. Sider (eds) *The New Simonides: Contexts of Praise and Desire* (Oxford: Oxford University Press, 2001), 148-63.

Bordaux, L. 'Lecture du Premier Stasimon des *Perses*, v. 532-97', in P. Ghiron-Bistagne, A. Moreau, J.-C. Turpin (eds) *Les Perses d' Eschyle, Cahiers du Gita* 7, 1992/93 (Montpellier: Université Paul Valéry, 1993), 70-80.

Borthwick, E.K. 'The 'Flower' of the Argives and a Neglected Meaning of *Anthos*', *Journal of Hellenic Studies* 96 (1976), 1-7.

Bourgeaud, P. *The Cult of Pan in Ancient Greece,* trans. K. Atlass and J. Redfield (Chicago: University of Chicago Press, 1988).

Brenne, S. 'Ostraka and the Process of Ostrakophoria', in W. Coulson et al. (eds) *The Archaeology of Athens and Attica under the Democracy* (Oxford: Oxbow Monographs, 1994), 13-24.

Brenne, S. 'T1: Ostraka', in P. Siewert (ed.) *Ostrakismos-Testimonien I*. Historia Einzelschriften Heft 155 (Stuttgart: Franz Steiner, 2002), 36-166.

Briant, P. *From Cyrus to Alexander: A History of the Persian Empire*, trans. P. Daniels (Winona Lake: Eisenbaums, 2002).

Brown, Stuart C. 'The Mêdikos Logos of Herodotus and the Evolution of the Median State', in A. Kuhrt and H. Sancisi-Weerdenburg (eds) *Achaemenid History III: Method and Theory* (Leiden: Netherlands Institute for the Near East, 1988), 71-86.

Brunt, P.A. 'The Hellenic League Against Persia', *Historia* 2 (1953/54), 135-63.

Burian, P. 'Tragedy Adapted for the Stage and Screens: The Renaissance to the Present', in P. Easterling (ed.) *The Cambridge Companion to Greek Tragedy* (Cambridge: Cambridge University Press, 1997), 229-83.

Burkert, W. *Structure and History in Greek Mythology and Ritual* (Berkeley: University of California Press, 1979).

Burn, A.R. *Persia and the Greeks* (London: Duckworth, 1984² with postscript by D.M. Lewis).

Cairns, D. '*Hybris*, Dishonour, and Thinking Big', *Journal of Hellenic Studies* 116 (1996), 1-32.

Caldwell, R. 'The Pattern of Aeschylean Drama', *Transactions and Proceedings of the American Philological Association* 101 (1970), 77-94.

Carriere, J.-C. *Le Carnaval et la Politique* (Paris: Les Belles Lettres, 1979).

Cartledge, P. *Agesilaos and the Crisis of Sparta* (London: Duckworth, and Baltimore: Johns Hopkins University Press, 1987).

Cartledge, P. *Greeks: A Portrait of Self and Others* (Cambridge: Cambridge University Press, 2002²).

Bibliography

Cassio, A. 'Old Persian MARIKA-, Eupolis *Marikas* and Aristophanes *Knights*', *Classical Quarterly* 35 (1985), 38-42.

Castellani, V. 'Clio vs. Melpomene; or why so little historical drama from Athens', in J. Redmond (ed.) *Themes in Drama*, vol. 8, *Historical Drama* (Cambridge: Cambridge University Press, 1986), 1-16.

Castriota, D. *Myth, Ethos, and Actuality: Official Art in Fifth-Century B.C. Athens* (Madison: University of Wisconsin Press, 1992).

Cawkwell, G. 'The Fall of Themistocles', in B.F. Harris (ed.) *Auckland Essays Presented to E.M. Blaiklock* (Auckland: Auckland University Press, 1970), 39-58.

Ceccarelli, P. 'L'Athènes de Périclès: un "pays de cocagne"? L' idéologie démocratique et l'*automatos bios* dans la comédie ancienne', *Quaderni Urbinati di Cultura Classica* 54 (1996), 109-59.

Chiasson, C. 'The Herodotean Solon', *Greek, Roman, and Byzantine Studies* 27 (1986), 249-62.

Chiasson, C. 'Herodotus' Use of Attic Tragedy in the Lydian *Logos*', *Classical Antiquity* 22 (2003), 5-36.

Clairmont, C. *Patrios Nomos: Public Burial in Athens during the Fifth and Fourth Centuries B.C.*, 2 vols (Oxford: BAR International Series 161, 1983).

Conacher, D. '*Persae*', in D. Conacher, *Aeschylus: The Earlier Plays and Related Studies* (Toronto: University of Toronto Press, 1996), 3-32.

Connor, W.R. 'Early Greek Land Warfare as Symbolic Expression', *Past & Present* 119 (1988), 1-29.

Connor, W.R. 'City Dionysia and Athenian Democracy', *Classica et Mediaevalia* 40 (1989), 7-32.

Couch, H. 'Three Puns on the Root *PERTH-* in the *Persae* of Aeschylus', *American Journal of Philology* 52 (1931), 270-3.

Couch, H. 'Proskynesis and Abasement in Aeschylus', *Classical Philology* 26 (1931), 316-18.

Craig, J. 'The Interpretation of Aeschylus' *Persae*', *Classical Review* 38 (1924), 98-101.

Croiset, M. 'Observations sur *Les Perses* de Timothée de Milet', *Revues des Études Grecques* 16 (1903), 323-48.

Csapo, E. 'The Politics of the New Music', in P. Murray and P. Wilson (eds) *Music and the Muses: The Culture of Mousikê in the Classical Athenian City* (Oxford: Oxford University Press, 2004), 207-38.

Dale, A.M. 'Interior Scenes and Illusion in Greek Drama', in A.M. Dale, *Collected Papers* (Cambridge: Cambridge University Press, 1969), 259-71.

Dale, A.M. *Metrical Analyses of Tragic Choruses: Fasicle I, Dactylo-Epitrite. Bulletin of the Institute of Classical Studies* Supplement 21.1 (London: University of London, Institute for Classical Studies, 1971).

Dean, W. 'Handel's *Serse*', in T. Bauman and M. Petsoldt McClymonds (eds) *Opera and the Enlightenment* (Cambridge: Cambridge University Press, 1995), 135-67.

Desmond, W. 'Punishments and the Conclusion of Herodotus' *Histories*', *Greek, Roman, and Byzantine Studies* 44 (2004), 19-40.

Detienne, M. *The Gardens of Adonis*, trans. J. Lloyd (Sussex: Harvester Press, 1977).

Detienne, M. *Dionysos at Large*, trans. A. Goldhammer (Cambridge, Mass.: Harvard University Press, 1989).

Detienne, M. and Vernant, J.-P. *Cunning Intelligence in Greek Culture and Society*, trans. J. Lloyd (Sussex: Harvester Press, 1978).

Devereux, G. *Dreams in Greek Tragedy: An Ethno-Pyscho-Analytical Study* (Berkeley: University of California Press, 1976).

Dewald, C. 'Wanton Kings, Pickled Heroes, and Gnomic Founding Fathers: Strategies of Meaning at the End of Herodotus's *Histories*', in D. Roberts, F. Dunn, and D. Fowler (eds) *Classical Closure. Reading the End in Greek and Latin Literature* (Princeton: Princeton University Press, 1996), 62-82.

Drew-Bear, T. 'The Trochaic Tetrameter in Greek Tragedy', *American Journal of Philology* 89 (1968), 385-405.

Dworacki, S. 'Atossa's Absence in the Final Scene of the *Persae* of Aeschylus', in G.W. Bowersock et al. (eds) *Arktouros: Hellenic Studies Presented to Bernard M.W. Knox* (Berlin: Walter de Gruyter, 1979), 101-8.

Easterling, P. (ed.) *The Cambridge Companion to Greek Tragedy* (Cambridge: Cambridge University Press, 1997).

Ebbott, M. 'The List of the War Dead in Aeschylus' *Persians*', *Harvard Studies in Classical Philology* 100 (2000), 83-96.

Ebeling, H. 'The *Persians* of Timotheus', *American Journal of Philology* 46 (1925), 317-31.

Ehrenberg, V. *From Solon to Socrates: Greek History and Civilization during the Sixth and Fifth Centuries B.C.* (London: Methuen, 1973^2).

Eitrem, S. 'The Necromancy in the Persai of Aischylos', *Symbolae Osloensis* 6 (1928), 1-16.

Else, G. *The Origin and Early Form of Greek Tragedy* (Cambridge, Mass.: Harvard University Press, 1965).

Erkelenz, M. 'Shelley's *Hellas* and Aeschylus' *Persians*', *Philological Quarterly* 76 (1997), 313-37.

Euben, J.P. 'The Battle of Salamis and the Origins of Political Theory', *Political Theory* 14 (1986), 359-90.

Evans, J. 'The Medism of Pausanias: Two Versions', *Antichthon* 22 (1988), 1-11.

Faraone, C. *Ancient Greek Love Magic* (Cambridge, Mass.: Harvard University Press, 1999).

Favorini, A. 'History, Collective Memory, and Aeschylus' *Persians*', *Theatre Journal* 55 (2003), 99-111.

Ferrari, Gloria, 'The Ilioupersis in Athens', *Harvard Studies in Classical Philology* 100 (2000), 119-50.

Finley, M.I. 'Empire in the Greco-Roman World', *Greece & Rome* 25 (1978), 1-15.

Finley, M.I. 'The Athenian Empire: A Balance Sheet', in M.I. Finley, *Economy and Society in Ancient Greece* (New York: Viking Press, 1982, edited with an introduction by B. Shaw and R. Saller), 41-61.

Fisher, N.R.E. *Hybris: A Study in the Values of Honour and Shame in Ancient Greece* (Warminster: Aris and Phillips, 1992).

Flintoff, E. '*Diplakessin* at Aeschylus' *Persians* 277', *Mnemosyne* 27 (1974), 231-7.

Flintoff, E. 'The Unity of the *Persians* Trilogy', *Quaderni Urbanati di Cultura Classica* 40 (1992), 67-80.

Flower, M. 'From Simonides to Isocrates: The Fifth-Century Origins of Fourth-Century Panhellenism', *Classical Antiquity* 19 (2000), 65-101.

Flower, M. and Marincola, J. (eds) *Herodotus Histories Book IX* (Cambridge: Cambridge University Press, 2002).

Foley, H. 'The Politics of Tragic Lamentation', in A. Sommerstein et al. (eds) *Tragedy and the Polis* (Bari: Lavante), 101-43.

Fontenrose, J. *The Delphic Oracle* (Berkeley: University of California Press, 1978).

Bibliography

Fornara, C. 'Some Aspects of the Career of Pausanias of Sparta', *Historia* 15 (1966), 257-71.

Fornara, C. 'The Hoplite Achievement at Psyttalia', *Journal of Hellenic Studies* 86 (1966), 51-4.

Fornara, C. *The Athenian Board of Generals from 501 to 404*. Historia Einzelschriften Heft 16 (Wiesbaden: Franz Steiner, 1971).

Fornara, C. 'Themistocles' Archonship', *Historia* 20 (1971), 534-40.

Fornara, C. *Herodotus: An Interpretative Essay* (Oxford: Clarendon Press, 1971).

Fornara, C. and Samons, L. *Athens from Cleisthenes to Pericles* (Berkeley: University of California Press, 1991).

Forrest, W.G. 'Themistokles and Argos', *Classical Quarterly* 10 (1960), 221-41.

Fowler, B. 'Aeschylus' Imagery', *Classica et Mediaevalia* 28 (1967), 1-74.

Frost, F. 'The Athenian Military before Cleisthenes', *Historia* 33 (1984), 283-94.

Frye, N. *The Anatomy of Criticism* (Princeton: Princeton University Press, 1957).

Gagarin, M. *Aeschylean Drama* (Berkeley: University of California Press, 1976).

Gantz, T. 'The Aischylean Tetralogy: Conjectured and Attested Groups', *American Journal of Philology* 101 (1980), 133-64.

Garland, R. *Surviving Greek Tragedy* (London: Duckworth, 2004).

Garvie, A, 'Aeschylus' Simple Plots', in R. Dawe et al. (eds) *Dionysiaca: Nine Studies in Greek Poetry by Former Pupils Presented to Sir Denys Page on his Seventieth Birthday* (Cambridge: Cambridge University Library, 1978), 63-86.

Georges, P. *Barbarian Asia and the Greek Experience: From the Archaic Period to the Age of Xenophon* (Baltimore: Johns Hopkins University Press, 1994).

Georges, P. 'Persian Ionia under Darius: The Revolt Reconsidered', *Historia* 49 (2000), 1-39.

Gillis, D. *Collaboration with the Persians*. Historia Einzelschriften Heft 34 (Wiesbaden: Franz Steiner, 1979).

Glover, J. *Cavalli* (London: B.T. Batsford Ltd, 1978).

Goheen, R. 'Aspects of Dramatic Symbolism: Three Studies in the *Oresteia*', *American Journal of Philology* 76 (1955), 113-57.

Golden, L. *In Praise of Prometheus: Humanism and Rationalism in Aeschylean Thought* (Chapel Hill: University of North Carolina Press, 1966).

Goldhill, S. 'Battle Narrative and Politics in Aeschylus' *Persae*', *Journal of Hellenic Studies* 108 (1988), 189-93.

Goldhill, S. 'The Great Dionysia and Civic Ideology', in J. Winkler and F. Zeitlin (eds) *Nothing to Do with Dionysos? Athenian Drama in its Social Context* (Princeton: Princeton University Press, 1990), 97-129.

Gombrich, E. 'Apollonio di Giovanni: A Florentine Cassone Workshop Seen Through the Eyes of a Humanist Poet', in E. Gombrich, *Norm and Form: Studies in the Art of the Renaissance* (London: Phaidon, 1971[2]), 11-28.

Gould, J. 'Hiketeia', in J. Gould, *Myth, Ritual, Memory, and Exchange: Essays in Greek Literature and Culture* (Oxford: Oxford University Press, 2001), 22-77.

Gould, J. *Herodotus* (London: Weidenfeld and Nicolson, 1989).

Gow, A.S.F. 'Notes on the *Persae* of Aeschylus', *Journal of Hellenic Studies* 48 (1928), 133-58.

Gow, A.S.F. 'Iunx, Rhombos, Turbo', *Journal of Hellenic Studies* 54 (1934), 1-13.

Green, J.R. *Theatre in Ancient Greek Society* (London: Routledge, 1994).

Green, P. *The Greco-Persian Wars* (Berkeley: University of California Press, 1996, reprint).

Gregory, J. (ed.) *A Companion to Greek Tragedy* (Oxford: Blackwell Publishing, 2005).

Griffith, M. 'Brilliant Dynasts: Power and Politics in the *Oresteia*', *Classical Antiquity* 14 (1995), 62-129.

Griffith, M. 'The King and Eye: The Rule of the Father in Greek Tragedy', *Proceedings of the Cambridge Philological Society* 44 (1998), 20-84.

Grundy, G. *The Great Persian War* (London: John Murray, 1901).

Haldane, J. ' "Barbaric Cries" (Aesch. *Pers*. 633-39)', *Classical Quarterly* 22 (1972), 42-50.

Hall, E. *Inventing the Barbarian: Greek Self-Definition through Tragedy* (Oxford: Oxford University Press, 1988).

Hall, E. 'Asia Unmanned: Images of Victory in Classical Athens', in J. Rich and G. Shipley (eds) *War and Society in the Greek World* (London: Routledge, 1993), 108-33.

Hall, E. 'Drowning by Nomes: The Greeks, Swimming, and Timotheus' *Persians*', in H. Khan (ed.) *The Birth of the European Identity: The Europe-Asia Contrast in Greek Thought*. Nottingham Classical Literature Studies, vol. 2 (Nottingham: Nottingham University Press, 1994), 44-80.

Hall, E. 'Aeschylus, Race, Class, and War in the 1990s', in E. Hall, F. Macintosh, and A. Wrigley (eds) *Dionysus since 69: Greek Tragedy at the Dawn of the Third Millennium* (Oxford: Oxford University Press, 2004), 169-97.

Hammond, N.G.L. 'The Conditions of Dramatic Production to the Death of Aeschylus', *Greek, Roman, and Byzantine Studies* 13 (1972), 387-450.

Hammond, N.G.L. 'Herodotus VII and the Decree of Themistocles', *Journal of Hellenic Studies* 102 (1982), 75-93.

Hammond, N.G.L. 'More on the Conditions of Production to the Death of Aeschylus', *Greek, Roman, and Byzantine Studies* 29 (1988), 5-33.

Hammond, N.G.L. 'The Expedition of Datis and Artaphrenes', in J. Boardman, N.G.L. Hammond, D.M. Lewis, and M. Ostwald (eds) *The Cambridge Ancient History*, vol. IV: *Persia, Greece and the Western Mediterranean c. 525 to 479 B.C.* (Cambridge: Cambridge University Press, 1988^2), 491-517.

Hammond, N.G.L. 'The Expedition of Xerxes', in J. Boardman, N.G.L. Hammond, D.M. Lewis, and M. Ostwald (eds) *The Cambridge Ancient History*, vol. IV: *Persia, Greece and the Western Mediterranean c. 525 to 479 B.C.* (Cambridge: Cambridge University Press, 1988^2), 518-91.

Hansen, O. 'On the Date and Place of the First Performance of Timotheus' *Persae*', *Philologus* 128 (1984), 135-8.

Hardwick, L. *Reception Studies*. Greece & Rome New Surveys in the Classics 33 (London: Oxford University Press, 2003).

Harmon, A. 'The Scene of the *Persians*', *Transactions and Proceedings of the American Philological Association* 63 (1932), 7-19.

Harrison, T. *The Emptiness of Asia* (London: Duckworth, 2000).

Harrison, T. *Divinity and History: The Religion of Herodotus* (Oxford: Oxford University Press, 2000).

Harrison, T. (ed.) *Greeks and Barbarians*. Edinburgh Readings on the Ancient World (Edinburgh: Edinburgh University Press, 2002).

Hartigan, K. *Greek Tragedy on the American Stage: Ancient Drama in the Commercial Theater 1882-1994* (Westport, Conn.: Greenwood Press, 1995).

Bibliography

Hartog, F. *The Mirror of Herodotus: Representation of the Other in the Writing of History*, trans. J. Lloyd (Berkeley: University of California Press, 1988).

Heath, M. *The Poetics of Greek Tragedy* (Stanford: Stanford University Press, 1987).

Helm, J. 'Aeschylus' Genealogy of Morals', *Transactions of the American Philological Association* 134 (2004), 23-54.

Herington, C.J. *Poetry into Drama: Early Tragedy and the Greek Poetic Tradition* (Berkeley: University of California Press, 1985).

Herington, C.J. *Aeschylus* (New Haven: Yale University Press, 1986).

Hesk, J. *Sophocles: Ajax* (London: Duckworth, 2003).

Hignett, C. *Xerxes' Invasion of Greece* (Oxford: Clarendon Press, 1963).

Holst-Warhaft, G. *Dangerous Voices: Women's Laments and Greek Literature* (London: Routledge, 1992).

Holtsmark, E. 'Ring Composition and the *Persae* of Aeschylus', *Symbolae Osloenses* 45 (1970), 5-23.

Hordern, J. *The Fragments of Timotheus of Miletus* (Oxford: Oxford University Press, 2002).

Hornblower, S. 'Panionios and Hermotimos (Hdt. 8.104-6)', in P. Derow and R. Parker (eds) *Herodotus and his World. Essays from a Conference in Memory of George Forrest* (Oxford: Oxford University Press, 2003), 37-57.

Horsfall, N. 'Aeschylus and the Strymon', *Hermes* 102 (1974), 503-5.

Hose, M. 'Response to Hall', in H.A. Khan (ed.) *The Birth of the European Identity: The Europe-Asia Contrast in Greek Thought 490-322 B.C.* Nottingham Classical Literature Studies, vol. 2 (Nottingham: Nottingham University Press, 1994), 81-9.

Hunter, V. *Past and Process in Herodotus and Thucydides* (Princeton: Princeton University Press, 1982).

Hutchinson, T. *The Complete Poetical Works of Shelley* (Oxford: Clarendon Press, 1904).

Immerwahr, H. *Form and Thought in Herodotus* (Cleveland: Case Western Reserve University Press, 1966).

Jameson, M. 'Waiting for the Barbarian', *Greece & Rome* 8 (1961), 5-18.

Jameson, M. 'The Provisions for Mobilization in the Decree of Themistokles', *Historia* 12 (1963), 385-404.

Janssen, T. *Timotheus Persae* (Amsterdam: Hakkert, 1989).

Johnston, S. 'The Song of the *Iunx*: Magic and Rhetoric in *Pythian* 4', *Transactions of the American Philological Association* 125 (1995), 177-206.

Jones, J. *On Aristotle and Greek Tragedy* (New York: Oxford University Press, 1962).

Kantzios, I. 'The Politics of Fear in Aeschylus' *Persians*', *Classical World* 98 (2004), 3-19.

Katz Anhalt, E. *Solon the Singer: Politics and Poetics* (Lanham: Rowman and Littlefield, 1993).

Keaveney, A. 'Xerxes' New Suit: Aeschylus, *Persae* 845-51', *Giornale Italiano de Filologia* 50 (1998), 239-41.

Kitto, H.D.F. *Greek Tragedy: A Literary Study* (London: Methuen, 1961³).

Knox, P. ' "So Mischievous a Beaste": The Athenian Demos and its Treatment of its Politicians', *Greece & Rome* 32 (1985), 132-61.

Konstan, D. 'Persians, Greeks and Empire', *Arethusa* 20 (1987), 59-73.

Konstan, D. *Pity Transformed* (London: Duckworth, 2001).

Kuhrt, A. 'Earth and Water', in A. Kuhrt and H. Sancisi-Weerdenburg (eds)

Achaemenid History III: Method and Theory (Netherlands Institute for the Near East: Leiden, 1988), 87-99.

Kurke, L. 'The Politics of *Habrosynê* in Archaic Greece', *Classical Antiquity* 11 (1992), 91-120.

Kurke, L. *Coins, Bodies, Games, and Gold: The Politics of Meaning in Ancient Greece* (Princeton: Princeton University Press, 1999).

Lang, M. 'Scapegoat Pausanias', *Classical Journal* 63 (1967), 79-85.

Larissy, E. 'Ahasuerus-Xerxes: *Hellas* as Allegory of Dissemination', *Essays and Studies* 45 (1992), 88-98.

Lattimore, R. 'Aeschylus on the Defeat of Xerxes', in *Studies in Honor of William Abbott Oldfather* (Urbana: University of Illinois Press, 1943), 82-93.

Lattimore, R. *The Poetry of Greek Tragedy* (Baltimore: Johns Hopkins University Press, 1958).

Lavelle, B. *Fame, Money, and Power: The Rise of Peisistratos and 'Democratic' Tyranny at Athens* (Ann Arbor: University of Michigan Press, 2005).

Lawler, L. *The Dance of the Ancient Greek Theatre* (Iowa City: University of Iowa Press, 1964).

Lazenby, J. *The Defence of Greece: 490-479 BC* (Warminster: Aris & Phillips, 1993).

Lefkowitz, M. *The Lives of the Greek Poets* (London: Duckworth, 1981).

Lenardon, R. 'The Chronology of Themistocles' Ostracism and Exile', *Historia* 8 (1959), 23-48.

Levine, D.B. 'Symposium and Polis', in T. Figueira and G. Nagy (eds) *Theognis of Megara: Poetry and the Polis* (Baltimore: Johns Hopkins University Press, 1985), 176-96.

Lewis, D.M. 'Themistocles' Archonship', *Historia* 22 (1973), 757-8.

Lewis, D.M. 'The Tyranny of the Pisistratidae', in J. Boardman, N.G.L. Hammond, D.M. Lewis, and M. Ostwald (eds) *The Cambridge Ancient History*, vol. IV: *Persia, Greece and the Western Mediterranean c. 525 to 479 B.C.* (Cambridge: Cambridge University Press, 1988²), 287-302.

Lincoln, B. 'Death by Water: Strange Events at the Strymon (*Persae* 492-507) and the Categorical Opposition of East and West', *Classical Philology* 95 (2000), 12-20.

Lloyd, A.B. 'Herodotus on Cambyses', in A. Kuhrt and H. Sancisi-Weerdenburg (eds) *Achaemenid History III: Method and Theory* (Netherlands Institute for the Near East: Leiden, 1988), 55-66.

Lloyd-Jones, H. *The Justice of Zeus* (Berkeley: University of California Press, 1971).

Lloyd-Jones, H. 'Problems of Early Greek Tragedy: Pratinas and Phrynichus', in H. Lloyd-Jones, *Greek Epic, Lyric and Tragedy: The Academic Papers of Hugh Lloyd-Jones* (Oxford: Oxford University Press, 1990), 225-37.

Lloyd-Jones, H. 'Notes on the New Simonides', *Zeitschrift für Papyrologie und Epigraphik* 101 (1994), 1-3.

Lonsdale, S. *Dance and Ritual Play in Greek Religion* (Baltimore: Johns Hopkins University Press, 1993).

Loraux, N. *The Invention of Athens: The Funeral Oration in the Classical City*, trans. A. Sheridan (Cambridge, Mass.: Harvard University Press, 1986).

MacDowell, D.M. '*Hybris* in Athens', *Greece & Rome* 23 (1976), 14-31.

Macintosh, F. 'Tragedy in Performance: Nineteenth and Twentieth Century Productions', in P. Easterling (ed.) *The Cambridge Companion to Greek Tragedy* (Cambridge: Cambridge University Press, 1997), 284-323.

Bibliography

Macleod, C. 'Clothing in the *Oresteia*', *Maia* 27 (1975), 201-3.

Macleod, C. 'Homer on Poetry and the Poetry of Homer', in C. Macleod, *Collected Essays* (Oxford: Clarendon Press, 1983), 1-15.

Manville, P.B. *The Origins of Citizenship in Ancient Athens* (Princeton: Princeton University Press, 1990).

Mastronarde, D. 'Actors on High: The Skene Roof, the Crane, and the Gods in Attic Drama', *Classical Antiquity* 9 (1990), 247-94.

Maurice, F. 'The Size of the Army of Xerxes in the Invasion of Greece in 480 BC', *Journal of Hellenic Studies* 50 (1930), 210-35.

McCall, M. 'Aeschylus in the *Persae*', in M. Cropp et al. (eds) *Greek Tragedy and its Legacy: Essays Presented to D.J. Conacher* (Calgary: University of Calgary Press, 1986), 43-9.

McGlew, J. *Tyranny and Political Culture in Ancient Greece* (Ithaca: Cornell University Press, 1993).

Meier, C. *The Political Art of Greek Tragedy*, trans. A. Webber (Cambridge: Polity Press, 1993).

Meiggs, R. *The Athenian Empire* (Oxford: Oxford University Press, 1972).

Michelini, A.N. '*Hybris* and Plants', *Harvard Studies in Classical Philology* 82 (1978), 35-44.

Michelini, A.N. *Tradition and Dramatic Form in the Persians of Aeschylus* (Leiden: Brill, 1982).

Mikalson, J. *Herodotus and Religion in the Persian Wars* (Chapel Hill: University of North Carolina Press, 2003).

Miller, A. '*Ingenium* and *Ars* in *Persae* 101-114', *Classical Antiquity* 2 (1983), 77-81.

Miller, M. *Athens and Persia in the Fifth Century B.C.: A Study in Cultural Receptivity* (Cambridge: Cambridge University Press, 1997).

Mitsis, P. 'Xerxes' Entrance: Irony, Myth, and History in the *Persians*', in P. Pucci (ed.) *Language and the Tragic Hero: Studies in Honor of Gordon Kirkwood* (Atlanta: Scholar's Press, 1988), 103-19.

Moles, J. 'Herodotus Warns the Athenians', *Papers of the Leeds International Latin Seminar* 9 (1996), 259-84.

Momigliano, A. 'Sea-Power in Greek Thought', in A. Momigliano, *Secondo Contributo alla Storia degli Studi Classici* (Rome: Edizioni di Storia e Letteratura, 1960), 57-67.

Moreau, A. 'L'oeil maléfique dans l'oeuvre d'Eschyle', *Revue des Études Anciennes* 58-9 (1976-77), 50-64.

Moreau, A. *Eschyle: la violence et la chaos* (Paris: Les Belles Lettres, 1985).

Moreau, A. 'Le songe d'Atossa. *Perses* 176-214. Éléments pour une explication de textes', in P. Ghiron-Bistagne et al. (eds) *Les Perses d' Eschyle, Cahiers du Gita* 7, 1992-93 (Montpellier: Université Paul Valéry, 1993), 29-51.

Moreau, A. 'La tétralogie des *Perses* a-t-elle une unité'?, in P. Ghiron-Bistagne et al. (eds) *Les Perses d' Eschyle, Cahiers du Gita* 7, 1992-93 (Montpellier: Université Paul Valéry, 1993), 120-44.

Moritz, H. 'Refrain in Aeschylus: Literary Adaptation of Traditional Form', *Classical Philology* 74 (1979), 187-213.

Morrison, J., Coates, J., and Rankov, N. *The Athenian Trireme* (Cambridge: Cambridge University Press, 2000[2]).

Mossé, C. *Alexander: Destiny and Myth*, trans. J. Lloyd (Baltimore: Johns Hopkins University Press, 2004).

Munson, V. 'Artemisia in Herodotus', *Classical Antiquity* 7 (1988), 91-106.

Murray, G. *Aeschylus, Creator of Tragedy* (Oxford: Clarendon Press, 1940).

Murray, O. 'The Greek Symposion in History', in E. Gabba (ed.) *Tria Corda: Scritti in onore di Arnaldo Momigliano* (Como: Edizioni New Press, 1983), 257-72.

Murray, O. 'The Ionian Revolt', in J. Boardman, N.G.L. Hammond, D.M. Lewis, and M. Ostwald (eds) *The Cambridge Ancient History*, vol. IV: *Persia, Greece and the Western Mediterranean c. 525 to 479 B.C.* (Cambridge: Cambridge University Press, 1988²), 461-90.

Nagy, G. 'Theognis and Megara: A Poet's Vision of His City', in T. Figueira and G. Nagy (eds) *Theognis of Megara: Poetry and the Polis* (Baltimore: Johns Hopkins University Press, 1985), 22-81.

Nagy, G. *Pindar's Homer: The Lyric Possession of an Epic Past* (Baltimore: Johns Hopkins University Press, 1990).

Neuburg, M. '*Atê* Reconsidered', in R. Rosen and J. Farrell (eds) *Nomodeiktes: Greek Studies in Honor of Martin Ostwald* (Ann Arbor: University of Michigan Press, 1993), 491-504.

Ober, J. *Mass and Elite in Democratic Athens: Rhetoric, Ideology, and the Power of the People* (Princeton: Princeton University Press, 1989).

Ober, J. 'The Athenian Revolution of 508/07 B.C.: Violence, Authority, and the Origins of Democracy', in J. Ober, *The Athenian Revolution: Essays on Ancient Greek Democracy and Political Theory* (Princeton: Princeton University Press, 1996), 32-52.

Ober, J. *Political Dissent in Democratic Athens* (Princeton: Princeton University Press, 1998).

Ober, J. 'Tyrant Killing as Therapeutic *Stasis*: A Political Debate in Images and Texts', in K. Morgan (ed.) *Popular Tyranny: Sovereignty and its Discontents in Ancient Greece* (Austin: University of Texas Press, 2003), 215-50.

Ogden, D. *Greek and Roman Necromancy* (Princeton: Princeton University Press, 2001).

Osborne, R. 'Archaeology and the Athenian Empire', *Transactions of the American Philological Association* 129 (1999), 319-32.

Osborne, R. *The Athenian Empire*. LACTOR 1 (London: LACTOR, 2000⁴).

Ostwald, M. *Nomos and the Beginnings of Athenian Democracy* (Oxford: Oxford University Press, 1969).

Ostwald, M. *From Popular Sovereignty to the Sovereignty of Law* (Berkeley: University of California Press, 1986).

Ostwald, M. 'The Reform of the Athenian State by Cleisthenes', in J. Boardman, N.G.L. Hammond, D.M. Lewis, and M. Ostwald (eds) *The Cambridge Ancient History*, vol. IV: *Persia, Greece and the Western Mediterranean c. 525 to 479 B.C.* (Cambridge: Cambridge University Press, 1988²), 303-46.

Padel, R. *Whom Gods Destroy: Elements of Greek and Tragic Madness* (Princeton: Princeton University Press, 1995).

Page, D. *Sappho and Alcaeus* (Oxford: Clarendon Press, 1955).

Parke, H.W. *Festivals of the Athenians* (Ithaca: Cornell University Press, 1977).

Parker, R. *Miasma: Pollution and Purification in Early Greek Religion* (Oxford: Clarendon Press, 1983).

Pavlovskis, Z. 'Aeschylus Mythistoricus', *Rivista di Studi Classici* 26 (1978), 5-23.

Pedrizet, P. 'Le Témoignage d'Eschyle sur le Sac d'Athènes', *Revues des Études Grecques* 24 (1921), 57-79.

Pelling, C. 'Aeschylus' *Persae* and History', in C. Pelling (ed.) *Greek Tragedy and the Historian* (Oxford: Clarendon Press, 1997), 1-19.

Pickard-Cambridge, A. *The Theatre of Dionysus in Athens* (Oxford: Clarendon Press, 1946).

Bibliography

Pickard-Cambridge, A. *The Dramatic Festivals of Athens* (Oxford: Clarendon Press, 1968², revised by J. Gould and D.M. Lewis).

Podlecki, A. *The Political Background of Aeschylean Drama* (London: Bristol Classical Press, 1999, reprint of 1966 edition).

Podlecki, A. 'Cimon, Skyros and "Theseus' Bones" ', *Journal of Hellenic Studies* 91 (1971), 141-3.

Podlecki, A. 'Three Passage in *Persae*', *Antichthon* 9 (1975), 1-3.

Podlecki, A. *The Life of Themistocles* (Montreal: McGill University Press, 1975).

Podlecki, A. *Perikles and his Circle* (London: Routledge, 1998).

Porter, J. *Studies in Euripides' Orestes* (Leiden: Brill, 1994).

Pritchett, W.K. 'The Transfer of the Delian Treasury', *Historia* 18 (1969), 17-21.

Pucci, P. 'Euripides: The Monument and the Sacrifice', *Arethusa* 10 (1977), 165-95.

Pucci, P. *The Violence of Pity in Euripides' Medea* (Ithaca: Cornell University Press, 1980).

Raaflaub, K. 'Herodotus, Political Thought, and the Meaning of History', *Arethusa* 20 (1987), 221-48.

Raaflaub, K. 'Stick and Glue: The Function of Tyranny in Fifth-Century Athenian Democracy', in K. Morgan (ed.) *Popular Tyranny: Sovereignty and its Discontents in Ancient Greece* (Austin: University of Texas Press, 2003), 59-94.

Raaflaub, K. *The Discovery of Freedom in Ancient Greece*, trans. R. Franciscono (Chicago: University of Chicago Press, 2004).

Reed, J. 'The Sexuality of Adonis', *Classical Antiquity* 14 (1995), 318-47.

Rehm, R. *The Play of Space: Spatial Transformation in Greek Tragedy* (Princeton: Princeton University Press, 2002).

Rhodes, P.J. *The Athenian Empire*. Greece & Rome New Surveys in the Classics 17 (Oxford: Clarendon Press, 1985).

Rhodes, P. J. *A Commentary on the Aristotelian* Athenaion Politieia (Oxford: Clarendon Press, 1993).

Robertson, N. 'The True Nature of the Delian League, 478-461 BC', *American Journal of Ancient History* 5 (1980), 64-96.

Robertson, N. 'The True Nature of the Delian League, 478-461 BC, Continued', *American Journal of Ancient History* 5 (1980), 110-33.

Robertson, N. 'The True Meaning of the Wooden Wall', *Classical Philology* 82 (1987), 1-20.

Robinson, E. 'Thucydidean Sieges, Prosopitis, and the Hellenic Disaster in Egypt', *Classical Antiquity* 18 (1999), 132-52.

Roisman, J. 'On Phrynichos' *Sack of Miletos* and *Phoinissai*', *Eranus* 86 (1988), 15-23.

Roller, L. *In Search of God the Mother: The Cult of Anatolian Cybele* (Berkeley: University of California Press, 1999).

Romilly, J. de *Magic and Rhetoric in Ancient Greece* (Cambridge, Mass.: Harvard University Press, 1975).

Rood, T. 'Thucydides' Persian Wars', in C.S. Kraus (ed.) *The Limits of Historiography* (Leiden: Brill, 1999), 141-68.

Rosenbloom, D. 'Shouting "Fire" in a Crowded Theater: Phrynichos's *Capture of Miletos* and the Politics of Fear in Early Attic Tragedy', *Philologus* 137 (1993), 159-96.

Rosenbloom, D. 'Myth, History, and Hegemony in Aeschylus', in B. Goff (ed.) *History, Tragedy, Theory* (Austin: University of Texas Press, 1995), 91-130.

Rosenbloom, D. 'From *Ponêros* to *Pharmakos*: Theater, Social Drama, and Revolution in Athens, 428-404 BCE', *Classical Antiquity* 21 (2002), 283-346.

Rosenbloom, D. 'Empire and its Discontents: *Trojan Women, Birds*, and the Symbolic Economy of Athenian Imperialism', in J. Davidson, P. Wilson, and F. Muecke (eds) *Greek Drama III: Essays in Honour of Kevin Lee*. Institute of Classical Studies Supplement 87 (London: Institute of Classical Studies, 2006), 245-71.

Rosenmeyer, T. *The Art of Aeschylus* (Berkeley: University of California Press, 1982).

Ruffel, I. 'The World Turned Upside Down: Utopia and Utopianism in the Fragments of Old Comedy', in D. Harvey and J. Wilkins (eds) *The Rivals of Aristophanes: Studies in Athenian Old Comedy* (London: Duckworth/Classical Press of Wales, 2000), 473-506.

Rutherford, I. 'The New Simonides: Toward a Commentary', in D. Boedeker and D. Sider (eds) *The New Simonides: Contexts of Praise and Desire* (Oxford: Oxford University Press, 2001), 33-54.

Rutherford, R.B. 'Tragic Form and Feeling in the *Iliad*', *Journal of Hellenic Studies* 102 (1982), 145-60.

Said, E. *Orientalism: Western Conceptions of the Orient* (London: Penguin Books, 1991, reprint of 1978 edition).

Saïd, S. 'Darius et Xerxès dans les *Perses* d' Eschyle', *Ktema* 6 (1981), 17-38.

Saïd, S. 'Tragédie et renversement: l'exemple des *Perses*', *Metis* 3 (1988), 321-41.

Saïd, S. 'Pourquoi Psyttalie ou comment transformer un combat naval en défaite terrestre', in P. Ghiron-Bistagne et al. (eds) *Les Perses d'Eschyle*, *Cahiers du Gita* 7, 1992-93 (Montpellier: Université Paul Valéry, 1993), 53-69.

Saïd, S. 'Herodotus and Tragedy', in E. Bakker et al. (eds) *Brill's Companion to Herodotus* (Leiden: Brill, 2002), 117-47.

Salanitro, G. 'Il pensiero politico di Eschilo nei Persiani', *Giornale Italiano di Filologia* 18 (1965), 193-235.

Sancisi-Weerdenburg, H. 'Exit Atossa: Images of Women in Greek Historiography on Persia', in A. Cameron and A. Kuhrt (eds) *Images of Women in Antiquity* (London: Routledge, 1993, revised edn), 20-33.

Sancisi-Weerdenburg, H. '*Yaunâ* by the Sea and Across the Sea', in I. Malkin (ed.) *Ancient Perceptions of Greek Ethnicity*. Center for Hellenic Studies Colloquia 5 (Washington, D.C.: Harvard University Press, 2001), 323-46.

Sansone, D. 'Aeschylus *Persae* 163', *Hermes* 107 (1979), 115-16.

Schenker, D. 'The Queen and the Chorus in Aeschylus' *Persae*', *Phoenix* 48 (1994), 283-93.

Schmidt, R. *Die Iranier-Namen bei Aischylos* (Vienna: Verlag der österreichischen Akademie der Wissenschaft, 1978).

Schütz, C. *In Aeschyli Tragoedias Commentarius*, vol. 2 (Halle, 1783).

Scott, W. 'The Mesode at *Persae* 93-100', *Greek, Roman, and Byzantine Studies* 9 (1968), 259-66.

Scott, W. *Musical Design in Aeschylean Theater* (Hanover: University Press of New England, 1984).

Seaford, R. *Reciprocity and Ritual: Homer and Tragedy in the Developing City-State* (Oxford: Oxford University Press, 1994).

Seaford, R. *Money and the Early Greek Mind: Homer, Philosophy, and Tragedy* (Cambridge: Cambridge University Press, 2004).

Sealey, R. 'The Origins of the Delian League', in *Ancient Society and Institutions. Studies Presented to Victor Ehrenberg on his 75th Birthday* (Oxford: Basil Blackwell, 1966), 233-55.

Bibliography

Segal, C. 'Catharsis, Audience, and Closure in Greek Tragedy', in M. Silk (ed.) *Tragedy and the Tragic: Greek Theatre and Beyond* (Oxford: Clarendon Press, 1996), 149-72.

Shapiro, A. 'Theseus in Kimonian Athens: The Iconography of Empire', *Mediterranean Historical Review* 7 (1992), 29-49.

Shapiro, A. 'Athena, Apollo, and the Religious Propaganda of the Athenian Empire', *Boreas* 24 (1996), 101-13.

Shapiro, S. 'Herodotus and Solon', *Classical Antiquity* 15 (1996), 348-66.

Shaw, P.-J. 'Lords of Hellas, Old Men of the Sea: The Occasion of Simonides' Elegy on Plataea', in D. Boedeker and D. Sider (eds) *The New Simonides: Contexts of Praise and Desire* (Oxford: Oxford University Press, 2001), 164-81.

Shear, T. Leslie Jr. 'The Demolished Temple at Eleusis', in *Studies in Architecture, Sculpture, and Topography Presented to Homer Thompson*. Hesperia Supplement 20 (Princeton: American School of Classical Studies at Athens, 1982), 128-40.

Shear, T. Leslie Jr. 'The Persian Destruction of Athens: Evidence from the Agora Deposits', *Hesperia* 62 (1993), 383-482.

Sider, D. 'Fragments 1-22 W²', in D. Boedeker and D. Sider (eds) *The New Simonides: Contexts of Praise and Desire* (Oxford: Oxford University Press, 2001), 13-29.

Siewert, P. 'The Ephebic Oath in Fifth-Century Athens', *Journal of Hellenic Studies* 97 (1977), 102-11.

Simms, R. 'Mourning and Community at the Athenian Adonia', *Classical Journal* 93 (1998), 121-41.

Simon, E. *The Festivals of Attika* (Madison: University of Wisconsin Press, 1983).

Slater, W. 'Symposium at Sea', *Harvard Studies in Classical Philology* 80 (1976), 161-70.

Smethurst, M. *The Artistry of Aeschylus and Zeami* (Princeton: Princeton University Press, 1989).

Smyth, H.W. *Aeschylean Tragedy* (Berkeley: University of California Press, 1924)

Snell, B. *Aischylos und das Handeln im Drama*. Philologus Supplementband 20 (Leipzig: Dieterich, 1928).

Sommerstein, A. *Aeschylean Tragedy* (Bari: Levante, 1996).

Spatz, L. *Aeschylus*. Twayne's World Authors Series (Boston: Twayne Publishers, 1982).

Stanford, W.B. *Greek Tragedy and the Emotions: An Introductory Study* (London: Routledge & Kegan Paul, 1983).

Stössl, F. 'Aeschylus as a Political Thinker', *American Journal of Philology* 73 (1952), 113-39.

Storey, I. *Eupolis: Poet of Old Comedy* (Oxford: Oxford University Press, 2003).

Strauss, B. *Fathers and Sons in Classical Athens: Ideology and Society in the Era of the Peloponnesian War* (Princeton: Princeton University Press, 1993).

Strauss, B. *The Battle of Salamis* (New York: Simon and Schuster, 2004).

Suter, A. 'Lament in the *Trojan Women*', *Mnemosyne* 51 (2003), 1-28.

Taplin, O. *The Stagecraft of Aeschylus* (Oxford: Clarendon Press, 1977).

Taylor, M. *The Tyrant Slayers: The Heroic Image in Fifth-Century B.C. Athenian Art and Politics* (Salem: Ayer Publishers, 1991²).

Thalmann, W. 'Xerxes' Rags: Some Problems in Aeschylus' *Persians*', *American Journal of Philology* 101 (1980), 260-82.

Thomas, R. *Herodotus in Context: Ethnography, Science, and the Art of Persuasion* (Cambridge: Cambridge University Press, 2000).

Thompson, H. 'Athens Faces Adversity', *Hesperia* 50 (1981), 343-55.

Tod, M. *Greek Historical Inscriptions*, vol. 2 (Oxford: Clarendon Press, 1962). Cited by document number.

Tuplin, C. 'Imperial Tyranny: Some Reflections on a Classical Greek Political Metaphor', in P. Cartledge and F.D. Harvey (eds) *Crux: Essays in Greek History Presented to G.E.M. de Ste. Croix* (London: Duckworth, 1985), 348-75.

Tuplin, C. 'Persians as Medes', in H. Sancisi-Weerdenburg, A. Kuhrt, and M. Cool Root (eds) *Achaemenid History VIII: Continuity and Change* (Leiden: Netherlands Institute for the Near East, 1994), 235-56.

Tuplin, C. *Achaemenid Studies*. Historia Einzelschriften Heft 99 (Stuttgart: Steiner Verlag, 1996).

Tuplin, C. 'Xerxes' March from Doriscus to Therme', *Historia* 52 (2003), 387-409.

Turner, E. *Athenian Books in the Fifth and Fourth Centuries B.C.* (London: H.K. Lewis, 1977²).

Unz, R. 'The Chronology of the Pentekontaetia', *Classical Quarterly* 36 (1986), 68-85.

Van Steen, G. 'Forgotten Theater, Theater of the Forgotten: Classical Greek Tragedy on the Modern Greek Prison Islands', *Journal of Modern Greek Studies* 23 (2005), 335-95.

Vermaseren, M. *Cybele and Attis* (London: Thames and Hudson, 1977).

Vermeule, E. *Aspects of Death in Early Greek Poetry and Art* (Berkeley: University of California Press, 1979).

Viator, T. 'The Stage History of Cibber's *Xerxes*', *Theatre Notebook* 46 (1992), 155-9.

Vlastos, G. 'Isonomia', *American Journal of Philology* 74 (1953), 337-66.

Wallinga, H.T. 'The Ancient Persian Navy and its Predecessors', in H. Sancisi-Weerdenburg (ed.) *Achaemenid History I: Sources, Structures and Synthesis* (Leiden: Netherlands Institute for the Near East, 1987), 47-96.

Watson, P. 'Apollonio di Giovanni and Ancient Athens', *Allen Memorial Art Museum Bulletin* 37 (1979/80), 3-25.

Webster, T.B.L. *Greek Theatre Production* (London: Methuen, 1970²).

Wees, H. van *Status Warriors: War, Violence and Society in Homer and History* (Amsterdam: Gieben, 1992).

Wees, H. van 'Politics and the Battlefield: Ideology in Greek Warfare', in A. Powell (ed.) *The Greek World* (London: Routledge, 1995), 153-78.

West, M.L. (ed.) *Hesiod: Works and Days* (Oxford: Clarendon Press, 1978).

West, M.L. *Studies in Aeschylus* (Stuttgart: Teubner, 1990).

West, M.L. *Greek Music* (Oxford: Clarendon Press, 1992).

West, M.L. 'Simonides Redivivus', *Zeitschrift für Papyrologie und Epigraphik* 98 (1993), 1-14.

West, S. and West, M.L. 'Sham Shahs', in M. Toher and M. Flower (eds) *Georgica: Greek Studies in Honour of George Cawkwell*. Institute of Classical Studies Bulletin Supplement 58 (London: Institute for Classical Studies, 1991), 176-88.

Wiles, D. *Tragedy in Athens: Performance Space and Theatrical Meaning* (Cambridge: Cambridge University Press, 1997).

Wilkins, J. *The Boastful Chef: The Discourse of Food in Ancient Greek Comedy* (Oxford: Oxford University Press, 2000).

Bibliography

Wilamowitz-Moellendorf, U. von. *Aischylos Interpretationen* (Dublin: Weidmann, 1966, reprint).

Wilson, J. 'Territoriality in the *Persians*', in M. Cropp et al. (eds) *Greek Tragedy and its Legacy: Essays Presented to D.J. Conacher* (Calgary: University of Calgary Press, 1986), 51-7.

Wilson, P. *The Athenian Institution of the Khoregeia* (Cambridge: Cambridge University Press, 2000).

Wilson, P. 'Athenian Strings', in P. Murray and P. Wilson (eds) *Music and the Muses: The Culture of Mousikê in the Classical Athenian City* (Oxford: Oxford University Press, 2004), 269-306.

Winnington-Ingram, R.P. 'Zeus in *Persae*', in R.P. Winnington-Ingram, *Studies in Aeschylus* (Cambridge: Cambridge University Press, 1983), 1-15.

Winnington-Ingram, R.P. 'A Word in *Persae*', in R.P. Winnington-Ingram, *Studies in Aeschylus* (Cambridge: Cambridge University Press, 1983), 198-9.

Wohl, V. *Love among the Ruins: The Erotics of Democracy in Classical Athens* (Princeton: Princeton University Press, 2002).

Young, T.C. '480/479 B.C. – A Persian Perspective', *Iranica Antiqua* 15 (1980), 213-39.

Zeitlin, F. 'The Closet of Masks: Role-Playing and Myth-Making in Euripides' *Orestes*', *Ramus* 20 (1980), 55-71.

Zeitlin, F. 'Playing the Other: Theater, Theatricality, and the Feminine in Greek Drama', in F. Zeitlin, *Playing the Other: Gender and Society in Classical Greek Literature* (Chicago: University of Chicago Press, 1996), 341-74.

Guide to Further Reading

Greek texts and commentaries

West, *Aeschyli Tragoediae* is the standard Greek text of Aeschylus' tragedies, though Page, *Aeschyli Septem*, remains useful for its readability. Broadhead is the fullest commentary on the Greek text of the *Persians* in English and contains appendices that may be helpful to readers who do not know Greek. Hall comprises an excellent introduction, Greek text, English translation, and commentary keyed to the translation. Sidgwick offers a good introduction, concise commentary on the Greek text, and a succinct appendix. Prickard's slightly earlier school text is also worth consulting. For those who read Italian, Belloni's introduction, translation, and commentary are lucid and thorough. Groeneboom's commentary (in Dutch, translated into German) is useful for its citation of parallel and explanatory texts from Greek literature. Also good is *Les Perses*, the Greek text and brief commentary in French prepared under the supervision of Jacqueline de Romilly.

Translations

The translations in this book are my own and keyed to West's Greek text of the play. The best translations to use with it are those which retain the line numbers of the Greek text. These include Benardete, a simple, accurate, and readable translation; Hall, which is faithful to the original; Podlecki, which also contains a commentary; Smyth, which is accurate and available on-line at http://perseus.tufts.edu/hopper/text.jsp?=Perseus:text:1999.01.0012

Lembke/Herington is a poetic adaptation of the original. Since the text has its own line numbers, it will be difficult to use with this book.

Basic tools

For information about theatre and festival in ancient Greece, Csapo/Slater and J.R. Green are invaluable. Simon and Parke offer short and useful accounts of the City Dionysia. Pickard-Cambridge, *Dramatic Festivals*, is the standard scholarly account. P. Easterling (ed.) *Cambridge Companion to Greek Tragedy*, is a handy resource for a number topics but is best on history of interpretation. J. Gregory (ed.) *A Companion to Greek Tragedy*, contains sound articles on a wide range of basic topics.

The Perseus website, edited by Gregory Crane (http://www.perseus.tufts.edu/hopper/), is an excellent resource. Another good website is the Stoa Consortium, which Ross Scaife edits (http://www.stoa.org/). Among the texts and information to be found on this site is the Suda-on-line, the Greek text and English translation by various hands of the tenth-century AD encyclopaedia.

Aeschylus: Persians

The Persian Empire and Xerxes' invasion of Greece

For the Persian empire, Brosius is the best place to start. She provides a well-organized selection of translated primary sources relating to the empire from 559 to 424 BC.

The study of the Persian empire has undergone a renaissance in recent decades. Briant's monumental history is a fruit of that rebirth as are H. Sancisi-Weerdenburg (ed.) *The Proceedings of the Achaemenid History Workshop. The Cambridge Ancient History*, vol. IV (second edition) provides articles of high quality. Kent remains indispensable for Persian inscriptions.

Good treatments of Xerxes' invasion in English include Grundy, Burn, P. Green, Lazenby, and Strauss. Young and Barkworth try to tell the story from the Persian perspective.

Columbia University's *Encylopaedia Iranica* (www.iranica.com/index.html), Livius (www.livius.org/persia.html), and achemenet.com (www.achemenet.com) are on-line resources useful for the study of Persia.

Athenian Empire

Osborne, *Athenian Empire*, selects, translates, and discusses the sources; it is the best starting point. Rhodes, *Athenian Empire*, offers a short, sensible narrative history of the empire. Meiggs is the best scholarly account. Robertson's articles on the 'True Nature of the Delian League' are a cogent provocation to the standard view.

Persians and others

Cartledge, 'Alien Wisdom: Greeks v. Barbarians', in *Greeks: A Portrait of Self and Others*, 36-62, is a good starting point. Hall, *Inventing the Barbarian,* examines the construction of the 'barbarian' in tragedy as way of defining the Greek identity. Harrison (ed.) *Greeks and Barbarians*, contains a number of useful articles. Georges, *Barbarian Asia*, offers historical analysis of Greco-Persian relations.

Aeschylus

Herington, *Aeschylus*, and Spatz are basic introductions to the playwright in English. Sommerstein is more detailed but still pitched to a wide audience. Winnington-Ingram, *Studies in Aeschylus*, offers literary analysis of Aeschylus' plays. Gagarin, *Aeschylean Drama* provides play-by-play exegesis from the perspective of intellectual history. West, *Studies in Aeschylus*, handles textual matters, but also contains a clear treatment of the structure of Aeschylus' tragedy. Taplin is exceptionally detailed, but indispensable for the staging of the plays.

Aeschylus' *Persians*

Smethurst and Michelini, *Tradition*, are the only book-length studies of the *Persians* in English. Smethurst compares the *Persians* and Zeami's *Sanemori*, analysing the structure, imagery, and strategies of allusion in the two dramas. Michelini studies the play from the perspective of the history of metre and dramatic form; she is good on verbal imagery and themes. Harrison, *Emptiness* of Asia, is a provocative historical reading of the play, which examines and critiques previous interpretations. A special edition of *Cahiers du Gita* 7 (1992/93) on the *Persians* contains a number of solid articles on the play.

Spatz's and Gagarin's chapters and Winnington-Ingram's essay are the best points of entry for the study of the *Persians*. Conacher offers a sober treatment of the play. Thalmann's and Saïd's articles are among the best analyses of the play. Good treatments of the political dimensions of the *Persians* can be found in Goldhill, 'Battle Narrative and Politics', Meier, and Pelling. Georges' chapter in *Barbarian Asia* and Harrison, *Emptiness of Asia*, offer strong historical readings.

Herodotus' *Histories*

Fornara, *Herodotus*, is the best place to start. Other good general treatments include Gould, *Herodotus*, and Immerwahr, *Form and Thought*. Raaflaub, 'Herodotus and the Meaning of History', is an excellent treatment of Herodotus' *Histories* as a way of understanding the time in which it was composed. Also worth consulting are the articles in E. Bakker et al. (eds) *Brill's Companion to Herodotus* (Leiden: Brill, 2002).

Reception

Hall's studies are fundamental for the *Persians*. Good general starting points include Hardwick, Garland, and Burian's and Macintosh's essays in *The Cambridge Companion*.

Lorna Hardwick has published a searchable database of late twentieth-century performances of Greek drama on the website of the Department of Classical Studies at the Open University of London. It can be accessed at http://www4.open.ac.uk/csdb/ASP/database.htm. Registration is required to search the database.

The Archive of Performances of Greek and Roman Drama at the University of Oxford, directed by Peter Brown, Edith Hall, and Oliver Taplin, has published a searchable database of productions (stage, screen, radio) on the web (http://www.apgrd.ox.ac.uk/database.htm). Registration is required.

Chronology

BC

c. **760–c. 550**: texts of Homer *Iliad* and *Odyssey*, and Hesiod *Theogony* and *Works and Days* are being written down.

c. **699–c. 647**: Deioces first king of Medes.

c. **646–c. 625**: Phraortes rules Medes.

c. **640–c. 479**: text of Theognis coming into formation.

c. **624–c. 585**: Cyaxares rules Medes.

614: Cyaxares takes Ashur.

612: Cyaxares takes Nineveh.

594: Solon's reforms at Athens.

c. **584–c. 550**: Astyages rules Medes.

561/60: Pisistratus seizes first tyranny at Athens.

559-530: rule of Cyrus the Great.

546/45: Cyrus defeats Croesus of Lydia. Persia assimilates Lydian empire.

534/33: traditional date for introduction of tragedy at Athens.

530-523: rule of Cambyses son of Cyrus.

527: Hippias succeeds Pisistratus.

525: Aeschylus born.

522-486: Darius rules Persian empire.

514: Hipparchus murdered by 'tyrant-slayers' Harmodius and Aristogiton.

513: Darius invades Scythia, bridging Thracian Bosphorus.

510: Pisistratidae expelled from Athens.

508/07: Clisthenes' reforms introduce democracy; formation of ten Attic tribes.

508-501(?): Athenians colonize Salamis.

507(?): Athenian envoys give earth and water to Artaphrenes.

506(?): Athenian hoplites defeat Boeotians and Chalcidians; Chalcis colonized.

501: democratic reorganization of City Dionysia; tragedy instituted (?).

501/500: Athenians reject Artaphrenes' ultimatum to reinstate Hippias.

500/499: abortive Persian/Milesian siege of Naxos.

499: Aeschylus' first tragedy.

499/98-494: Ionian Revolt.

499/498: Ionians, Athenians, and Eretrians attack Sardis; city and temple of Cybebe burned.

494: battle of Lade.

494: siege and destruction of Miletus.

493: Persian reprisals against Chios, Lesbos, Tenedos and rebellious mainland cities. Phoenician fleet gains control of western side of Hellespont; Persians take eastern side.

493-91(?): Phrynichus' *Capture of Miletus*.

492: Mardonius' sea-borne invasion of northern Greece.

211

490: Persians attack Naxos and Cyclades, proclaim Delos sacrosanct, sack Eretria. Athenian and Plataean hoplites defeat Persians at Marathon.

489/88: Miltiades' failed siege of Paros.

488-81(?): war between Athens and Aegina.

486: comedy instituted at City Dionysia.

486-465: rule of Xerxes.

484: Xanthippus ostracized.

483: Xerxes has canal cut behind Mount Athos. Themistocles persuades Athenians to use surplus silver to build fleet of 100 triremes.

483/82: Aristides ostracized.

480: May: Xerxes marches from Sardis to Greece; August: battles of Thermopylae and Artemisium; September: battle of Salamis.

479/78: summer: battle of Plataea, battle of Mycale; autumn/winter: siege of Sestus and crucifixion of Artayctes. Athenians dedicate cables from Xerxes' bridges.

478(?): Simonides' *Plataea*.

478/77: Greeks liberate Western Anatolia; Pausanias recalled to Sparta; foundation of the Athenian empire.

476(?): Phrynichus' *Phoenician Women*.

476: siege and enslavement of Eion; 'Eion epigrams'; colonization and first Athenian disaster at Eion(?).

475: capture and enslavement of Scyros; 'discovery' of Theseus' bones.

***c*. 470**: Aeschylus stages *Women of Aetna* in Sicily to commemorate Hieron's refoundation of Catana as Aetna; restaging of *Persians* in Sicily (?).

474(?): Athenian war with Carystus.

472: Aeschylus' *Persians*.

469-66(?): battle of Eurymedon; destruction of Phoenician fleet.

467: Aeschylus' *Seven against Thebes*.

465(?): capture and 'enslavement' of Naxos.

464: disaster at Drabescus in Thrace.

463: capture and indemnification of Thasos; seizure of mines.

463: Aeschylus' *Suppliants*.

461: reforms of Ephialtes; ostracism of Cimon.

460/59-454: invasion of Egypt; total defeat.

458: Aeschylus' *Oresteia*.

456: Athenians complete long walls. Aeschylus dies in Gela, Sicily.

454: Athenians stockpile tribute at Athens(?); first tribute lists inscribed and displayed.

443: panhellenic colony, Thurii, on site of Sybaris.

427-416(?): Pherecrates' *Persians*.

426(?): revival of Aeschylus' *Persians* at Athens.

426-415(?): Herodotus' *Histories* published.

425: Aristophanes' *Acharnians*.

424: Aristophanes' *Knights*.

422: Aristophanes' *Wasps*.

421: Eupolis' *Maricas*.

417-411(?): Eupolis' *Villages*.

415: Euripides' *Trojan Women*.

415-413: Athenian invasion of Syracuse.

408: Euripides' *Orestes*.

405: Aristophanes' *Frogs*.

405: battle of Aegospotami; Athenian fleet captured.

404: Athens surrenders to Sparta; long walls dismantled; fleet reduced to twelve ships.

404-358: Artaxerxes II King of Persia.

c. **400**: Choerilus' *Persian Wars*.

400-394: Sparta and Persia at war.

400-375(?): Metagenes' *Persians of Thurii*.

399-395(?): publication of Thucydides' *History*.

396-394: Agesilaus' invasion of Persian empire.

396-394(?): Timotheus' *Persians*.

394: battle of Cnidus: defeat of Spartan navy by newly funded Persian navy under the command of Conon of Athens.

331/30: Alexander the Great sacks and burns Persepolis.

205: Pylades performs Timotheus' *Persians* at the Nemean Games.

31: battle of Actium.

c. **19**: posthumous publication of Vergil's *Aeneid*.

2: Augustus stages naval battle between 'Athenians' and 'Persians'.

AD

c. **500**: *Persians* selected with *Prometheus Bound* and *Seven against Thebes* to form 'Byzantine triad'.

1339: Boccaccio's *Theseid of the Wedding of Emilia*.

1360: Boccaccio's *Fates of Illustrious Men*.

c. **1423**: tenth-century AD vellum manuscript of Aeschylus' seven plays arrives in Italy.

1453: Turks capture Constantinople.

1461: Apollonio di Giovanni receives commission for *Xerxes' Invasion of Greece* and *Triumph of the Victorious Greeks*.

1518: first book edition of Aeschylus' plays.

1571: battle of Lepanto; reading of *Persians* in Italian translation on Zacynthus.

1585: *Oedipus the King* restaged at Vicenza, Italy.

1654: Francesco Cavalli's *Xerxes* performed in Venice.

1660: performance of Cavalli's *Xerxes* after Louis XIV's wedding.

1694: Bononcini's *Xerxes*.

1699: Colley Cibber's *Xerxes*.

1738: Handel's *Xerxes* premières in London.

1815: Anonymous *Xerxes the Great* or *The Battle of Thermopyle*, produced in Philadelphia.

1821: Greek revolt from the Ottoman empire.

1822: Shelley's *Hellas*.

1902: papyrus of Timotheus' *Persians* discovered in Abusir, Egypt.

1939: BBC reading of Gilbert Murray's translation of *Persians*.

1942: revival of *Persians* in Göttingen, Germany.

1946-49: Greek civil war.

1947: Greek theatre production of anti-communist *Persians* to celebrate union of Dodecanese with Greece.

1951: Tzvalas Karousos directs leftist prisoner performance of *Persians* on island of Aï Stratis.

1960-69: Mattias Braun's adaptation of the *Persians* received as anti-war play.

1967-74: military dictatorship in Greece.

1970: John Lewis' adaptation of the *Persians* performed at St George Church, New York.

1971: Takis Mouzenidis' *Persians* performed at Epidaurus.
1974: Circle Repertory production of the *Persians*.
1991: First Gulf War.
1993: Peter Sellars' *Persians* premières in Robert Auletta's adaptation.
2003-: Second Gulf War.
2004: Ellen McLaughlin's adaptation of the *Persians* first performed.

Glossary

allotrios: 'alien', 'someone else's'; opposed to *oikeios* 'one's own'.

anapaest: two-beat metrical foot of the form ∪∪−; marching anapaests are spoken/recited in two metra, ∪∪− ∪∪−/∪∪− ∪∪−, called anapaestic dimeter. Lyric anapaests are metrically more flexible and sung to a melody.

anaphora: the repetition of words at the beginning of sentences, verses, or clauses.

anthos: literally 'blossom' or 'flower', designates the best, most conspicuous, or most lustrous part of anything. The word also refers to what grows or emerges on or from the surface of something else, such as the nap of fine cloth, froth on the sea or on wine, patina on bronze, and smoke from fire.

antistrophe: literally 'turning back' or 'about', the term refers to the second stanza in a pair metrically corresponding stanzas. See under **strophe**.

archê: 'beginning', 'origin'; also the term for empire or right to rule. See under *telos*.

aretê: 'virtue', 'excellence', 'nobility'.

Atê/atê: Goddess of destructive delusion/subjective state of delusion and objective result of disaster.

charis: 'gratitude', 'favour', or 'grace'. It designates the favours one does for another and the debt of gratitude owed in exchange.

dactyl: two-beat metrical foot of the form −∪∪.

daimôn: divine power or spirit; the divine force that determines a person's fortune.

dêmos: 'people'; democracy means 'domination by the people'; also means 'village'.

deus ex machina: literally 'god from a machine', so called because at the end of tragedies a god appeared hoisted into the air on a crane, or *mêchanê*, to resolve irresolvable conflicts and to prophesy the future outside of the drama.

drachma, mina, talent: drachma = 4.3 g of silver on the Athenian standard; 100 drachmae = 1 mina, 430 g of silver; 60 minae = 1 talent, 25.8 kg of silver.

drama: the source of our word 'drama', in ancient Greek it means 'a thing done', an action of consequence which demands reciprocation. *Drama* entails *pathos*, 'suffering', of greater magnitude.

ekplêxis: literally a 'striking out', it refers to mental and emotional 'astonishment'.

eleutheria: 'freedom' in the sense of belonging to a free *oikos* and *polis* − not being the slave or subject of another.

epode: a stanza rhythmically independent of a strophic/antistrophic pair, which either marks the end of an ode or a thematic and metrical break within it.

215

euthynai: the procedure by which Athenians held public officials who handled money accountable.

exodos: choral song of exit from the orchestra.

habros: 'lovely', 'delicate', 'luxurious', 'desirable'. A keyword of Greek lyric poetry of the seventh and sixth centuries BC, it becomes pejorative after the Persian Wars and is associated with enervating material excess.

harmamaxa: a covered chariot associated with the effeminate luxury of the Persians, it is referred to in the *Persians* as a 'tent on wheels', and may be in the orchestra during the *kommos*, symbolizing the absence of the men who accompanied it – according to Herodotus, 22,000 of Persia's finest soldiers.

hêbê: literally 'youth', but meaning the 'prime of life'. The word designates men of military age and nubile women.

hegemony: literally, 'military leadership' (*hêgemonia*), command with the power to compel allies to follow wherever the 'leader' (*hêgemôn*) leads. Common privileges include occupying the right wing in battle and imposing friends and enemies on allies.

hoplite: a heavily armoured infantryman characteristic of Greek land warfare; the product of Greek political and social structures in which land ownership and the duty to protect it are integral to citizenship.

hybris: violent disregard for the honour of another, including the gods; violent and fruitless expenditure of energy with the intent to damage another's person or property.

hypothesis: literally, 'plot', the term refers to the summary of a play appended to a manuscript. The *hypothesis* often includes plot, setting, characters, date, and whether the play won first prize.

iamb: one-and-a half-beat metrical foot of the form ∪–. Lyric iambic is a flexible metre based on the form x–∪– (x = either – or ∪) and sung to a melody.

iambic trimeter: the basic spoken metre of drama, composed of three iambic dimeters: x–∪–/x–∪–/x–∪– (x = either – or ∪).

Ionians: according to Herodotus, an indigenous people of the Aegean who adopted Greek language and culture. The most prominent Ionian city is Athens, which claimed to be the mother city of Ionians who colonized Western Anatolia and the Aegean islands, planting further colonies in the Black Sea, southern Italy, and Sicily. 'Ionia' designates Ionian city-states in Western Anatolia (such as Miletus), but sometimes stands for all the Greek city-states of Western Anatolia, which included the other branches of the Greeks, Aeolians and Dorians. The Ionians proper formed a loose union of twelve cities, called the duodecapolis, which assembled at the Panionion near Mycale.

Ionic *a minore*: a lyric metre based on the form ∪∪– –.

isonomia: literally 'equality of law', but more generally, equal access to power which implies majority rule and accountability for office-holders; sometimes a synonym for democracy.

iunx: the wryneck, a bird whose head can swivel 360 degrees. Tied to a wheel and spun, it was used in Greek erotic magic to win back a lost lover. *Iunx* can also refer to the wheel itself or stand more generally for a love incantation.

kenning: a figurative expression which substitutes for a noun, such as 'the sweat of the fount of Bromius' for 'wine'.

kleos: literally something 'heard' or said about someone; 'glory', 'good-repute', 'renown' which lends mortals a form of immortality.

216

kommos: sung lament between actor(s) and chorus.

koros: means 'fullness' or 'satiation' in Homer, then comes to mean 'insatiability'. It is associated with *hybris* and *atê*.

kosmos: 'order' or 'social order'; it also means 'ornament', and refers to ceremonial clothing. It can also suggest honour or glory. Philosophers used it to mean 'world order', in the sense of our cosmos.

lecythia: lyric trochaic metre of the form $-\cup-\text{x}-\cup-$ (x = $-$ or $\cup$).

Mede(s): an Aryan people like the Persians, who consolidated power in Iran before the Persians. The Greeks often conflated them with the Persians.

medism: collaborating with the Persians.

oikeios: 'of one's *oikos*', 'one's own', 'part of one's nature'; opposed to *allotrios*.

oikos: household and family including land, slaves, and property.

olbos: quality of wealth which implies prosperity, happiness, divine favour, blessedness and the capacity to transmit these to future generations.

ostracism: a democratic institution first practised in 488/87 at Athens. The citizen body dissolved into ten tribes and each citizen deposited a sherd with the name of the citizen he would most like to go into exile for a decade. If 6,000 sherds were cast, the man whose name turned up on the most of them went into ten-year exile, though his house and property remained intact in Attica. The Athenians voted to hold an ostracism two to three months before it was held.

parodos: the 'side entry' to the orchestra; choral entry song of a drama.

pathos: 'suffering'.

pelanos: a porridge-like ritual offering containing meal, olive-oil, wine, which can be burned or poured to the ground.

plêthos: 'number', 'large number', 'majority', 'population', 'mass or masses'.

ponos: 'labour', 'toil', 'suffering'; the labour value of symbolic capital (nobility, virtue, gratitude, glory).

ploutos/Ploutos: richness of the soil and its produce; wealth. The god embodying these goods.

pothos: 'longing', desire for what is absent.

proskynêsis: Persian social ritual by which inferiors bow to superiors from their knees; Greeks considered it a ritual marking the divinity of the Great King since they bowed this way only before gods.

scholium: a marginal comment in a manuscript. These comments preserve information about an ancient text and the history of its interpretation.

skênê: literally, 'tent', the word for the stage-house in the Athenian theatre, a wooden building used to represent palaces, temples, and other structures.

stichomythia: literally, 'talking in lines', a dialogue conducted mainly in one-line utterances, but sometimes including half-lines and statements of up to three lines.

stasimon: a stationary choral song, delivered but not addressed to the audience. In the *Persians*, the first stasimon begins with an anapaestic prelude before modulating to lyric iambic and lyric dactylic. The second stasimon is sung in lyric dactylic metre.

strophe: literally 'turning' and so thought to refer to the dance movements of a chorus, the term refers to the first stanza of a pair of stanzas – *strophê* and *antistrophê* – of corresponding metrical shape.

telos: 'endpoint'; 'realization', 'fulfilment', 'payment'.

tribe: Greek *phylê*, at Athens, a group of citizens united by fictionalized kinship in the worship of an eponymous hero; derived from clusters of villages in the three major geographical regions of Attica, the city, the plain, and the coast.

Attica was divided into ten tribes, which were the organizational basis for Athenian society. The Council, the hoplite army, generalships, ostracisms, public burial, and dithyrambic choral competitions were structured by tribe.

trireme: warship with hull, bronze ram, and small deck, powered by three banks of 30 oars on each side; 200 men comprised a full complement, 180 rowers and 20 crew, marines, and archers.

trochaic tetrameter: spoken metre composed of four trochaic measures, the final measure lacking a syllable: $-\cup-x/-\cup-x/-\cup-x/-\cup-/$ (x = $-$ or $\cup$).

Index

Index

catharsis 135, 141-2

Cavalli, Francesco *Xerxes* 158

chariot and *hybris* 49-50, 73; and *olbos* 51-2, 153; Assyrian 43, 49; curtained (*harmamaxa*) 131-2; of the day 63, 69; of the sun 158; *see also* Queen, Xerxes, yoke

chorus and *atê* 43-4, 46; and Darius 47, 56, 87-8, 90, 101-2, 114-15; and female choruses 45, 56; and free speech 54, 81, 126; and imperialism 40-6, 101-2; and messenger 63-4, 81; and *pathos* 39, 137-8; as citizens 63, 126; as 'the trusted' 54, 77; attitudes of 40-3; council of 48; exclamations of 45, 79, 87, 134; hymn of 86-8, 132; laments of 45, 63-4, 79-82, 122-38; language of 43-4, 81, 127; perspective of 50; premonitions of 54, 89; prophecy of 81; *proskynêsis* of 50, 81, 83; robes of 137-8; *see also* epode, parodos, stasima

chorus leader 77, 85

Cibber, Colley *Xerxes* 158-9

comedy 154-6

cosmos 37, 76, 107, 112, 135, 142, 145

Croesus 51, 123

Cybebe/Cybele 19-20, 22, 23, 84, 104-5, 146, 152

Cyrus *passim* 17, 93, 98-100, 121, 155

daimôn (divinity) and *koros* 109, 131, 134; as character 99; as fiend 77, 91, 126, 139-40; Darius as 85; of Persians 43, 77; *see also* Xerxes

Darius *passim*; and cure 84, 86, 114-16; and Golden Age 110, 114, 116, 155; and principles of drama 46, 89, 105-6, 108-9; and prophecies 89, 91; and Solon 108-9, 114-5; and sympotic poetry 114-15; as focalizer 102-3; as god 86-7, 102, 110; as mortal 86; authority of 114; conquests of 116-21; costume of 88; entrance of 86, 88-90; epithets of 47, 116; historical 102-3, 111, 143;

interpretations of 146-7; *olbos* of 86, 94, 101, 110; parting words of 114-15; pity of 56, 74, 88, 95, 103, 147; praise of 87, 110, 116; prophecies of 103, 106-9, 111; recognition of 89, 97; tomb of 47, 85-6; *see also* chorus, Xerxes

day/night 68, 71, 76, 78, 85

Delian League 31-2; *see also* Athenian empire

Delphic Oracle 43, 48, 64, 67, 91, 107, 108

Demeter and Kore 15, 84

demos 17, 19, 33, 58, 98, 112

Dionysus 14, 84, 151, 152, 161

Dorian(s) 49, 53, 54, 107, 110, 151; *see also* Sparta

Eion 32-3, 118; epigrams 76-7

epinician 142, 145

epode 43-4, 88, 111

equality (*isonomia*) Athenian 18, 72-3; in Eion epigrams 33; in Ionia 19; Persian lack of 57-8, 72-3, 147; versus monarchy 18, 36-7, 99

Erinyes 92, 113-14, 127

erotic magic 130-1

eunuch 20, 33-4, 39

Eupolis *Maricas* 154, 161; *Villages* 17

Euripides *Andromache* 125; *Orestes* 149; *Trojan Women* 21

eye 'evil' 53, 130; of gods 49-50; of house 52, 65, 153; of the night 71; of snake 49; of trireme 53; 'trusted' 130-1, 153; *see also* verbal imagery

fear and dramatic reality 45-6, 127; and lament 153; and military posturing 40; and wealth 51-2; as deferring *pathos* 39; as tragic emotion 11, 22, 78, 124-5, 141; of barbarian sailors 46, 68-9; of chorus 43, 45-6, 47, 90, 137; of Darius 93; of Queen 50-2, 57, 83, 90-1

fish/fishing 41, 46, 59, 71, 81, 130

freedom (*eleutheria*) and Ionians 32; and Persian Wars 27, 60, 70; and poverty 75; as life-giving light 69;

Index